STOW – WADEBRIDGE – POLZEATH – PORT IS   BOSCASTLE
FORD - BARNSTAPLE – BRAUNTON – WOOLA
GWATER – BURNHAM-ON-SEA – WESTON-
N BEACH – SEVERN VIEW – BERKELEY –
F DEAN – LYDNEY – SEDBURY CLIFFS – CHEPSTOW –
WYE – KINGTON – KNIGHTON – NEWCASTLE-ON-CLUN – MONTGOMERY
H – PRESTATYN – MOSTYN – FLINT – CONNAH'S QUAY – QUEENSFERRY
ON-LE-WILLOWS – ASHTON-IN-MAKERFIELD – WIGAN – STANDISH –
BAY – CARNFORTH – MILNTHORPE – OXENHOLME – KENDAL – LAKE
E PASS – BROTHERS WATER – ULLSWATER – POOLEY BRIDGE – PENRITH
IRK – ABBOTSFORD – MELROSE – GALASHIELS – STOW – FOUNTAINHALL
STLE, OLD & NEW TOWNS, HOLYROOD & ARTHUR'S SEAT) – GRANTON–
INLITHGOW - POLMONT – FALKIRK – STENHOUSEMUIR – BANNOCKBURN
DRYMEN – BALMAHA – MILARROCHY – LOCH LOMOND – ROWARDENNAN
RUM – BRIDGE OF ORCHY – INVERORAN – RANNOCH MOOR – HEAD OF
OCH LINNHE – CORPACH – LOCH EIL – GLENFINNAN (LOCH SHIEL) –
RISAIG (LOCH NAN CEAL) – MORAR (WHITE SANDS) – LOCH MORAR –
OCHY BRIDGE – LOCH LOCHY – LAGGAN – LOCH OICH - ABERCHALDER
MNADROCHIT – URQUHART BAY – BLACKFOLD – INVERNESS – BUNCHREW
VANTON – ALNESS – INVERGORDON – TAIN – EDDERTON – ARDGAY –
VER – HELMSDALE – ORD OF CAITHNESS – BERRIEDALE – DUNBEATH
SO – CASTLETOWN – DUNNET – MEY – GILLS BAY – JOHN O'GROATS –
STOW – WADEBRIDGE – POLZEATH – PORT ISAAC – TINTAGEL – BOSCASTLE
FORD - BARNSTAPLE – BRAUNTON – WOOLACOMBE – ILFRACOMBE – COMBE
GWATER – BURNHAM-ON-SEA – WESTON-SUPER-MARE – CONGRESBURY
N BEACH – SEVERN VIEW – BERKELEY – SLIMBRIDGE – FRAMPTON-ON-
F DEAN – LYDNEY – SEDBURY CLIFFS – CHEPSTOW – TINTERN ABBEY –
WYE – KINGTON – KNIGHTON – NEWCASTLE-ON-CLUN – MONTGOMERY
H – PRESTATYN – MOSTYN – FLINT – CONNAH'S QUAY – QUEENSFERRY
ON-LE-WILLOWS – ASHTON-IN-MAKERFIELD – WIGAN – STANDISH –
BAY – CARNFORTH – MILNTHORPE – OXENHOLME – KENDAL – LAKE
E PASS – BROTHERS WATER – ULLSWATER – POOLEY BRIDGE – PENRITH

Ice Cream, Cakes and a
Very Long Walk

*The journal of Peter Youngs' walk
from Land's End to John O'Groats*

Peter Youngs

Ice cream, Cakes and a
Very Long Walk

Peter Youngs

ISBN 978-1-909660-46-5

A CIP catalogue record for this book
is available from the British Library.
Published 2015 Tricorn Books
131 High Street, Portsmouth, PO1 2HW

Printed & bound in the UK

A relation used to take the family on country walks, but she did like to try and lead them on short-cuts. When they found themselves stuck on banks of muddy ditches, and tried to climb over fences, scratching themselves on barbed wire to get out, only to find a bull in the field, causing them to retreat and search for another route, they decided that they had ended up facing a much longer walk than was originally planned.

Ice Cream, Cakes and a
Very Long Walk

CONTENTS

PREFACE

*T*o adapt a statement made by Jerome K Jerome in *Three Men on the Bummel* (an account of a cycling tour in Germany), I would not suggest that anybody use this book on its own as a walking guide for getting from Cornwall to the north of Scotland, or anywhere in between, and they would need good maps and guide books, as I had.

Although I had been fascinated all my life, by stories of people who had walked from Land's End to John O'Groats, and I much enjoyed reading their books, I never seriously thought I would have the opportunity to undertake such a project. However, in June 2010 I read a story in *The News* by a cyclist who had completed it – as usual I thought 'how marvellous, but I shall never do it' – but then I stopped and thought again. My circumstances had very recently changed – I was shortly due to take part-retirement, and I currently had no family ties as in the past. Why shouldn't I try the project? I have been a keen long-distance walker for many years.

I discussed it with my brother, but I remember I was rather a while getting to the point. I was going on about, 'There is something I very much want to attempt ... A walk project ... It would be so interesting ... I've been thinking a lot about it ...' He said, 'I was wondering whatever you were going to come out with – I thought you were going to tell me you were off to the Himalayas!' And then, re. Land's End to John O'Groats, 'Well, why not give it a go?'

So, between August 2010 and March 2014, I walked the length of Britain (in between other commitments and interests,) including a lot of detours to other interesting areas, a total of 1,535 miles (the most direct route is about 870 miles). Over three years and seven months I completed the journey of 107 days of walks (average 14 to 15 miles daily).

I did each section consecutively, and always returned to the exact spot I had reached the previous time, so there were no gaps anywhere; I did not even take ferries across estuaries – I walked inland until I could cross rivers. I chose south to north – Cornwall is marvellous, but I wanted to save the very best till last and I regard the Scottish Highlands as the jewel in the crown.

As the account of the walk is taken from rough notes that I wrote up in journals at the time I covered the various areas, it comes across very much as a series of experiences, impressions and meditations, sometimes on information not checked out – 'I think', etc, and there is some repetition on subsequent days which it is difficult to eliminate sometimes.

The account relives my feelings at the time. My interest in the project grew constantly throughout – hence more detail and description as I progressed northward. Maybe, therefore, I haven't done justice to some southerly areas I crossed, many of which were some of the most beautiful. I have added a few extra photos for these areas, to compensate. The maps at the beginning of each section are sketch maps and are therefore not intended to be drawn to scale. They serve to provide a general indication of the areas covered. The book, (as per the journals) treats the John O'Groats goal as a slightly 'open' secret, till the last day. Until then, I do not admit to the obvious intention.

My thanks to so many people I know for their interest and encouragement, particularly my brother, his wife and all their family and connections, and various other friends. My brother lent me maps; one of my nephews gave me a huge map of the UK to hang up, and I added stickers at all interesting points I reached; and all the others contributed with various offers of help too, or with the valuable encouragement to reach my goal and publish this book.

My thanks too, to the publishers who gave me so much assistance in sorting out rather muddled sections of my notes, and help in many other ways.

North Cornwall & Devon, & Somerset Coast Paths
(including northern half of SW Coast Path)
368 miles

Day 1
16/8/10

Land's End — Sennen Cove — Cape Cornwall —
Pendeen Watch — Rosemergy
(15 miles approx)

*A*s an introduction, I now summarise the journey to Land's End. Yesterday — taxi to Cosham (Portsmouth), train to Westbury, a further train via Castle Cary to Taunton, and an express train, but calling at Tiverton Parkway, Exeter St David's, Newton Abbot, Totnes, Plymouth, Liskeard, Bodmin Parkway, Par, St Austell, Truro, Redruth, Camborne, St Erth and Penzance.

The ride between Exeter and Penzance, I think, is one of the loveliest train journeys in Britain. The coastal section through Dawlish and Teignmouth, the views of the Dartmoor peaks between Newton Abbot and Plymouth, and the magical Cornish scenery through the heart of the county, so unspoilt, from Saltash to Penzance, with the additional benefit of glorious summer sunshine, have left very happy memories. But this is supposed to be a 'book' about a walk. Perhaps a very short book, I wonder, or perhaps quite a long one?

So, now for the day in question. I had been taken by taxi from the very good B&B guest house, where I was staying, and this morning I stepped forth from Land's End at 9.30 am into a world of purple heather, rocks and boulders - many of which needed careful negotiation, including some scrambling — and the ever-present Atlantic Ocean, stretching far away. Very warm sunshine early in the day was replaced later with some sea mist and cool breezes. It was difficult to predict progress, as up and down gradients are often very steep, and very frequent, and the coastal path can be very indirect at times, no doubt for good reasons. But if it was a tough walk, it was also outstandingly beautiful — both factors tend to cause delays; it was too lovely to rush through too fast, and I took some short extra detours sometimes.

Mostly the walk was high up on the cliffs with dramatic views to the sea below. Sometimes it descended through coves, sandy and warm. But almost everywhere was utterly unspoilt and revealed the charm of Cornwall — a county of magical scenery with its cliffs, hills, moors, villages, towns, fishing ports and its history.

A summary of my route — Sennen Cove, soon after Land's End; somewhat later, Cape Cornwall on a rocky headland. If I hadn't been so busy eating blackberries, a Kit-Kat, and vanilla-and-wild-cherry ice cream, I might be able to tell you something about it (history, tourism etc.).

At Levant (and other places), there was much evidence of the old Cornish mines (tin, etc.), ruined buildings, also restoration work. At Pendeen Watch I saw the lighthouse, quite close up. The descent and ascent either side of Portheras Cove seemed particularly steep and rough going, but well worthwhile.

I finally followed a path inland, around 5.30 pm, to the small settlement of Rosemergy, and had lemonade at a farmhouse, where teas were being served; and took a bus back to Penzance, which also detoured into Marazion, with good views of St. Michael's Mount – an irrelevant, but well worthwhile, part of the programme.

Interestingly of course, the coastal path of North Cornwall is part of the South West Coast Path, which starts at South Haven Point, Dorset and finishes at Minehead, Somerset (or vice-versa).

Day 2
17/8/10

Rosemergy – Zennor – St Ives – Carbis Bay – Hayle
(17 miles approx)

*A*nother taxi ride – to Rosemergy, of course – and I started walking about 10.15 am. But the day had started with rain and mist, and there were still no improvements. Rather than go out to the coast again and see nothing of the beauty of the scenery there, or wait for the weather to clear and so lose valuable time, I decided on what I think was the best option – I walked by the direct road route to St Ives. I was still able to enjoy some limited views of the rugged, hilly Cornish landscape, and I saved myself quite a lot of time – the road is fairly near the coast, but a much quicker alternative. In fact the weather did eventually clear when I reached St Ives (via Zennor).

I couldn't help thinking of a poem – I know nothing of the background of it, but I have repeated it from childhood:

'As I was going to St Ives,
I met a man with seven wives.
The seven wives had seven sacks,
The seven sacks had seven cats;
The seven cats had seven kits.'

The question asked at the end is:

'Kits, cats, sacks, wives –
How many were going to St Ives?'

I have since heard the answer may be 'none' - they were all coming *from* St Ives! (Won't attempt to draw a picture of this scene, although it could be interesting.)

As I have mentioned – improvement in weather. As I reached a high summit on the road – the last and highest on my route, I think – there was St Ives ahead and below, the mist lifting and the coastline northwards beginning to take shape. And the rest of the day was quite sunny.

St Ives itself was exceptionally busy, with traffic and people everywhere. I won't quote the verses this time, but 'The Floral Dance', which I learned once, is a piece of music, the words to which refer to 'that quaint old Cornish town'. With its steep narrow streets, and fine old buildings, this seemed like the town. I did some shopping, and walked to the quay and the sands, and had a snack.

I had thought I would have liked a ride on the St Ives to St Erth branch railway, but there was no need anyway, because the North Cornwall Coast Path, on which I continued, follows the line for almost all the route. I walked via Carbis Bay, along and up and down the cliffs, and watched the trains. The path also runs above Porth Kidney Sands, to Lelant, after which I reached main roads and crossed the River Hayle to Hayle (5.15 pm).

I caught a train back to Penzance, in good time to write postcards at the guest house in the evening - a very full and interesting day, again. Reflecting on the day, one particular memory impresses me – when the weather cleared, and I looked north-east from St Ives, I could see headland after headland . . . about six or seven, I should think – probably to as far as twenty-five or more miles away. With the sun shining on the distant cliffs, it was a very beautiful sight.

DAY 3
18/8/10

HAYLE – GWITHIAN – GODREVY POINT – PORTREATH
(15 miles approx)

I left Penzance by train, with all my luggage, alighted at Hayle, and went to my 'new' B&B accommodation in the town; very good again.

So I was able to re-commence walking at 11.00 am. I had completed the detour round the estuary yesterday, but just had to follow round the north side of Hayle harbour, and then walked along the sands and cliffs, and among the sand dunes, through Towans and Gwithian, to the higher cliffs at Godrevy Point – good views from the top. I looked down to the small Godrevy Island, with its lighthouse.

I then continued on the very high cliffs at Navax Point, and above tiny coves far below - with such names as 'Hell's Mouth' and 'Dead man's Cove' they certainly did not look like the safest places to be! Thence, I followed the coast path above the high North Cliffs and I think I got a very distant view of Lundy Island, far up, and off, the coast.

So far the walking has been, compared with some earlier sections, really easy. But the last section, into Portreath, broke this pattern completely. At Carvannel Downs there are two significantly steep descents, with corresponding ascents, and a further very steep descent to Portreath.

The only other thing I observed, which I had not realised, is how clearly Redruth and Camborne towns can be seen in the distance, about midway between Godrevy and Portreath.

Portreath was quite busy, with visitors to the port and sands today. I had a Cornish clotted cream tea. Throughout the walk, I have to say I have acquired a distinct taste for blackcurrant-and-clotted-cream ice creams, which seem to appear throughout Cornwall with delightful regularity.

I reached Portreath around 4.45 pm, spent a while there, and then travelled to Redruth by taxi and on to Hayle by bus.

Apart from one light shower, the weather has been very pleasantly sunny, and windy too.

DAY 4
19/8/10

PORTREATH – PORTHTOWAN – ST AGNES HEAD –
TREVAUNANCE COVE – PERRANPORTH
(15 miles approx)

I took a bus from Hayle, which got me to Portreath, for 11 am for the start of today's walk. After the initial climb up to the cliff tops, I followed a comparatively level section beside MoD fencing, which warned of the importance of keeping to the path, because of mines. The typical beauty of the north Cornish coast continued here and throughout the day, as glorious as ever. I soon came upon another two very steep descents, similar to yesterday, with their corresponding ascents!

And the situation was repeated at Porthtowan (where I indulged in the favourite ice cream, plus a Kit-Kat) and Chapel Porth – both small sandy coves set in the rugged coastline.

Indeed, the 'ups and downs', or the 'downs and ups' continued at intervals throughout the day – providing dramatic and delightful views, of course. I climbed up to Wheal and up to St Agnes Head, just able to get the best views of it and from it, before some change in the weather. The bright morning changed to a windier and rather wet afternoon, and these conditions lasted into the evening, but visibility did remain quite good.

From the wild summit of St Agnes Head, I continued to a rather similar Newdowns Head and then down to Trevaunance Cove. There were no other settlements of any significant size (as far as I could see in the mist) and I was blown past Perranporth Aerodrome - I am not sure if it is in use or not, but I did see the sign.

Suddenly the view of Perranporth opened up below me. There were quite a lot of people about, despite the rain. Equally suddenly (most conveniently) a bus for Truro appeared as I entered the village, and I was taken there forthwith, including a scheduled tour with two official bus stops in the grounds of the very modern Royal Cornwall Hospital. Truro looked a fine city with an impressive cathedral – not at all modern, unlike its hospital. If only I knew my history books as well as I know my ice creams, I could make this part of my record so interesting.

Anyway, I took an express bus from the bus station through lovely old Truro, back to Hayle, to my B&B, and listened to the rain getting heavier.

Day 5
20/8/10

Perranporth – Ligger Point – Holywell – Kelsey Head – Newquay
(14 miles approx)

*A*fter an extremely good breakfast that filled me up well for the day, I took a bus again from Hayle, via Portreath and St Agnes, to Perranporth. I started walking at about 11.45 am, and proceeded along the sands (Perran Beach), then up into the sand dunes to avoid the incoming tide – these dunes are known as Penhale Sands. I avoided the danger of the tide only to find notices on the dunes – MoD warnings about unexploded mines! But further reading assured me that by keeping to the way-marked path I was in no danger from them.

The wind grew very strong and rain (not so much as yesterday) followed. The usual steep descents/ascents followed at intervals through the day, with a few areas being quite high and flat.

I followed the route via Ligger Point, Penhale Point, Holywell, Kelsey Head, Pentire Point West and Crantock Beach, along which I walked – all coastal entirely.

At the River Gannel Estuary, I had the choice of crossing to Newquay by a small ferry-boat (but I felt I would still like to say I had walked all the way to Newquay); taking a longer detour inland to a bridging point (it seemed an unnecessary diversion of considerable length); or fording the river, which I felt was the best option, and very direct. The tide was receding, and I followed this official route of an ancient walkway, now a bridge for walkers and cyclists, but submerged under the water. I got across safely and was very soon in the centre of Newquay.

I explored parts of the town – the Esplanade, and the town centre – where I found a teashop, which I much enjoyed visiting, needless to say.

I had completed the walk at 5.15 pm, having checked with the bus station that I could get a direct service to Truro again. So this I did, via Perranporth and the grounds of the Royal Cornwall Hospital again. I then took a bus on to Camborne, and another to Hayle for B & B again, memorable for very good breakfasts and for showing a very great interest in my walks. So I felt very happy to have covered the route from Land's End to Newquay in this holiday. Tomorrow I would have to return home.

So, just a few comments on the return journey back to Hampshire. Really it is a repeat of the introductory section to Day 1 – but in reverse direction. The main difference was the weather – mist and rain in the West Country. I was therefore most pleased to have enjoyed the sunshine so much on the trip to Cornwall.

Coming back, only half of St Michael's Mount was visible, showing how low the cloud was. But conditions improved – also I had good connections at Taunton and Westbury. I reached Penzance from Hayle by bus, and I took a taxi from Cosham to home.

I wrote about many happy memories in the introduction to Day 1 – the journey to Penzance – certainly I've got very many more of them now!

Day 6
4/10/10

Newquay — Watergate Bay — Mawgan Porth — Bedruthan Steps — Porthcothan Bay
(17 miles approx)

*N*eedless to say, it is wonderful to be in Cornwall again. Firstly, a quick summary of the journey to Newquay.

Yesterday I took a taxi to Cosham, and train to Salisbury, where I had lunch at the station café. I then took a train which called at Tisbury, Gillingham, Templecombe, Sherborne, Yeovil Junction, Crewkerne, Axminster, Honiton, Feniton, Whimple, Exeter Central and Exeter St David's.

The weather was wet for the earlier part of the day, and fields and hillsides looked very lush and green. The gold and red autumn colours of the trees added to all this beauty. There was some flooding in the Axminster area, after the heavy rain.

I changed to the Penzance train at Exeter St David's (journey was as Day 1, with rougher sea at Dawlish and Teignmouth, and I alighted at Truro). The bus then took me to Newquay - I had a look around the town, and booked in for B & B; very good accommodation again.

Now for today's walk – the main 'problem' was getting away from Newquay!

But there were good reasons. The proprietors of the B&B very correctly told me about parts of Newquay which were well worth seeing. It is a large town, with quite a number of headlands and beaches. I finished off from last holiday, and also checked at the bus station for this holiday. The harbour was quite scenic, as were parts of the town itself. Views from Pentire Point East were good, and near the town centre was a beach with very high cliff-type rocks, one with a house on, accessed by a high, narrow bridge, and insular at high tide. I met a man and a Filipino lady, who I talked to for a while. He told me that I looked a typical Englishman, and that he would like to photograph me with the Filipino lady, as they were working on a research project about England – to be included in their publication. So I agreed to this and it was all very discreetly conducted.

After all this, I headed northwards up the coast, just after 1 o'clock. It seemed some time ago that the cries of the gulls had awakened me in the morning, but it was well worth getting the 'feel' of this Cornish town. The autumn colours and the cool air provided a different atmosphere to the generally warm and busy character of the last holiday in August in the area. Weather today was very good, with plenty of sun and clear views.

I proceeded along the North Cornwall cliff-paths, with steep descents and ascents, from time to time to sea level and up again. Walked via Porth, Whipsiderry, Watergate Bay, Griffin's and Beryl's Points and Mawgan Porth, where I had a snack and break.

After this, the paths became rougher and steeper, and the scenery even more spectacular – quite as good as the last holiday. I walked via Trenance Point, Trerathick Point and Carnewas, and passed Bedruthan Steps – a series of large high rocks, just off the coast. There are fine examples of herringbone walls in this area, too – like this:

This very rugged coast abounds with stories of shipwrecks, so a walker told me – more so, I gather, than a lot of the rest of the county. I could well imagine.

I continued via Park Head and Porth Mear to Porthcothan Bay, which I reached at 6.15 pm. It was a remote sandy bay with a very small village, but on a bus route – so after having soup and coffee at an inn, there I caught the 556 service – nearly an hour's ride – in darkness, through increasingly narrow lanes much of the time; it seemed very circuitous and all, as I like it, very Cornish. I alighted,close to the B & B at Newquay.

DAY 7
5/10/10

PORTHCOTHAN BAY – TREVOSE HEAD – TREVONE BAY – STEPPER POINT – PADSTOW – WADEBRIDGE
(22 miles approx)

*A*fter a very good breakfast, I took a bus along the coast road including, which is quite usual, a detour to Newquay Airport, and I alighted at Porthcothan Bay, so resumed the walk at about 11 am. It was quite windy and cloudy, but sunnier later on. I climbed the cliff path above the bay, getting good views of the Atlantic breakers rolling in. The walk wound above Fox, Warren and Pepper Coves, before descending to Treyarnon Bay, Constantine Bay and Booby's Bay – plenty of sand to see, and to cross. Climbing then resumed up to Trevose Head (with good view of lighthouse), after which there were downs and ups – Polventon Bay, Cataclews Point, Harlyn Bay and Newtrain Bay – and at Trevone Bay I stopped for a meal.

The next section featured some really steep gradients in very regular succession – past Round Hole and Gunver Head, and above Butter Hole and Pepper Hole – to a very good viewpoint at Stepper Point, above the River Camel Estuary, with very clear vistas up and across the river.

After this, I was walking on the south side of the Camel for the rest of the day. Initially, it was very wide and the sea was rough, and the tide was high. Gradients were now mainly downward, and the path became much flatter. The route ran via Hawker's Cove, Harbour Cove and Gun Point, into Padstow. Padstow is just the sort of place I like – 'olde-worlde', compact, narrow streets, busy quayside, a harbour full of boats, and plenty of old stone buildings. And also three scoops of wild-cherry ice cream. Which reminds me that I failed to mention – yesterday I had a vanilla, a strawberry with clotted cream, and a blackcurrant with clotted cream – ice creams, of course.

It was very fortunate that I reached Padstow tourist office just before it closed. I was therefore able to ascertain that the Camel Trail was five miles in length as far as Wadebridge, where a bus would leave at 8 pm, which connected at St Columb Major with another which went to Newquay. I would therefore just have time to walk on to Wadebridge.

So this I did. It really was a beautiful autumn evening, and the Camel Trail, which I followed, was the course of the old railway, which used to link with many other West Country lines and, ultimately, London Waterloo. I started at the old Padstow station and reached Wadebridge just as it was getting dark. It looked a fine town, but I will hope to tell you more tomorrow morning, when I should see it better.

The trail walk was so peaceful and tranquil, winding along beside the River Camel, with at least one impressive bridge over a creek. Sometimes in cuttings, sometimes on embankments, but always quite level, and the views across the tidal river to the other side of the valley were wonderful.

I was just in time for the 8 o'clock bus at Wadebridge, and the connection to Newquay. A long day, with a lot of walking today!

Day 8
6/10/10

Wadebridge — Rock — Polzeath
(12 miles approx)

*M*y very good breakfast eaten, I took a bus along the coast again but through to Padstow, where I changed to the Wadebridge service. Alighting there, I proceeded to my latest B&B to book in, a most delightful large old 17th Century house. High ceilings, large and high windows, sloping floors etc!

At 1 o'clock, I started out on today's walk, having 'wandered' through the charming old town – as lovely as Padstow, I think (though not a fishing port on the coast). I saw that at least part of the railway station is preserved.

The walk necessitated using roads and lanes on the north side of the Camel Estuary, and I looked across to last evening's walk on the south side. Proceeded via Bodieve, Trewornan, Gutt Bridge, Dinham and Trevelver. Here I made a small mistake. I tried to take a short-cut on a path linking two lanes, only because I felt like a change from lane-walking. But some signs had been removed, and when I realised it was useless to work out the route, I returned to the lane again, before risking losing much time.

This reminded me of a story a schoolteacher liked to tell us, years ago. She taught us maths very ably, but always warned us against not following laid-down procedures in detail. She illustrated her point thus: (As far as I remember.)

A relation used to take the family on country walks, but she did like to try and lead them on short-cuts. When they found themselves stuck on banks of muddy ditches, and tried to climb over fences, scratching themselves on barbed wire to get out, only to find a bull in the field, causing them to retreat and search for another route, they decided that they had ended up facing a much longer walk than was originally planned.

I can hear the final conclusion, as the teacher's voice resonated over the classroom ringing in my ears now – 'Never take short cuts in mathematics!'

So, back to theme of my walk, again. I passed Cant Farm, Porthilly Cove and then stopped at Rock, which is opposite Padstow, on the estuary. I had appropriate food and drink at a café. I then walked on the official path of the North Cornwall coast again, having completed my detour, and avoided the ferry crossing. The path took me along the shores and sands mostly, and around Bree Hill and past Daymer Bay to Trebetherick and along the cliffs to Polzeath. Very good clear views across the Camel, again in bright autumn sunshine.

I was just right for catching the last bus back to Wadebridge at 6.10 pm, and returned to the 17th Century B&B for the night.

A rather shorter walk today, after 22 miles yesterday!

Day 9
7/10/10

Polzeath – Pentire Point – Port Quin – Port Isaac – Port Gaverne
(10 miles approx)

The old house I'm staying in is very impressive – as is the breakfast. But I dragged myself away for a lovely early-morning walk to Wadebridge town and back, and later caught the bus to Polzeath, where I continued the walk from last evening, at about 10.15 am.

The fine weather lasted well again today, and I followed the coast path up the cliffs, past New Polzeath, and right up to Pentire Point, with clear views all around – the Camel Estuary and surrounding areas. I continued along and up and down, following the coastal cliff paths – Com Head, Carnweather Point (here I met two walkers who pointed out Hartland Point to me, now faintly visible up the distant coast – a famous summit above the North Devon shore), Trevan Point and Doyden Point – and then descended to Port Quin.

If I thought that section of the coast was rather tough, how can I describe the next? I should think from Port Quin to Port Isaac must be about the most spectacular, and testing part of the whole SW Coast Path. But then, I don't really know, do I? Anyway, this section, of about three or four miles was quite unforgettable. You climb and climb, with a precipitous drop to the sea on the left, and high hills and a fine fence on the right. I suppose it was quite nice to feel the fence was there to hold on to, or indeed to flee through! I thought it would have been very nice if it were on my left between me and the sheer drops! I seemed to cope all right though, thoroughly enjoying this most impressive scenery – the cliffs were very high right through to Port Isaac and the views quite amazing.

But there were countless twists and turns, the fence always there, the sheer drop often there, constant climbs and descents all the time, and much was steps – goodness knows how many at a time. You will understand why today's mileage was low – I made slow, but very happy progress. The relevant names are Kellan Head, Scarnor Point, Varley Head and Lobber Point.

There was eventually a very fine view down to Port Isaac itself, and when there I rewarded my efforts with ice creams (2), fancy cakes (2), and water and coffee, quite abundantly. I took a little time to explore this very quaint old fishing port and harbour – it is itself very hilly and very delightful.

I finally walked up the streets and paths and along the cliff-path, to the very nearby Port Gaverne, into which I descended at about 5 pm.

I caught the last bus back to Wadebridge again, and returned to the B&B.

Day 10
8/10/10

Port Gaverne – Tregardock Cliff – Trebarwith Strand – Tintagel
(12 miles approx)

I walked into Wadebridge town again and caught the bus to Port Garverne and started walking – still in the fine weather – at about 10.30.

The coast path on today's section was as attractive as ever – some parts similarly spectacular as yesterday's, but not much with very sheer cliffs very near the path. The ups and downs were still pretty frequent, beautiful, and on a significant scale (steepness and length involved).

Route was via Tresungers Point, Bounds Cliff, Rainie Point, Delabole Point, Dannonchapel, Tregardock Cliff, the Mountain (and it felt like it), Start Point and Backways Cove – to the summit, above Trebarwith Strand, which afforded quite a dramatic view of this little port and village – so picturesque. Down in this village I stopped for the usual kind of snack then climbed the corresponding height to the summit on the north side. The cliff-path continued on an easier scale to this morning, but the views were outstanding still, culminating (after Penhallic and Dunderhole Points and Glebe Cliff) with a fine view of Tintagel Head, or 'Island' and Castle on it.

The very wild, rugged coast here seems appropriate for the stories connected with King Arthur. (Tintagel is traditionally held to be his birthplace, and seat of power, and the seat of power of his Knights of the Round Table.)

So I enjoyed a walk around the village in mid-afternoon, followed by afternoon tea in a shop, and later caught a bus to Camelford, where I changed to the Wadebridge service, and back to the 17th century 'base'. Tintagel, I would also comment, would seem an appropriately memorable place to end this week of such pleasant walking.

Well – a summary of the return journey the following day: I took an early bus via Bodmin to Bodmin Parkway station, where I enjoyed refreshments in a café up in the old signal box. Also saw steam trains as well as regular services. My train took me right through to Westbury – via Plymouth, Exeter St David's, Taunton and Castle Cary. Further train to Cosham, and taxi home. It really has been a wonderful holiday again.

Perhaps just a humorous note to finish on. I am impressed, this week, by how rarely I have had to cross areas where cattle or horses graze. I admit that when I'm walking alone I feel a little wary, and keep by the fences if I feel the animals appear too interested in following me. Being away from the path, but able to jump over the fence if necessary, is perhaps a bit unconventional, and could land me in a lot of brambles, stinging-nettles, mud and water sometimes. But the peace of mind! (Much as I do like animals really.) But I'm getting away from the humorous note:

> A true story: A lady was out walking with her husband, and crossing a field. She asked him if one of the animals there was a bull. He assured her it was not. The animals were all cows. The lady felt so grateful that she approached the one in question, patted it on the nose, affectionately, and said – 'Hello, old chap!'

Day 11
22/11/10

TINTAGEL – ROCKY VALLEY – BOSCASTLE – BUCKATOR – CRACKINGTON HAVEN
(15 miles approx)

I will proceed with the usual introduction to a rather shorter holiday in the West Country this time, due to temporary pressure on my time. If it had been last week I think it would have been a holiday, not just in the west, but in the Wet Country, though. There had been quite severe flooding in parts of Cornwall (mainly in the south), including a landslip which blocked the main railway line for a while.

As I travelled by train yesterday, the countryside did look wetter, and the rivers fuller, the further west I got. I took trains as follows:

1. Cosham to Westbury
2. Westbury to Taunton
3. Taunton to Plymouth
4. Plymouth to Bodmin Parkway

The journeys and connections went well. The 'usual' joys of the coastal and Dartmoor views in Devon, and the inspiring Cornish scenery, were experienced. I took a taxi from Bodmin Parkway to Wadebridge, and another from Wadebridge to Camelford, where I had a B&B, in very good accommodation, again.

So now for today. I took a bus to Tintagel, where I resumed the walk from October, commencing at 9.45 am. Certainly the first thing that struck me was the sudden change from summer to winter in the place since last time. No holidaymakers, tourists, swimmers, surfers; a number of cafés etc closed; and a cold, dry and fairly sunny day today. But I think there is a beauty in every season, and the winter is an excellent time of the year for enjoying brisk, invigorating walking, often in clear, frosty or snowy conditions; berries to be seen, giving a Christmas touch, and plenty of other causes for exulting over the glorious heritage in the countryside.

I walked through Tintagel and down to the coast and castle again, then proceeded along Smith's Cliff, and above Bossiney Haven, and down into Rocky Valley. Here, especially, and also elsewhere, the beauty of the torrents and waterfalls (so full) was very impressive after the heavy rain of last week.

Continued along Trevalga Cliff and Forrabury Common, and then down to Boscastle harbour and quay. I followed along to this picturesque village, noting how it must have changed since the extremely severe floods of 2004. I saw where a bridge had been replaced, and the river course seems to have been widened. Some buildings, badly damaged, appear to have been removed or rebuilt.

In the Visitor Centre, I watched a video of the actual flooding and afterwards, as seen at the time on television in the news presentation. It was a truly alarming sight, including scenes of people being airlifted from upper floors of flooded buildings into rescue helicopters; and a considerable number of vans and cars being swept away in the flood waters into the sea – many were never recovered, and many were damaged almost beyond recognition. (I did not see it on TV at the time.)

I talked to a lady, an inhabitant, who witnessed the scenes at the time and was watching the video, and expressed my concern and sympathy. She said her house was not affected, but her daughter's was flooded. She felt they owed so much to a local coastguard who realised very quickly that they were on the verge of a major incident, and who immediately alerted the rescue services, and thus probably prevented any fatalities. It was really wonderful, miraculous, providential that no one died.

My walk continued via Penally Hill, Pentargon, Fire Beacon Point, Buckator, Rusey Cliff, High Cliff and Cam, to Crackington Haven, which I reached around 4.45 pm. This last section from Boscastle was quite tough-going, with extremely steep ascents and descents, and extremely scenic coastal views. I had coffee at the end of the walk, at a café, just before it closed, but I had to wait a while for my bus, which took me back, via Boscastle and Tintagel, to Camelford.

Another glorious day!

Day 12
23/11/10

CRACKINGTON HAVEN — DIZZARD POINT — WIDEMOUTH BAY — BUDE
(11 miles approx)

*A*fter a typically good breakfast to set me up, I proceeded to the bus stop again, and the bus transported me to a point near Crackington Haven, from whence I walked to the exact point I reached on the walk yesterday. Having also enjoyed soup and coffee at the café there, I set off on foot again at about 11.30.

The weather was sunny, but the air cold, the views clear, and the Atlantic Ocean looked remarkably calm. From the start, I could see Lundy Island and Hartland Point.

Again, the ups and downs were very steep, most particularly on the earlier part of the walk. I walked via Castle Point, Cleave, Chipman Point, and the one which seemed a really tough ascent from a low valley – Dizzard Point. A notice at the top interestingly recorded that it was 132 miles to Minehead, Somerset and 500 miles to Poole, Dorset. Then on via Cancleave, Millook, Penhalt Cliff and Wanson, to Widemouth Bay, where I was walking on the sands for the first time today – so far, cliff path walking has been pretty much the norm.

It was around this area that the gradients were becoming considerably easier – gradually. So I continued along 'easier' cliffs – to Phillip's Point, Upton, Efford Down and Compass Point, to Bude Haven, and I took the bridges over the canal and river into Bude itself. Had a good walk around the town – quite bustling and thriving, I felt – and quite sizeable. I visited some shops, and enjoyed tea and cakes in a café. Thus I concluded today's walking at about 5 pm.

I took a bus back from the Strand at 5.25. By which time it was quite dark, and it also came on to rain heavily – so I didn't see too much of the semi-coastal route back to Tintagel and Camelford. But I was fortunate in that the rain only persisted while I was in the bus. Dry weather resumed before I alighted and walked back to the B&B.

Bude, of course, is quite near the Devon border, indeed, the most northerly coastal town in Cornwall. So – another landmark reached on this rather short, but extremely enjoyable holiday.

Some notes on the return journey the next day: had taxi direct to Bodmin Parkway. Train journeys were as going to Cornwall except no change at Taunton. And it is lovely to reflect on having covered so much of the NORTH of Cornwall on the SOUTH WEST Coast Path. Note this can sound a rather confusing combination of the points of the compass.

But it does remind me of a true story. A man received a letter from a friend in New South Wales, Australia. So the friend used the initials in his address – NSW, Australia, on the letter. The recipient told his friends that he had a letter to read to them, from NORTH SOUTH WEST Australia!

And one other final comment on this mini-holiday of mine. Have you noticed what was missing? Ice creams. Sounds a rather serious state of affairs. You may therefore be sure that the weather had really been getting cold.

DAY 13
10/2/11

BUDE – COOMBE – MARSLAND VALLEY – MEAD CORNER
(12 miles approx)

*H*ere is the introduction to this holiday – the summary of the day before. It is, of course, a very lovely time of the year, with the prospect of spring just round the corner. A lot of snowdrops to be seen in the countryside, leading me to think of crocuses, daffodils, primroses, bluebells, ice creams. I am picking up a theme from the end of Day 12.

I travelled to Cornwall on 9th February, 2011, by car this time – it seemed a good idea while winter timetables were still in force for public transport services. I left around 9 am, and drove on the M27 to the New Forest, and then on bypasses around Bournemouth, Dorchester and Bridport, to the Axminster area, where I spent a very enjoyable afternoon with family connections, including a good lunch at the large, old, stone-built farmhouse into which they have recently moved – Victorian, and some of it older. It was very interesting being taken round it, seeing how they are restoring it, enjoying the views over the rural Devon landscape and walking round the attached old farm-buildings, garden and paddock. Talking, too, about family, friends, churches, farms etc.

About 4 pm, I resumed my car journey, taking the Honiton and Exeter bypass, and on to the north side of Dartmoor, and into Okehampton, and on to Hatherleigh, Holsworthy and Bude – a total day's journey of about 200 miles. Saw some fine countryside, although some areas were quite misty, and of course, darkness fell by about 6 pm.

And now for today. The guest house B&B accommodation is very good indeed. Filled with a good breakfast, I started walking around Bude, shopping, seeing a few areas of the town I didn't visit last time, and I happened to go into a store, and happened to see it had a café, and I happened to have coffee, toasted sandwiches and an ice cream sundae (vanilla, with caramel sauce, whipped cream and chocolate flake – in a very large glass). There is little doubt I am addicted to cafés. If they are in front of me, I seem to have to go in them.

I started the main part of the walk around 12 o'clock. It was a wet day – but then, if you never see wild, rugged Cornwall in the rain, or wind, or both, you have never really seen it in all its 'moods'. It did brighten up a little, later, though.

My route was mainly on the cliff tops – with all the usual steep ups and downs. I walked via Crooklets, Maer Down, Menachurch Point, Sandy Mouth, Warren Point and Duckpool. (Saw a lot of lambs, with sheep, on this section.)

I diverted inland at Duckpool, to see the very scenic little village of Coombe. It really is a Cornish gem – a picturesque mill house and a cluster of little cottages, a rippling stream and ford and woodland areas. I then continued on a slightly inland route, similarly attractive from time to time. I headed north past GCHQ Bude to Stanbury Cross and James's Cross and to the very pretty Marsland Valley. On crossing the river there, I crossed from Cornwall into Devon. I continued up the wooded slopes, to Mead Corner, which I reached at about 5 o'clock. At this point, I emerged from the trees, which make the Marsland Valley woodland so attractive.

I walked on after, to Welcombe Cross, in the gathering dusk, and caught a bus back to Bude to return to the B&B.

Day 14
11/2/11

Mead Corner – Embury Beacon – St Catherine's Tor – Hartland Quay
(8 miles approx*)

There are some days when a lot of extra walking is done to get from where the bus stops to the start of the walk; and from the end of the walk to where the bus picks up from – this was one such day!* (And I didn't want to leave my car parked anywhere lonely.) Indeed, I recall a story of a conversation, as follows:

Mr X: Can you tell me how to get to town A, from here?
Mr Y: Well, if I was going to town A, I wouldn't go from here at all!

But my 'extra' walking was very enjoyable too, even if it didn't directly contribute to progressing along the intended walk. 'Extra' walking is not recorded above.

Having had a look round Bude again, I took the 11.30 bus from the Strand. The 'look round' involved shopping, and a repeat performance of yesterday's visit to the café in the department store. The ice cream today was of more moderated proportions however, but only because I didn't want to miss the bus.

The bus took me to Welcombe Cross, and I repeated yesterday evening's walk, in the opposite direction to Mead Corner, where I really began The Walk at about 1 o'clock.

I proceeded into Mead itself, in a little rain, which soon became a lot of rain, but lessened very much, later. Continued past Strawberry Water, and then up a very steep path which joined the coast path near Chisel Ridge. There were very few walkers out today. Indeed I only met, I think, two people to speak to, just before the 'ascent'. These were two ladies, locals, and they showed a great interest in my walk; one of them said, with heartfelt enthusiasm, that I would find it most enjoyable up at Hartland Quay, today — it will look so bleak! They gave me very helpful information about the route, and the amount of time to allow.

Now back to the route — mainly on the cliff tops. I continued via Knap Head, Embury Beacon, South Hole (Nabor Point), Sandhole Cliff, Mansley Cliff, Milford Common and Swansford Hill. The path then followed a scenic inland 'Valley Route' to Speke Mill, and a cliff top route over St Catherine's Tor to Hartland Quay. One feature of part of the cliff-walking today, in the rain and mist, was that from the height of these North Devon cliffs, I heard the roar of the waves below but, in this weather, when looking down, have been unable to see the sea.

Also, the impressions I have so far gained are that while the North Cornwall cliffs look very rugged, there is a grandeur about the North Devon cliffs which is also quite distinctive and appealing.

As the lady said, Hartland Quay did look very bleak, but I like to see these places in all seasons and all weathers, and I appreciated the bleakness, the rain, mist and wind, and the absence of crowds of tourists.

I had coffee and crisps in the warm, welcoming pub, which I arrived at around 4.15 pm, having completed another section of coast. I then continued on my 'additional walk' to get the 6.10 pm bus back from Hartland village — and certainly a very pleasant walk on a hilly, winding Devon lane.

The bus duly returned me to Bude, and I walked back to the very good B&B guest house again. What would the weather be like tomorrow?

DAY 15
12/2/11

HARTLAND QUAY — HARTLAND POINT — W. & E. TITCHBERRY — WINDBURY HEAD — CLOVELLY
(13 miles approx)

After another very good breakfast, I went round the Bude shops, emptying a shelf in one of them of its 18 lemon slice cakes with lemon icing, plus I added to this three chocolate caramel slices.

I drove the car up to Hartland village, where I found suitable parking. Then walked through to Hartland Quay which looked totally different today. Clear sunshine and only a few clouds in the sky – indeed, it stayed fine all day – windy, with quite impressive waves crashing on the beaches. Yes, very different weather to yesterday – and there were more walkers around.

I started out on the coast walk, again, around 12.45, from the Quay. The section from here to Hartland Point was, unquestionably, very tough going, and very scenic, especially in this good weather. But various people had already warned me. It was almost continuously alternate - very steep ascents and very steep descents. Probably it was one of the hardest, and most spectacular sections of the SW Coast Path. So my progress was slow.

Lundy Island could now be clearly seen. From the Quay to the Point, the main locations passed were Warren Cliff, Blackpool Mill and Blegberry, Upright and Blagdon Cliffs. The views of Hartland Point lighthouse were good. Red Devon clay was now in evidence, very noticeable when I passed molehills.

After Hartland Point, the route was quite different. Progress really seemed fast. Through the following areas, it was just easy cliff-top walking – almost flat, a lot of it: North Cliff, W & E Titchberry Cliffs, Gawlish, Fatacott, Exmansworthy and Beckland Cliffs and Windbury Head. At one point though, I descended into and ascended from a remarkably scenic area of wooded valley – but not very steep. The path crossed a gurgling stream and I felt surrounded with green foliage of most beautiful delicate shades. Ferns etc. I should have concentrated on identifying what they all were. Perhaps I was preoccupied with thinking of how beautiful too, the lemon-icing sliced cakes, and chocolate caramel slices must be looking in my rucksack.

Windbury Head is a small hill, the site of an ancient hill fort, now with Dartmoor ponies grazing on it. But after this hill, and again at Mouth Mill, the path descended into exceptionally deep valleys, almost to, or onto the beach - the views were tremendous, the valleys well wooded with high trees.

The 'easy' gradients resumed again after this, all the way to the top of Clovelly. I walked through some more woods – quite extensive. These were Snaxland Wood, Gallantry Bower and Rushbush Copse.

I had wondered if I would arrive at Clovelly in the sun or the rain. In fact I reached it in the semi-dark – a fine evening (6 o'clock) and a real atmosphere to this 'Gem of North Devon', with the lights coming on in this quiet, peaceful but outstandingly quaint and beautiful village. I walked down its very steep cobbled streets and steps, marvelling at the 'olde-worlde' architecture, where no traffic was permitted. I don't think I've ever seen anything anywhere quite like Clovelly. It was so unspoilt, and I would say, unique. I reached the quay and beach, phoned for a taxi to pick me up from the 'top', and climbed back up again.

The taxi took me back to Hartland, and I drove my car from there, back to Bude. A particularly enjoyable day!

I think I should also mention the noticeable kindness of the proprietors of my B&B. They phoned around that morning and obtained a whole list of taxi numbers for me, and even said I could phone them for help, if necessary. It really was a very good guest house.

Day 16
13/2/11

Clovelly — Buck's Mills — Peppercombe — Green Cliff — Westward Ho!
(14 miles approx)

I started out a little later today, having had due rest, good food and a careful study of maps. It is always confusing when you have two maps for the next sections of the walk, one being 2½ inches to the mile, and the other 1¼ inches to the mile!

I am reminded, on the subject of the scale of maps, of this true story of a lady who enjoyed going on motoring trips very much, but sometimes felt a little apprehensive about the distances involved. She would then ask if she could have a look at a map of the area — 'one of the ones that makes everywhere look nice and near!'

I drove to Clovelly, found suitable parking, and commenced walking at about 11.45 am. I couldn't resist one more walk down the cobbled streets to the quay and beach, and back up to the top again. Talking to one of the locals, I learned that the coast of South Wales can only be seen on a very clear day — certainly not today. It had rained quite a lot overnight, and today was cloudy, but mainly dry, throughout. The coast around Croyde, between Barnstaple and Ilfracombe, 'up' the Devon coast, could be clearly seen, however. Lundy Island was still quite clear too.

My route now took me high along the tops of the cliffs for a good while. Snowdrops, catkins and gorse were thriving during this holiday. Most definitely a foretaste of spring.

The first part of the walk wound, like a forest drive, up in the woodland. This was, in fact, called 'the Hobby Drive'. Further on, there were some really magically scenic sections — after the rain, everywhere was looking very lush and green. The narrow path wound through more woods, where ferns, ivy and moss abounded.

Further on still there were the usual very steep ups and downs, sometimes with very little level walking at all, and sometimes the path came right down to, or nearly to, the rocky shore.

The order of the points or places after the Hobby Drive, was as follows: Barton Wood, Buck's Mills, Worthygate and Sloo Woods, Peppercombe, Rowden, Babbacombe, Westacott and Cockington Cliffs, Green Cliff, Abbotsham and Cornborough Cliffs and, I think Kipling Cliff – I was rather excited when I saw the sign as I thought it might have been Kipling cakes.

After many ups and downs, the final coastal section was quite level, and apparently the course of a disused railway.

I thus reached Westward Ho! at about 6 pm, and as with Clovelly yesterday, in semi-darkness. It can be a little eerie in wooded sections in such conditions, and I wondered if I should call it, at such times, not the Coast Path, but the Ghost Path. It will, I expect, be easier to describe Westward Ho! in tomorrow's daylight. I saw lights, buildings and sea tonight. I returned by taxi to Clovelly, and thence drove my car to Bude. A very interesting day.

Day 17
14/2/11

Westward Ho! – Northam – Appledore – Bideford – Instow – Fremington – Barnstaple
(15 miles approx)

*A*fter today's very good breakfast, I went round the Bude shops, and then headed off in the car for Westward Ho! With fine, clear, sunny weather today, I was able to see what I couldn't of it yesterday when it was too dark. Fine sands and rocks, Atlantic breakers rolling in impressively, and the usual hotels, shops and dwellings. There were hills behind, and a golf links adjacent. Sunshine, a good wind blowing, and chill in the air, gave a nice feel to the place.

I started the walk around 12.15. Views of lambs, and views of daffodils, from time to time, made it feel like early spring. The route started off in streets and lanes, via Northam, Watertown and Appledore, which is particularly attractive. I explored the quay, and climbed the hill on which part of it is built, gaining fine views of Westward Ho! and across the river estuaries to the Croyde area, northwards. The Rivers Torridge and Taw 'join' at the estuary, to flow into the sea. The views across to Instow were very good too.

I followed the coastal path beside the River Torridge, via Burrough and Cleave Farms, into the fine old town of Bideford, with its excellent many-arched, old stone bridge over the Torridge. Just before crossing it, I heard someone call me; it was the taxi man who had taken me back to Clovelly last night. He was walking his dog. He gave me some useful information about my route while we were talking.

So I crossed the bridge to East-the-Water, the other side of the river. The path took me to the old Bideford railway station there, which had been nicely restored, and there was some old stock on the tracks. I was now on the Tarka Trail (memories of book about the otter), which is the old railway course, now used by walkers and cyclists, and I walked this all the way to Barnstaple (9 miles). It goes further too. So, on the level for all this distance, I made much faster progress – I almost felt like the Atlantic Coast Express!

It was a truly delightful walk, initially running beside the River Torridge, (opposite the side I had just walked up). It then followed close to the River Taw, to Barnstaple. There were restored stations at Instow and Fremington, a tunnel and a bridge over a creek. At Barnstaple, it was difficult to see in semi-darkness, where I was routed onto another path or where the railway used to go. I soon found myself in the town's streets and the town centre. This was the third night running (but I am a walker) when I have reached my destination after lighting-up time. The lights of Barnstaple could be seen from some distance back, very attractive the sight, and reflected in the river. My arrival time – 6.30 pm.

I made my way to the bus station, caught the service via Bideford back to Westward Ho! and drove back to Bude.

Today's route was interesting and different – partly urban, and a mixture of streets, lanes, paths and old railway.

I am reminded, again, of another of my true stories about a 'certain lady'. The conversation went like this:

Walker: I'm hoping to go on a walk today.
Lady: I hope it's not a lonely walk.
Walker: On no. I shall hope to follow some well-used roads.
Lady: I hope they're not busy, dangerous roads!

So – just the usual notes on my return journey the following day. I drove back to Barnstaple in the morning to visit the tourist information centre, as I had been too late yesterday. I also wrote and posted most of my postcards while in the town – but of course got home before them.

Then drove back home, without leaving time to have ice creams – what are things coming to? But I had a good journey – I seemed to bypass everywhere though. The general route was: the areas of N & S Molton and Tiverton, the M5 and Exeter, Honiton and Axminster bypasses – and along the coast, as on 9th February, 2011 – Dorchester, M27 etc. I reached home about 6.30 pm.

Quite a lot of rain fell today but driving conditions were pretty good.

Once again, a very happy and memorable holiday. Cornwall completed, and Devon started.

DAY 18
27/3/11

BARNSTAPLE — CHIVENOR — WRAFTON — BRAUNTON — SAUNTON — CROYDE BAY
(12 miles approx)

*H*ere begins another rather short holiday — rather a lot to do at home with gardening etc. Firstly, the usual introduction.

On 26th March, 2011, I took a taxi to Cosham, followed by an interesting selection of train journeys. The first was from Cosham to Eastleigh, the next was via Winchester to Basingstoke and then another train, calling at Andover, Salisbury, Tisbury, Gillingham, Templecombe, Sherborne, Yeovil Junction, Crewkerne, Axminster, Honiton, Pinhoe, Exeter Central and Exeter St David's. And my last train on the Tarka branch line took me on, calling at Crediton, Yeoford, Copplestone, Morchard Road, Eggesford, Umberleigh and Barnstaple. This Tarka Line was exceptionally delightful, crossing through the heart of Devon, from south to north. Very scenic river valley routes, and a real atmosphere of an old-fashioned branch line, the train calling at picturesque old stone stations.

This 'friendly' train was of few coaches, diesel-powered, and packed with local people talking quite non-stop. Also, the three-hour journey from Basingstoke to Exeter was most pleasantly memorable — glorious countryside views throughout. Spring really seems to have begun, daffodils and primroses are appearing, and the weather is sunny, warm and calm.

I took a walk round Barnstaple and a bus to a farm near Fremington (not far to go), where I settled in for B&B for the night.

So today — 27th March — after good rest and food at this lovely quiet, picturesque working farm, I took the bus into Barnstaple, and after seeing a little more of the town, I picked up the Tarka Trail again, from the last holiday, and commenced walking about 11 am on it.

The weather was extremely lovely again — a little misty, but warmer, still and dry, and as calm as yesterday. I continued the walkers' and cyclists' route on this old railway trail, past the partly preserved old Barnstaple Town station — the station I alighted at yesterday was the old Barnstaple Junction station. The route today continued beside the River Taw, on the opposite side to the last part of the walk on 14th February, 2011. A very lovely and level walk, it was about six miles in length. It turned inland from the tidal river for the last section, past Chivenor and Wrafton, before entering Braunton, which is apparently the largest village in England, but I got the impression of a busy, old-fashioned little town.

I had a real midday treat in Braunton — a delightful ice cream with the title 'Exotic Explosion'. (Orange and vanilla.) I continued my walk by the direct road route to the village of Saunton. I feel tempted to compose a limerick now:

A fine large village is Braunton,
And there's very fine sands at Saunton,
But after my roam,
And I'm on my way home,
Will it be quite so nice, passing Taunton?

I will add an old-fashioned footnote, of the sort they used to write years ago, after a cartoon joke, to ensure no ill-feeling was meant:

The writer of this limerick hastens to add that Taunton is nevertheless an exceptionally fine town with extremely good amenities, and particularly good railway connections to London and most parts of Britain.

Now, back to the walk! At this point, there were good views of the extensive and very high coastal sand dunes, called Braunton Burrows. I walked down to Saunton beach, enjoying good views of the extensive sands; also enjoyed soup, cakes and more ice creams at a café.

The coastal path was now getting very hilly and steep, as Saunton Down, partly cliff, was reached – excellent views down to the sea. I continued down to Croyde Bay, and walked along the sands there.

I completed the walk at about 5 pm, phoned for a taxi, whereby I was transported back to Braunton, and I enjoyed a cup of coffee at an hotel there. I caught a bus back to Barnstaple and another back to my B&B. A wonderful day again.

Day 19
28/3/11

CROYDE BAY – BAGGY POINT – WOOLACOMBE –
MORTE POINT – LEE BAY – ILFRACOMBE
(15 miles approx)

After eating a good breakfast, I took a bus into Barnstaple again and changed to another which took me on via Braunton, to Croyde Bay. The driver was most obliging, and, as he knew I wanted to buy a morning paper, suggested to me (without me asking), at the stop in Croyde village, that he wait on at the bus stop while I go to a newsagents in the next street – which I did, by following his directions. He explained to the one other passenger what was happening – both were quite happy to wait!

On reaching Croyde Bay at 11 am, I started today's walk – the weather was just as lovely as yesterday – with the same mistiness. I proceeded over

Middleborough Hill, to Baggy Point and Whiting Hole, Putsborough Sands and Vention and then to Woolacombe, partly on the cliffs, partly in the sand dunes, and partly on the sands – very fine sands on this stretch of coast.

Woolacombe was a very pleasant hillside resort; I enjoyed the scenic blend of colours – of brown, pink and white – in my three-scoop ice cream (chocolate, strawberry ad vanilla) at a café.

I walked on, along the cliffs, above Barricane Beach to Morte Point, Rockham Bay and Bull Point; there is a lighthouse there, but happily, not a bull. On this section of coast, one should be able to see the coast of Wales in the distance, but the mist prevented this today. I met, in this area, if I might put it this way, a dog taking a lady for a walk. This was certainly the impression I got. The very lively little animal appeared to be providing plenty of power to tow its owner along on its lead, and she happily followed. I had opportunity to ask her about views across to South Wales, and she confirmed what I have stated.

There was quite a lot of steep descending /ascending of the cliffs, again, on this piece of coast, particularly down into Lee Bay, and up again, after. I walked on to Flat Point, and Torrs Park, another very high point, from which I descended by Torrs Walk, a remarkable series of zigzags – I should think at least 10, the path being built into the cliff, with fine views down to the sea, and gorse, heather and daffodils growing. Thus I descended to Ilfracombe – I gained good views of the town, and got a good impression of the resort with its seafront areas, gardens and hotels. I reached the bus station around 6 o'clock; a bus was just due to leave for Barnstaple, so I duly boarded and was taken via Mullacott Cross and Braunton, thence – where I changed to a local bus for my B&B.

Once again, a very much-enjoyed day.

And just the comments on the return home, the next day. I spent the morning in Barnstaple, as my train did not leave till midday. Without going into too much detail, I visited various buildings, enjoyed various foods, and, particularly ice cream, of various flavours.

The weather was rather cloudier. The train ride from Barnstaple to Exeter was a repeat of 26th March in the opposite direction, but included an additional stop at Kings Nympton. I then took a fast train from Exeter St David's, calling only at Taunton and Castle Cary, before I alighted at Westbury. Then I took a train to Cosham and taxi home.

Yes – another very pleasant mini break. Now back to the garden!

DAY 20
18/4/11

ILFRACOMBE – HELE – WATERMOUTH – COMBE MARTIN –
GREAT HANGMAN CAIRN – HOLDSTONE DOWN
(12 miles approx)

*N*ow for another mini break, following quickly after the last one.
Firstly, yesterday: according to the usual custom, taxi to Cosham. Then three rail journeys: firstly Cosham to Salisbury; secondly, on to Exeter St David's, as on 27th March from Salisbury onwards, but the train called at Feniton and Whimple, and not Pinhoe; and thirdly, the delightful cross-Devon branch line on to Barnstaple, as described last time. But this time the train stopped at Crediton, Eggesford, Kings Nympton, Portsmouth Arms and Umberleigh.

I got a good bus connection at Barnstaple to Ilfracombe (via Braunton), and made my way to a very nice B&B guest house, high up in the town. I then popped out for another walk around the town, and was as impressed as on 28th March. A lighter and warmer evening though. But the weather was as misty as last time – the sea mist prevented views of Wales still, but there was a lovely calm atmosphere – weather dry and sunny. The latest attraction, of floral character, was bluebells. So far I have seen plenty in bloom – the countryside looks in the prime of spring.

And now for today. I enjoyed a very good breakfast at this guest house/hotel. Then I walked down the very steep hill into Ilfracombe High Street, shopped and continued to the seafront, and areas adjacent, to make sure I had really 'done' the town. And before starting the walk proper, at about 10.15 am, I visited the Tunnels. There were three I was able to walk through. They were built in, I think, Victorian times, to enable the new novel idea of sea-bathing to be enjoyed with adequate privacy, and, initially there were separate beaches (isolated coves), for males and females. The tunnels enabled bathers to walk beneath the cliffs, from the town to the 'private' beaches. In about 1850, the railway was built from London to Bristol and crowds of holidaymakers travelled there and were then ferried in large boats down the Bristol Channel to the popular, emerging holiday resort of Ilfracombe.

Today's walk took me via Capstone Point, part of the harbour area again, Hillsborough Fort (a steep climb here, to these Iron Age earthworks) and Beacon Point. Here I met a guy (walking his dogs) who gave me useful information about my route. His local knowledge was good on tides, good viewpoints, amounts of time to allow on sections of the coast path etc. There were some high spring tides, so it was useful to know when and where to be careful when walking at sea level. Because of the constriction of the Bristol Channel, there is a very high tide range between peak and low, and the Severn Bore, the mini-tidal wave, is significant but only noticeable in the River Severn. As he said, there is always a Severn Bore at all high tides, but not very conspicuous at 'lower' highs – and always created by the geographical constrictions.

I continued via Hele Village and Bay, Samson's Bay, Widmouth Head, Watermouth (good views of Watermouth Castle), Napps, Golden Cove and Sandy Bay, to Combe Martin. I stopped for – should I really mention the word yet again? They were in double cones, one coconut flavour, and one clotted cream with vanilla flavour. And when consumed, I immediately indulged in a repeat performance on the same scale exactly.

Thus adequately refreshed, I left the delightful coastal village by another steep climb – at this point, a notice informed me I had entered Exmoor National Park and in due course, the character of the scenery developed more to heather-covered, high cliff-top moorland. Please excuse the two mo(o)r(e)s. I walked on cliffs, very high summits and very steep ascents and descents again – via Lester Cliff, Little Hangman, Great Hangman Cairn (complete with a fine high stone cairn) and Holdstone Down.

The walk was thus completed at about 5 pm, and I took a taxi back to Combe Martin, and bus to Ilfracombe. The weather has been really wonderful – just like yesterday, but due to the sea mist, still no views of the coast of Wales.

I did another walkabout in Ilfracombe, had soup and cheesecake in the garden of a seafront café, and returned to my guest house.

Day 21
19/4/11

Holdstone Down – Heddon Valley – Woody Bay – Lee Bay – The Valley of Rocks – Lynton & Lynmouth
(12 miles approx)

Breakfast duly enjoyed, I reflected on the day's plans. I thought two things seemed pretty sure, like fixed points in a changing scene: i) that I wouldn't see the coast of Wales, and ii) that I would eat ice creams, considerably in the plural. I was right, on both.

The sea mists that were limiting views across the Bristol Channel were however providing a lovely weather atmosphere still – as already described. No rain, no wind. Calm, sunny.

So – I took the 9.40 am bus from Ilfracombe to Combe Martin, and the same taxi driver as yesterday, drove me back to Holdstone Down. I started walking around 11 o'clock – via North Cleave, High Cliff and East Cleave and reached a fine viewpoint above the Heddon Valley, seeing Hunter's Inn (a well-liked landmark) and district, a long way below. I followed the steep descent to the valley, and steep ascent up, after to the cliff-top path, and on to Great Burland Rocks and West Woodybay Wood – to Woody Bay itself – a very steep winding lane took me down through the very scenic green woods, to the remote sandy and rocky shore, a magical spot below the huge cliffs down which a fine waterfall ran.

I returned to the cliff top and rejoined the coast path, following all this fine Exmoor/cliff-edge scenery. I walked via Crosscombe Wood, Crock Point, Lee Bay (with good views of Lee Abbey), and into the Valley of Rocks – this was a spectacular sight. Enormous rocks, and enormous sections of high hills of rock and huge cliff-like rock structures overlooked this inland valley. But the coast path directed me back from these sights afterwards, following high above the shore, and this area of lofty rock cliffs was also impressive. And so I reached Lynton and Lynmouth.

Along this section I met two very friendly tourists – a chap from Colorado, and another from Quebec. They were most enthusiastic about the Valley of Rocks, and wanted to accompany me for nearly all the rest of the walk, to hear all about Britain and its walks. I had my photo taken with them, and found them very entertaining company. They were with a coach party.

I explored Lynton – a quaint old town at the top of a high hill, and took a cliff path close to the Lynton and Lynmouth Cliff Railway – it ran on a very steep gradient, linking the two towns – it was a cliff lift and has survived for many years.

I also explored Lynmouth, at the foot of the hills and at the mouth of the River Lyn. It had a very rocky beach, and was also a quaint old town. But of course it was famous for having been struck by most powerful flood waters in 1952. I went round a kind of museum there, exhibiting many photos of the severe damage to the town. Sadly, between 30 and 40 people drowned that night. Buildings and vehicles were swept away by the raging River Lyn, swollen dramatically by exceptionally intense rain from Exmoor. Prince Philip visited the town soon after.

I completed my walk about 4.45 pm, then took a bus to Blackmoor Gate, another to Barnstaple and another to Ilfracombe. I had soup and cheesecake again, at the same café as yesterday. And, oh yes, without going into details – ice creams: two eaten at Lynton, two at Lynmouth, two at Barnstaple and one at Ilfracombe – as far as I remember. (There could have been more.)

So I returned to the guest house in the twilight, after another wonderful day. And my return journey, 20th April: I noticed an amusing card on a table, while enjoying breakfast, before I left: 'If you would like to have breakfast in bed, you must sleep in the kitchen'.

I took a bus to Barnstaple, train (calling at Umberleigh, Eggesford, Copplestone, Yeoford, Crediton and Exeter St David's), a further train calling at more or less the same stops as on 17th, to Salisbury – and the third train, to Cosham for taxi ride, thence to home – with very pleasant holiday memories.

LYNTON & LYNMOUTH — COUNTISBURY — THE FORELAND —
GLENTHORNE PLANTATIONS — COUNTY GATE
(8 miles approx)

So now for the next mini break — another short holiday, due to many and varied commitments. Firstly though, 21st May.

I took the car this time, as there was a family wedding to attend first, in East Devon. I left around 10.45, and drove on M27 to Bournemouth, Dorchester and Bridport bypasses, reaching the Axminster area around 1.30 pm. It was a fantastic day, with a very good service at the village church. Plenty of music too — I think my favourite was 'Crown Him with many crowns'. We proceeded to the delightful rural farmhouse, as described on 10th February, for the reception. Thus from the picturesque old church to the picturesque old farmhouse, gardens and grounds. We enjoyed drinks, afternoon tea, a hog-roast, speeches etc, in the marquee. The weather was fine and I met plenty of family connections and other friends. I had to leave a little early though, and even so, only just reached the guest house at Lynton by about 11 pm. I used the M5 from Exeter to Tiverton, and then the North and South Molton areas — rather wet and dark at the end of the journey.

Today - first a good rest, an appetising breakfast, and a later start. I treated myself to a ride on the spectacular Lynton and Lynmouth Cliff Railway — down and back up — as referred to, see 19th April, 2011.

My walk from Lynton and Lynmouth, both of which towns I explored again, began around 12.30pm. The weather was sunny, but wind very strong at times. I still haven't been able to see the coast of Wales!

My coast path route took me up the very high cliffs, past Point Perilous (get past this one quick, I thought), to Countisbury, Butter Hill, The Foreland, Kipscombe Enclosure and Chubhill Wood. Then I came to three rather interesting names — Sir Robert's Chair (apparently a small rock headland), Desolation Point, and Desolate. My crazy sense of humour — I wondered, did Sir Robert buy himself such an expensive chair and other luxuries, that the poor who lived on his estate financially reached the point of desolation (Desolation Point), and indeed eventually became Desolate?

I continued on a more sensible note through Wingate Combe to Glenthorne Plantations. In this area there are masses of rhododendron bushes in bloom — a magnificent sight — and scenic conifers and deciduous woodlands.

After this, I took a path inland to the main road at County Gate, for a bus back. County Gate, interestingly, was the Devon/Somerset county border — hence the name. So I entered (just) Somerset today. Cornwall and Devon are now completed.

I felt justified in celebrating at the County Gate café, with blackcurrant-crumble ice cream (two scoops) and iced raspberry and elderflower cake with clotted cream (one very large slice)!

Having completed the walk at 4.15 pm, I rode in the bus back to Lynmouth and walked the steep climbs up to Lynton for B&B.

Yes, a wonderful couple of days, again!

Day 23
23/5/11
COUNTY GATE — CULBONE — PORLOCK WEIR — PORLOCK BEACH — PORLOCK
(10 miles approx)

*B*ed and breakfast having been much appreciated, I drove from Lynton and Lynmouth to County Gate, and commenced walking about 10.30 am.

The weather was extremely windy today but in sheltered areas it was amazingly calm and quiet. Sunny most of the day, but rain in the afternoon – a day of contrasts.

The other item of note was that today, I really felt sure I saw the coast of Wales! At several points between Lynmouth and Culbone the land was very faint, but the clear weather at these parts of the day just made viewing possible. There seemed to be very distant buildings and chimneys but appearing very small. 'Success' at last!

I took a path from County Gate back to the coast path where I had left it yesterday. Between here and Culbone there were constant minor diversions from the original paths due to landslides, quite a lot recently, and the risk of more. The extensive woodlands continued nearly all the way to Porlock Weir, and were very green despite much dry weather recently. Foxgloves were appearing too. The route generally followed along the tops of very high cliffs.

I walked through Yenworthy, Embelle and Culbone Woods, reaching the tiny hamlet of Culbone, and its tiny church. It is thought that parts of this building are of Saxon origin, and it looked very picturesque. Then I continued through Yearnor Wood and descended (at one point, through an old stone tunnel) on steep gradients to sea level and open flat country – very different to the enormous cliffs of the Exmoor coast. But there were still plenty of high hills around.

I proceeded via Worthy, Porlock Weir (with its quaint quayside buildings), and along Porlock Beach (very stony), and then inland over the marshes, and into Porlock itself – a fine old village. I concluded the walk at a very good teashop, around 2.30 pm, in the rain, but found great solace in soup, and a clotted cream tea, and of course, ice cream.

Caught the bus back to County Gate, via the very long steep Porlock Hill (up it)! Then I transferred to my car and drove back to Lynton and Lynmouth – I also drove out to Watersmeet in the evening and enjoyed extra walking there – it was exceptionally beautiful and I could not resist a visit. Rocks, rivers meeting, impressive waterfalls and enormously high well-wooded cliffs. Then returned to B&B, well pleased.

Perhaps I could conclude, as the subject seems to have preoccupied me very much, with a summary of expectations of seeing the Welsh coast:

AREA	COMMENTS	OUTCOME
Hartland Point	Informed it is possible to see it	No view
Clovelly	Informed quite often seen clearly	No view
Morte Point	Informed I should be able to see it	No view
Ilfracombe	Informed it was visible this morning	No view
Ilfracombe again	'We saw the lights of Wales last night'	No view
Combe Martin	'It should be visible'	No view
Lynton/Lynmouth	'You can usually see it'	No view
Lynton/Lynmouth	'You can usually see it'	Saw Wales

So, I am also tempted to quote a true incident, in a different context, about the 'certain lady' I write about in this book. It was just that she had visited her opticians, but the one who usually checked her eyes was not available then. Later, when she visited again, and he was able to do a vision check, she told him: 'Last time I came here, I couldn't see you!'

Day 24
24/5/11

PORLOCK – BOSSINGTON BEACH, VILLAGE AND HILL – SELWORTHY BEACON – MINEHEAD
(13 miles approx)

Note: 319 miles since leaving Land's End on SW Coast Path

After enjoying good accommodation and refreshments again, I drove from Lynton and Lynmouth to Porlock Hill (a very steep descent, partly 1:4) and to Porlock.

Then started today's walk about 10.45 am and enjoyed fine, breezy, sunny weather all day. I proceeded beside Bossington Beach – here and all through the day, the views of the Welsh coast were really clear (between Porthcawl and

Barry). Continued through the very pretty village of Bossington and climbed via Hurlstone Combe to the top of Bossington Hill. Then on via Selworthy Beacon and on a long stretch of high, open and quite level moorland, a little inland from the coast, until the edge of Minehead. I entered a very well wooded area, very scenic, before getting views of the town. Descended zigzag paths, very steep, on wooded cliffs, and thus reached Minehead harbour.

This really was a landmark – it was the northern end of the 630 miles South West Coast Path from Poole, via Land's End, of which I have now walked approximately half – from Land's End. I now have to search for another path to follow!

However, for the moment, I decided to see all I could of Minehead, so I continued in the same direction – perhaps I should refer to the walk now as an 'eastward' - and later, as a 'northward walk'. So I 'did' the Strand (beach and sands), the town centre – all attractive – and, particularly interesting to me, the railway station: this was the terminus of the independently run West Somerset Railway – which operated with steam trains – one of which I saw arrive. Very delightfully nostalgic! The line is a very good length, from just outside Taunton. (So I concluded the walk about 3.15 pm)

The bus stop for my return journey was most ideally situated very close to, and between, the points where I saw steam trains enter the station, and the ice cream shop! I didn't mind waiting half an hour for the bus. I think I need to say no more.

I accordingly returned by bus to Porlock and drove my car back up the very long, steep Porlock Hill, and back to Lynton and Lynmouth. I did some shopping and enjoyed fish-cakes, cup of tea, blackcurrant-and-cream ice cream and apple juice at a local fish and chip shop.

Again, returned to B&B, well pleased.

DAY 25
25/5/11

MINEHEAD – DUNSTER BEACH – BLUE ANCHOR – WATCHET
(8 miles approx)

Although this was the day to return home, I realised I should be able to include some more walking first, as my drive back to Hampshire was not now such a great distance as on earlier sections.

I left the B&B, well refreshed, driving via Porlock Hill and village to Minehead, whence I resumed the walk at about 10.45 am and enjoyed good clear weather and views – it was sunny and dry.

My route took me on a new coast path here on, the West Somerset Coast

Path to start with, quite flat, and I followed past Butlins and alongside the golf course, via The Warren, to Dunster Beach – and good views of parts of the village, particularly the beautiful old Dunster Castle, were to be enjoyed. The West Somerset Railway curved toward the coast soon after at Blue Anchor, where I paused to see the well-preserved old station, and watched a diesel (three-coach) rail bus pass a steam-hauled six-coach train.

The path followed close to the sands and beaches all the time, but now rose on the cliffs – I walked on via Cridland's Copse and Fox Covert, to Watchet, where the railway rejoined the coast again, and I saw the station and another train, a rail bus again. The cliff gradients were much less steep now, and there were pleasant woods on this section.

I descended into Watchet, a really charming little town, quite unpretentious though – an old-fashioned fishing port, and the harbour was particularly quaint. Time of arrival about 2 pm.

It had been very pleasant on today's walk, hearing the chugging and whistling of steam trains in the distance. Also, it had been particularly interesting to see yet more of the South Wales coast. Even clearer views today. The shape of the Bristol Channel was now much more in evidence – with hills, and possibly mountains, visible on the Welsh side, and flat land, and lower cliffs on the English side – I was probably looking at the areas of Burnham-on-Sea and Weston-super-Mare – also, the Quantock Hills were very clear, and extremely near now.

I caught a bus back to Minehead, and then drove home, taking a cross-country route via Taunton, Ilminster, Crewkerne and Dorchester and back to the M27 etc. I really should mention that I had a very good tea at Maiden Newton en route – including a fruit-crumble and the obvious.

Again, a very lovely holiday, and if people ask me how far I have got now, and I say I've got to Watchet, that will sound the same as 'I've got to watch it' – and perhaps some confusion?

Day 26
4/6/11

WATCHET – WEST QUANTOXHEAD – BICKNOLLER COMBE – CROWCOMBE GATES – TRISCOMBE COMBE – PLAINSFIELD – SPAXTON – BRIDGWATER
(18 miles approx)

It now seemed to be workable – and hopefully, for the foreseeable future, to continue the 'eastward', then 'southward' and later 'northward' walk on a day trip basis, rather than staying away overnight. The route is so much nearer to home, at present.

After rising very early, and driving to Cosham station, I caught the first train of the day (6.19 am), to Bristol Temple Meads (via Southampton Central, Salisbury, Warminster, Dilton Marsh, Westbury, Bradford-on-Avon, Bath Spa – and other stops), where I had the added pleasure of seeing a steam train depart. I changed to an express train to Taunton (non-stop), via Bedminster, Nailsea, Yatton, Highbridge and Bridgwater, and took a taxi across to Watchet (and here I saw yet another steam train, at the West Somerset Railway station).

I have to say, believe it or not, that due to coincidences of circumstances, I did not eat a single ice cream today. There was just nowhere selling them when I had time to stop. But I lived on snacks throughout, including the bottled water I carry, and an 'emergency' supply of chocolate éclair sweets. Not very many left in the pocket at the end of the day! Also, I consoled myself that what may have been lacking today in ice cream pleasures was made up for in steam train pleasures.

But I must get on with the real objective of the day: the walk was really wonderful, with really fine weather, very little rain and quite strong winds. I left Watchet at about 11.15 am – this included a quick look round the charming little old town – and walked to Doniford, along the coast and then struck inland to St Audries and West Quantoxhead, where I took the Coleridge Way and gradually ascended the beautiful Quantock Hills, via Weacombe and Haslett, and up Bicknoller Combe, where the word 'gradually' should be replaced by 'steeply'. I reached a summit – this was now the Macmillan Way West path – and followed along the top of the Quantock Hills, an open ridge, with excellent views of the Bristol Channel to the north, and the Welsh and English coasts, and various ranges of hills; and to the south, fine views of the valley between Taunton and Minehead, and the hills beyond. This route followed via Black Ball Hill, Halsway Post, Crowcombe Park Gate, Crowcombe Combe Gate, Fire Beacon, Great Hill, and Triscombe Combe (the top of).

From here, I turned northward and descended a long, steep, very beautiful lane, amid coniferous woods, rhododendrons and bracken, via Dibble's Elbow (a hairpin bend) and Cockercombe, to the village of Plainsfield. And, after this, it was road walking all the way to Bridgwater – but pleasant, quiet, quite minor roads and attractive rolling landscapes around.

I passed beside Hawkridge Reservoir – good views over this large 'lake' – and continued via Spaxton, Four Forks, Danesborough and Durleigh, into Bridgwater, and the pleasant old town centre, reached about 6.15 pm.

I caught a bus back to Taunton, walked to the station, and took an express train back through Bridgwater etc to Bristol Temple Meads, and a very late train back to Fareham (same route as in the morning - fast service again) and a local train to Cosham – hence home by car about 11.45 pm.

A good full day – I slept well! Really, it has been once again so enjoyable and memorable.

Day 27
6/6/11

Bridgwater — Pawlett — West Huntspill — Highbridge — Burnham-on-Sea — Berrow — Bleadon — Uphill — Weston-super-Mare
(23 miles approx)

I couldn't resist trying another trip like Saturday 4th June, as soon as possible. So, again rising very early, I drove to the station, and caught the first train, which called at more or less the same stations to Bristol Temple Meads. I just, by the 'skin of my teeth', caught a semi-fast train, which called at the larger stations on the same route as Saturday, but also took the 'loop' line into and out of Weston-super-Mare en route, and called there too. But I alighted today at Bridgwater, of course. It didn't seem that long since I left Cosham station really, at the early hour.

Fine weather prevailed again — sunshine! A cloudy start contrasted with a windy finish. I started walking around 11 o'clock but seemed to take some time getting out of Bridgwater. I saw more of the town centre and the River Parrett — and the canal. But I got a bit confused by the ring road system, and went the long way round to the main Highbridge road, which I then followed. It was a busy road, with good pavements generally, but I had to go through some miles of industrial areas before getting into the open countryside.

I detoured off from the main road at times, once in the pleasant rural areas, and followed lanes through villages, with views of the Quantock Hills one way, and the Mendip Hills the other — the country I followed through was generally flat. I think it is known as the Somerset Levels — rather like Dutch scenery, intersected with dykes.

I walked via Dunball, Walpole, Pawlett, Stretcholt and West Huntspill, where I met one of the locals walking his dog. He (the man, not the dog, of course) told me how cyclists (recently), and walkers too, quite often pass through this area, en route between Land's End and John O'Groats, or vice-versa. Very interesting. He also took some photos of me on my camera.

I continued via Alstone to Highbridge and thence to Burnham-on-Sea, a sizeable holiday resort, with quite extensive sands — and some mud. The views of the English and Welsh sides of the Bristol Channel continued to be interesting. I enjoyed some good snacks, not the least, Exotic Explosion ice cream.

I turned somewhat inland, through Berrow, Ford Common, and past Animal Farm. And on to Hope Farm — all very pleasant, if a little busy, country lanes — one of which followed by the main railway for about a mile. So I reached Bleadon Level and Bleadon village, joining the main road for a while before returning to the coast via the picturesque wooded area of Uphill.

I concluded this long walk along Weston-super-Mare seafront, seeing fine

old hotels of ___e, the sands, the pier, the Wheel, and the town itself,
and the rail___ch I reached around 7 pm.

It t___ long journey home. The train back to Bristol Temple
Meads (___sea etc again) ran slightly late, and I just missed my
connec___our for the last train to Portsmouth Harbour, which didn't
stop a___ basically the same type of fast service as on Saturday, and
same___I alighted at Fareham again but had to wait over half an
ho___minutes past midnight to Cosham — thence, car and home,
a___

___m very happy with it all, again!

Severn River Estuary, Bristol, Gloucester & Forest of Dean

105 miles

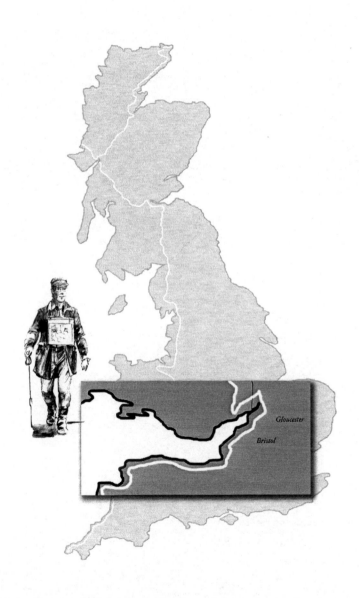

Day 28
18/6/11

Weston-super-Mare — Weston Woods — Worle — Ebdon — Hewish —
Congresbury — Cleeve — Backwell — Flax Bourton — Long Ashton —
Ashton Gate — Bristol (Temple Meads)
(25miles approx)

Yes, now for a further day trip. I followed the procedure of first train from Cosham to Bristol Temple Meads, with a good connection again, on to Weston-super-Mare (semi-fast).

From here, I started the walk about 10 o'clock in heavy showers and strong winds. But it was sunny later. I soon reached the seafront, which I followed northwards on sands or promenades for a little, still enjoying good views of the English and Welsh sides of the Bristol Channel — and the weather coming across it.

My route was via Knightstone, where I left the coast for the rest of the day, proceeding to Worlebury Hill and Weston Woods, where I gained some height in the pleasant woodlands, but then descended to Kewstoke and on to the flat areas — at Worle. I enjoyed my main snack of ice cream and iced cakes. I don't beware of the ice — not that sort.

I continued through Ebdon, Bourton (along pleasant country lanes) and Hewish (here I reached the main A370 road to Bristol, pavemented, and I followed it nearly to Bristol). It is rare to use such a route as this, but the lanes and footpaths in this area are extremely winding, and really it was a pleasant section of countryside too — so I did not mind.

I walked via Congresbury, Cleeve, Brockley, Backwell, Farleigh and Flax Bourton, before leaving the A370 for quieter routes again, through the large old village of Long Ashton — it did seem quite 'Long' getting through it, after about 20 miles of walking today. I suddenly got a very clear view of the City of Bristol ahead and below, and into it I gradually descended — through Ashton Gate — and I walked along about two miles of Bristol's streets. The terraces of stone-built houses, the ascents and descents, shops, warehouses, a considerable length section alongside the River Avon, and a distant view of the impressive Clifton Suspension Bridge which crosses the Avon Gorge — were the interesting highlights of this section.

Eventually I saw the famous Temple Meads railway station, a fitting climax to the day, and a convenient place to end the walk, for my train journey home. (I reached it around 7.30 pm.)

Some people would say — what about all the interesting sights of Bristol? The City Centre and goodness knows what else?

I suppose if someone said to me 'you really must see a certain town — it is so old — a castle there of Roman, Saxon and Norman construction combined — moat full of water all round it, a working drawbridge … genuine Tudor houses standing in their own grounds … some of the most famous gardens in England … complete old town walls preserved from the year dot … etc', my first question in view of my interest in the subject would be – but has it got a railway and a station?

So – just a few comments on Bristol Temple Meads station. It was one of the finest railway stations I had ever seen – for grandeur and size. Apparently one of Brunel's 'works', it certainly rivals London's terminus stations, and I wondered if it might be described as the jewel in the crown of the Great Western Railway. Built in, I assume, West Country stone, it has, I think a number of towers, including a clock tower, 13 railway platforms, imposing entrance hall, a fine restaurant and a long uphill approach road. The sense of history and atmosphere was wonderful!

I therefore enjoyed waiting for my train, surveying the extent and size of the many buildings – and eventually left on one of the later fast services, on the usual route, changing at Fareham, and finally alighting at Cosham. Drove home, which I reached around 11 pm. What a wonderful day again!

Day 29
25/6/11

BRISTOL (TEMPLE MEADS) – TEMPLE GATE – CITY CENTRE – WHITELADIES ROAD
– WESTBURY-ON-TRYM – COMPTON GREENFIELD –
SEVERN BEACH – AUST – SEVERN VIEW
(19 miles approx)

I did a repeat performance of the last three days, using the very early train from Cosham to Bristol Temple Meads.

Then the procedure changed. I started straight out on the walk, just before 9 am. Today's weather was mixed – somewhat cloudy, at times windy and sunny, with light rain occasionally. As would have been gathered from Day 28 comments, the next most important thing was to see the old city centre of Bristol (joke!).

I walked past fine old buildings including the Grand Hotel, Guildhall, the Cathedral Church – particularly ornate. Crossed a fine old bridge, too, with good views of the river, then entered the newer part of the centre. I went round in circles somewhat, finding myself again in the Temple Gate area, near where I first started. I have recorded that it took me a long time to get out of Newquay, and Bridgwater. Much more so Bristol because of its size.

The newer part of the centre was impressively and attractively laid out too. I reached the Cotham area, and Whiteladies Road – a considerable length, with its many fine shops – amid an architecturally attractive residential area of older, stone-built West Country type houses, spaciously arranged. The buildings on the west side of Whiteladies Road seem to belong to Clifton, and those on the east, to Redland. I climbed upward to, and through, Westbury Park (nice trees and lawns), and then descended to Westbury-on-Trym. Time for a quick break here.

I sat on a seat outside the shops, eating a snack. A gentleman came past, smiled (no idea who he was, but something seemed to have impressed him). He said, 'You're enjoying that, aren't you?' 'That', need I tell you, was a chocolate Cornetto ice cream.

I then continued via Brentry and Catbrain, along quite pleasant main roads before reaching lanes, paths and open country. At the village of Compton Greenfield, I got good views of the Welsh coast and one of the two Severn road bridges — and of the River Severn itself. Around this area, I was entering Gloucestershire. Continued via Dyer's Common.

I reached the coast of the Severn Estuary itself at the small town of Severn Beach, and from here I followed the Severn Way coastal footpath (it goes inland a bit, at times).

This was a very interesting section, which I walked as far as Severn View. Throughout, with clear weather, and a high tide, the wide River Severn, and in open country, and distant views across to Caldicot, Chepstow and district (Wales), there was plenty to enjoy.

I followed the sea wall, soon passing under the more southerly of the two River Severn road bridges — both amazing feats of recent engineering, each about two or three miles long, very high above the water. Interestingly, too, just prior to this 'southerly' bridge, I must have crossed over the River Severn railway tunnel, which is longer. I proceeded thence via New Passage, after which the path ceased to be concreted, and detoured a little inland, across marshes, at Northwick.

Soon had very good views of the 'northerly' River Severn road bridge, and continued via Old Passage to Aust. I came on to higher land at Severn View, beside the motorway where it reaches the bridge. Very good views across, again. Here, had I wanted to, I could have taken the walkway beside the road all the way across to Chepstow, Wales — about an hour's walk — and bus back. But — oh no! My dislike of high buildings and bridges took over. I love mountains, hills and cliffs generally — but not this bridge — so high, so long!

I remember a limerick:

> A person whose surname was Clare,
> Was sure he could fly in the air,
> So he climbed a tall tree
> And then cried, 'Dearie me!
> I think it's much safer down there!'

I would have been in no danger of course, but, turning away from the bridge to the

English soil, I seemed to feel it was 'much safer back there!'

So, after food and drink at Severn View Services, I returned by bus to Bristol bus station. (Walk finished about 4.30 pm – but I had another, through the city again to Temple Meads railway station.) I caught the 7.23 pm train to Fareham, usual route, another train on to Cosham, and drove home.

Very pleasant memories; no nightmares afterwards about high bridges – just thought about hopefully walking further in the direction of Wales, and telling myself that if I was to go via Gloucester, I would see much more that is worth seeing anyway, than if I had crossed the Severn Bridge (!).

DAY 30
4/7/11

SEVERN VIEW – OLDBURY SHORE – BERKELEY – WANSWELL – HALMORE – SLIMBRIDGE
(18 miles approx)

Again – what seems now the usual procedure – car to Cosham, and train to Bristol Temple Meads, early and speedy. I then took a bus to Bristol bus station and a further bus to Severn View.

I started walking, thence, at about 10.45 am – the weather was distinctly warmer. I was very glad of cooling breezes off the tidal Severn, and I certainly missed them later in the day when I was walking further inland. The sunshine was glorious however, the tide quite high in the Severn, and the views across to Wales, and also England now, across the 'other' side; and of England on 'this' side, were generally most attractive.

Gloucestershire was such a delightful county to walk in – I rather felt in the 'Heart of Old England'. I felt like singing, 'O Peaceful England', or of 'England's Green and Pleasant Land'. Such a tranquil day, and hardly a ripple on the Severn. Indeed, the only noise at times, which was as music to my ears, was of the trains in the distance – interestingly there are main railway lines on both sides of the Severn – from Gloucester to Bristol; and from Gloucester via Lydney and Chepstow to Severn Tunnel Junction. It was in these areas I heard the trains, which across the water often looked like toy models. Oh yes, there was another noise which was as music to my ears – in the shops, the gentle purring of the freezers which contained the ice cream! I do sound as if I'm getting quite 'carried away'.

Views which came up quite impressively in the earlier part of the walk, by the river, were of hills in Wales and England and of the town of Lydney across the water; and of the Cotswold Hills on 'this' side, which continued to get increasingly clear.

My route, from the higher vantage point of Severn View, took me down to the flat riverside path (again, the Severn Way), via Littleton Warth, Pillhead Gout, West End, Oldbury Shore, and past the power station and Hills Flats to Severn House Farm; then past the further power station and Hamfield Farm, where I changed to an inland route, seeing some picturesque villages. Berkeley, reached via Hook Street, was the first. I stopped for a snack and enjoyed too, a close view of the grand old Berkeley Castle, in its stony glory.

I continued through winding rural lanes, through the little villages of Wanswell and Halmore, to Moorend and to Slimbridge, my last village of today's programme. I hope to get a better view of it next time – I had to rush a bit, doing some additional walking for a mile or two, to Cam and Dursley station. (My walk had finished around 6.30 pm.)

Despite a 'rush' to the station, I did miss a train, but the next one was not too long coming. This one sped me back via Yate etc to Bristol Temple Meads, and I caught the last train, also fast, back to Fareham, and another to Cosham, for car and home – after midnight.

Another very long and very happy day.

DAY 31
11/7/11

SLIMBRIDGE – PATCH BRIDGE – FRAMPTON-ON-SEVERN – SAUL JUNCTION – PARKEND BRIDGE – QUEDGELEY – GLOUCESTER
(15 miles approx)

Yes – another repeat performance – Cosham by car, Bristol Temple Meads by train – early and speedy again. Also, 'all change' at Bristol. I continued thence on a fast running train, calling at Filton Abbey Wood, Bristol Parkway and Yate, before stopping at Cam and Dursley, where I alighted.

I returned (walked) thence to Slimbridge – the same additional mileage, in the opposite direction, same route as last Monday evening.

Then started today's walk about 10.45 am, enjoying the beauty of Slimbridge village in weather very similar to last time – decidedly warm, with plenty of lovely sunshine. I followed a lane to Shepherd's Patch, and at Patch Bridge, joined the footpath to follow the Gloucester and Sharpness Canal (the earlier part on which I walked was also more of the Severn Way) and in fact, apart from a small detour, followed the canal all the way to Gloucester. It was a most peaceful, tranquil route indeed, but I therefore saw very little of the River Severn – however it was a well worthwhile alternative.

The canal was quite wide, and very much used by pleasure boats of all sizes.

The distant views were, to the left, what I assume to be the Malvern Hills and to the right, the Cotswolds again. The delightful rural setting of the canal - everywhere around it very flat, and meadows and woodland very scenic - made the immediate views most inspiring.

The path was on the north/west sides of the canal, i.e. the left, and I continued to Splatt Bridge, which I crossed to explore the highly attractive village of Frampton-on-Severn. It was genuinely old, and not only unspoilt but uncommercialised – a real picture-postcard/chocolate-box type Gloucestershire village – distinctive church, thatch and stone cottages, large areas of village greens, and ponds. Truly idyllic! I thought of a poem I learned at school, of somewhere thoroughly typically English, and rural – a fictitious name given, I think, 'Grantchester', with two lines included:

> 'The church clock stands at ten to three
> And is there honey still for tea?'

However I had to push on. I rejoined the canal path around Saul Junction – a junction of waterways (not a railway junction, I'm afraid – boo-hoo-hoo!) but a very busy area for boating, with a marina.

After this, I walked into much quieter areas, with very few boats or people, and passed Parkend Bridge – but a little later on things changed yet again. I came to residential areas at Hardwicke and onwards. Quedgeley is about 99% on the opposite side of the water. I passed Rea and then entered Gloucester. Here, things got more industrial, but after Hempsted I saw the impressively preserved historic docks – fine old waterside buildings – gained views of the majestic cathedral tower, and by about 4.30 pm, I had completed the walk in the grand old city centre, with its many important shops too.

I enjoyed indulging in the usual refreshments such as orange juices, lemon meringue pie, and needless to say, strawberry and vanilla ice creams – among other delightful delicacies – mainly at the end of the day. Caught train from Gloucester station, which transported me at speed, via Yate etc, to Bristol Parkway and Bristol Temple Meads, where I changed to the Portsmouth service, fast as usual, and with the further change at Fareham for Cosham, and car, and home at about 11 pm. Then, happy dreams!

Day 32
19/7/11

GLOUCESTER — OVER — CALCOTT'S GREEN — MINSTERWORTH — CHAXHILL —
WESTBURY-ON-SEVERN — LITTLEDEAN
(14 miles approx)

*T*he Cosham etc first paragraph of Day 31 can again be restated here, except the fast train to Bristol Temple Meads was followed by my taking a further fast train right through to Gloucester – after Cam and Dursley. I commenced my walk around 11 am.

Earlier on, I referred to taking a 'northward' walk but today, due to geography of the Severn Estuary, it was beginning to become more of a 'southward' walk, by comparison.

The weather was quite an interesting mixture today. Why do we sometimes tend to be so ungrateful for it? It all worked out to be a perfect average of mixtures, for which we should be thankful! It would be easy to say that when the sun was out it was a bit too hot, when the showers came they were a bit too wet, when the wind blew it was a bit too much, and when it stopped it was a bit too humid! When it started to rain, I thought it was hardly worth putting a waterproof coat on, but when my shirt was really wet I thought, 'how silly'. I put the coat on and the rain stopped. I thought – I won't bother to take it off though, but got too hot, took the coat off, and the rain accordingly started again – should I bother to put the coat on again? On reflection, I think it's easy to want to be too fussy about the weather – I have very happy memories of it, really.

Well, now about where I walked – I much enjoyed seeing more of the fine old City of Gloucester, particularly the quaint old streets and shops, and the majestic cathedral, close-up this time. I crossed the bridge to the west side of the River Severn, and followed the Gloucestershire Way from Over, through the meadows, and beside the railway, via Moorcroft and farms. I met a local farmer sitting by a gate with his sheep dog. We couldn't understand at first why the dog was barking at me. But I had just cut my hand slightly (on some wood), and was holding it well up to reduce bleeding. The poor dog probably thought I was shaking my fist at it. I plastered my hand, lowered my arm, and we made friends! The farmer and I talked about the rural scenes around us. He did infer it was nice to talk to someone who was genuinely interested in the countryside – he said crowds of 'townie' people often came through, completely ignoring the scenery around and talking non-stop about all sorts of other things!

I walked on via Calcott's Green to Minsterworth, where the path followed the bank of the River Severn for a short distance. Here I met two guys and had an interesting conversation about the Severn Bore. (See also Day 20). One of these chaps had recently seen a very high series of waves, coming right to the top of the bank. These sorts of conversations really don't Bore me (!)

All these villages were so picturesque, especially the little cottages in them. Also, the views of the River Severn, as I proceeded down the valley, were very good. The tide was high, and the river was widening a lot now – and winding a lot. Good views of the hills around in all directions still, and I think just a glimpse of some Welsh mountain peaks to the north-west.

I walked via Chaxhill (now following country roads) and Westbury-on-Severn, and had good views there of the very beautiful Water Gardens of Westbury Court. I then climbed the winding road, via Elton, up the wooded hillside of the start of the Forest of Dean district, to the scenic old town of Littledean (arrived 5.15 pm – just right for the bus back).

So I was transported back by similar routes to Gloucester bus station, and I walked on to the train station with a pause for another good snack – 'usual' diet! The train trips back were as in the morning but the opposite way – of course – via Bristol etc – except there was a diversion via Eastleigh instead of the Netley route, and I changed trains at Fareham for Cosham – and so, to car, to home, to bed. A great day, again.

Day 33
23/7/11

Littledean – Cinderford – Forest of Dean (Speech House – Cannop Ponds – Parkend – Whitecroft – Norchard) – Lydney
(14 miles approx)

I wonder if I should write at the moment, 'I drove to Cosham, and took a train to Bristol Temple Meads, unless otherwise stated'? Well, there is no 'otherwise stated' today. But I changed to a cross-country express train at Temple Meads (Manchester-bound), which took me fast, only calling at Bristol Parkway, to Cheltenham Spa, where I transferred again – to a more local train 'back' to Gloucester. I then walked to the bus station for the service on the direct Day 32 route, to Littledean – here, I alighted.

And now, the walk began (11.30 am.) (Do I hear you say – wasn't it 11.30 pm, after all the events of the preceding paragraph?)

The weather – very pleasant – a mixture of sunshine and clouds. And the route – as last time, still more of a southward direction and even eastward, temporarily. For most of the day, I enjoyed the beauty of the Forest of Dean. Certainly extensive; as far as I could see largely deciduous; and many of the roads and lanes were unfenced. Sheep roamed everywhere freely, as may other animals

58

– certainly deer do – although I didn't see them. The woodland was generally very thick, with very few clearings.

My route – from Littledean, I followed the winding road up a steep hill to Cinderford – a sizeable town, which is also very hilly, enabling me to enjoy good views of the Forest of Dean ahead, and again the River Severn tidal estuary – and the Cotswold and Malvern Hills. I then walked via Stockwell Green, Ruspidge and beside a very scenic Forest of Dean road (and I detoured further too, into the woods at times) to the very imposing old Speech House – now a hotel. A grand building indeed. I should have 'read up' a bit more about it than just the good menu on the board outside.

I continued to Cannop and the two very beautiful, tranquil Cannop Ponds. I had left roads by now, enjoying the forest paths which took me beside these ponds, which were quite large. Plenty of picnickers here today. I followed beside Russell's Inclosure, and eventually came out on a country road at Parkend. Here I was able to experience another of the attractions of the Forest of Dean – although I was now more on the borders of it – the Dean Forest Railway. Trains were running today too on this independently run line

I took roads and lanes which followed the railway, all the length of it to Lydney Junction. Walked beside Parkhill Inclosure to Whitecroft. Here, the timing was good. A chap was just opening the level-crossing gates. He told me a train would be through very soon. They were running diesel-hauled services and a station was in process of construction at Whitecroft. I had an excellent view of the train – a fine locomotive pulling three well-occupied GWR livery coaches.

Then walked via New Mills to Norchard station. Would you believe it, saw another train – I think, the same one returning, on the high-level station section. The low-level station seemed to house a lot of stock. Both levels were immediately adjacent. I walked on to Newerne and Lydney, and its small Town station, and through the streets to its Junction station, which was impressively laid out, and extensive sidings too, with even more stock than at Norchard. This station was immediately adjacent to the main line Lydney station on the Cardiff to Gloucester route, and I was just right for the 5.24 pm Nottingham-bound cross-country express on which I travelled back to Gloucester. Very good views across the wide River Severn, en route and a fast non-stop running train.

I caught another fast-running train via Yate etc to Bristol Temple Meads, and the 'usual' fast service to Fareham, and 'slow' service to Cosham – then car, home. The only delay on this journey was at a shop, for the purpose of buying two more ice creams for supper, to add to the many joys of the day!

Section 3

Offa's Dyke Path and nearby areas (English/Welsh borders, South to North Wales, including the Black Mountains) 236 miles

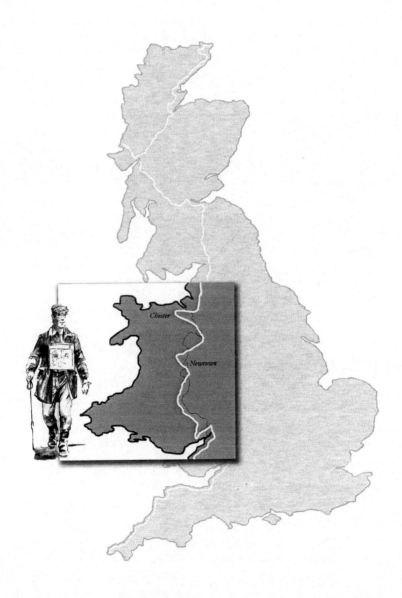

Day 34
29/7/11

Lydney — Aylburton — Alvington — Woolaston — Tidenham — Sedbury
Village — Sedbury Cliffs — Tutshill — Chepstow
(13 miles approx)

Note: 486 miles since leaving Land's End — crossed from England to Wales today

Should I say - 'Needless to say' — car to Cosham, fast train to Bristol Temple Meads? After this, I took the Manchester express to Cheltenham Spa, again — and a fast running train, calling only at Gloucester, to Lydney where I alighted for the commencement of the walk, around 11 am.

Light rain was falling, but it cleared during the day. Nevertheless it stayed quite misty, which really provided quite an atmosphere. The views of the widening River Severn Estuary as the day went on — of the tidal waters, expanses of sand, some mudflats, and the distant coastline on the other side, partly shrouded, or limited in fogginess - had a mysterious charm, I thought.

Leaving Lydney, I enjoyed views of the Dean Forest Railway again, also seeing St Mary's Halt, a very small station between the Town and Junctions stations surrounded by scenic woodland.

I followed the main Lydney to Chepstow road for most of the day — this was really not boring, with wide grass verges and banks, and good paths through scenic old villages, plus views of unspoilt country all around — the Severn, the hills etc. One highlight en route should be mentioned: I tasted an ice cream with a mixture of three flavours I had never had together before — chocolate, caramel and coconut. Now you couldn't call a walk like that 'boring'!

I passed through the picturesque villages of Aylburton, Alvington and parts of Woolaston, with their excellent stone buildings, mellowed into the country scenes over time — old churches, cottages, pubs, farms and so on. And then on through the hamlets of Stroat and Wibdon, and part of the village of Tidenham, similarly lovely — and then off the main road to Tump Farm and Sedbury, equally scenic.

Then things got more exciting for me — I reached the start of Offa's Dyke Path at Sedbury Cliffs, which overlooked the Severn, with views across to Aust, and the M48 motorway bridge. I felt I must start 'doing' this walk, at least following its general route. I had been doing a southward walk again, so I now changed back to a northward.

Offa's Dyke is of course an ancient earthwork that criss-crosses the present borders of England and Wales, from the south to the north Welsh coasts. The dyke probably dates from the 8th Century, and is named after King Offa. It is some sort of historic frontier (but evidence tends to be either lacking or conflicting as to

63

detail) between the Mercian and Welsh kingdoms, and its high bank is sometimes very clear, and sometimes virtually untraceable now. Sometimes there is a deep ditch to the west of the bank. The present path keeps company with the old dyke for over half its length.

So I joyfully walked the path from Sedbury Cliffs, up or down, through woodland and fields and around Sedbury itself to the cliffs above the River Wye, and Tutshill, getting fine views of the river, and of Chepstow and its ancient castle. But I then left the path, and descended between fine old stone houses and walls to river level, and crossed the Wye on the narrow road bridge, to see the grand old town of Chepstow itself, following the old streets to the station — where a train for Gloucester via Lydney pulled in at the moment I arrived, (about 4.30 pm.)!

By walking over the River Wye bridge into Chepstow — another cause for excitement to me — I had transferred not just from Gloucestershire to Monmouthshire, but from England to Wales. Also, it had been quite interesting on the Dyke Path, asking locals for confirmation of the route. They seemed to take a real delight in helping, and were clearly used to assisting individuals and groups.

So I returned by a speedy train to Gloucester, another speedy one to Bristol Temple Meads (and good snacks at both stations) and the usual fast and slow trains to Fareham and Cosham respectively — and good old car home.

One other thought came to my mind on this wonderful day. Just a bit amusing, about the 'certain lady' I refer to. I once drove her with her husband, through Eastbourne, and he wanted to walk a little of the South Downs Way, which starts there. I felt like him today, when I wanted to feel I had set foot on the start of Offa's Dyke Path. But she said, at Eastbourne, that her husband (as to the South Downs Way) wanted to be taken there, because he wanted to put his foot 'in it'! (A lot of difference between the use of the words 'on' and 'in'.)

Day 35
9/9/11

CHEPSTOW — WOODCROFT — WINTOUR'S LEAP — DENNEL HILL —
JAMES'S THORNS — DEVIL'S PULPIT — TINTERN ABBEY
(8 miles approx)

There has been a longer gap since the last walk, compared with recent trends — due to a hernia operation I had on 19th August. All seems to be going well, but I did a shorter mileage this time, as a precaution.

After my drive to Cosham station, and my fast train ride to Bristol Temple Meads, I alighted for a business appointment near the station, and was able to get back to the station in time for the 10.48 train from Portsmouth, which calling at

Filton Abbey Wood only took me on to Newport (South Wales) via the Severn Tunnel, beneath the river. If my map calculations are correct, the tunnel is about four miles long – remarkable – and a very interesting experience. On entering Wales, the other end, we passed Severn Tunnel Junction station, non-stop, and I alighted at Newport. I noted the bi-lingual railway signs and notices in English and Welsh, and enjoyed listening to station announcements at Newport in both languages too. After a snack on the station, I boarded a further train, to Chepstow, again via Severn Tunnel Junction.

So I made rather a late start (1.15 pm), walking out from Chepstow – the views of the town, and the countryside I covered showed up to good advantage on this warm fine summer's day. I crossed back on the narrow road bridge (see 29th July, 2011), to the English side of River Wye, and followed up the spectacular Wye Valley, along Offa's Dyke Path again. Quite a hilly walk, set in scenery of sloping meadows and woodlands with views of very grand country mansions standing in their own grounds – especially beautiful with autumn colours appearing.

The walk ran between the Rivers Severn and Wye - the distant Severn, so huge, contrasted with the sharply meandering Wye, with its precipitous 200-foot high limestone cliffs below the walker.

The route ran via Woodcroft, Broadrock, Wintour's Leap (said to have been named after a Royalist leader, who escaped his pursuers by leaping over the cliff to the Wye below), Dennel Hill, James's Thorns, Shorn Cliff and Devil's Pulpit, where there was a magnificent view of Tintern Abbey, majestic although ruined, and of the valley around. Shortly after, I took a steep path down to Tintern village and abbey, losing my way at one point, and consequently taking rather a long detour! Reached Tintern about 5.30 pm.

I caught a bus to Chepstow, a train to Newport, and returned thence on a fast Portsmouth train, via the Severn Tunnel again, Bristol Temple Meads etc – the usual route, but changed at Southampton Central to a train which stopped at Cosham – and so, albeit late, to home again.

Certainly a marvellous day! And interestingly, it is just over a year since I set out from Land's End.

Day 36
16/9/11

TINTERN ABBEY — CASWELL WOOD — BROCKWEIR — BIGSWEIR —
COXBURY FARM — REDBROOK — KYMIN — MONMOUTH
(10 miles approx)

I seem to be steadily increasing my walking mileages, after my 'op'.
I took the very early (6.15 am) train from Cosham, fast service via Salisbury, Bristol Temple Meads etc and of course through the Severn Tunnel again – reached Newport (South Wales) at 9.25 am, and transferred very conveniently to the 9.27 which 'deposited' me at Chepstow at 9.48. I also had a good bus connection to Tintern Abbey, and I started my walk around 10.45.

Fine weather prevailed, thankfully, except for one short shower, in the afternoon. Having enjoyed a close-up view of the abbey, and a quick tour of Tintern itself, I embarked on the long steep climb up to Offa's Dyke Path, rejoining it where I left it a week ago. I followed it through Caswell Wood to the Brockweir Valley, where there is a choice of routes as far as Bigsweir. I chose the Wye riverside route, rather than 'over the hills'.

So I descended the valley to Brockweir – a very charming little village at the foot of this open-meadow type hillslope, and much enjoyed walking alongside the River Wye for some miles – it flows, quite sizeable and fast, below very high, steep coniferous-forested hillslopes on each side, pleasant villages, both sides too. I walked past Coed-Ithel Weir and Bigsweir House and Bridge – then the route climbed high into the woods, and the Dyke Path followed the high summits – via Creeping Hill, Coxbury Farm and Highbury Wood.

Then the descent to the river again, at Redbrook, and ascent to Duffield's Lane, and the particularly fine, high viewpoint at Kymin, from which I saw clearly Monmouth town and the River Wye in the foreground, and the Black Mountains in the distance. Really quite dramatic!

So I again descended steeply, via Garth Wood and May Hill, to Monmouth and the Wye (arrived 5 pm). I should elaborate. The only part of Monmouth I actually reached was the name board, to inform me I was entering it, and I think some Welsh – and a bus stop. But as I needed to catch the bus back, and it was due to reach that stop very soon, it seemed wiser not to explore further, and perhaps lose my way – and lose the bus. I will, all being well, 'do' Monmouth properly, next time. I did however have to declare a state of 'Ice Cream Crisis' – of which, more shortly.

The bus took me back down the Wye Valley (Tintern etc) to Chepstow, and I walked to the station, where I caught a train to Severn Tunnel Junction, and got a quick connection, thence, on a fast service through the tunnel to Bristol Temple

Meads etc to Fareham – and a slow train to Cosham, and my medium-speed car home. (10 pm.) End of ice cream crisis.

('Ice Cream Crisis' was declared at 5 pm.) I had had no chance to buy one. I forgot to buy one at Cosham, a shop on the way home had just closed, but the store just near my house was still open. They say 'everything comes to those who wait'. It was a most delicious vanilla tub ice. Perhaps all the better for the wait for it. It crowned a day, well worth crowning!

DAY 37
1/10/11

MONMOUTH – KING'S WOOD – HENDRE FARM – LLANVIHANGEL-YSTERN-
LLEWERN – ONEN – TAL-Y-COED – LLANTILIO CROSSENNY
(9 miles approx)

*T*he most interesting item of note today, I suppose, was that in England and in Wales, the highest temperatures ever recorded in October were logged! It felt like it too, at times – but a glorious sunny day, ideal for views. So I experienced a situation unique since weather records began. And maybe before.

My journey to South Wales was not of course unique at all, but as always, so enjoyable, but it is repetitive when written down – I almost say in my sleep – car to Cosham, fast train to Bristol Temple Meads and through the Severn Tunnel to Newport; then slower train to Chepstow; then bus via the Wye Valley to Monmouth.

I remember reading a book about some holidaymakers, I think set in Germany. The comment was made that fortunately, they had reached a small town at which they stayed overnight, so small, that it was possible to 'do' it, i.e., see all the sights, historic buildings etc – in the morning following – which left all the rest of the day to enjoy themselves.

Probably many tourists are like that, the 'ritual' of observing everything the guide book tells you to look out for is usually itself enjoyable but if taken too seriously, can prevent the sense of relaxation and freedom which may be experienced by 'doing your own thing' after.

Happily, this 'conflict of priorities' does not seem to trouble me. Walking is my objective, but I made the point, previous Day (36) that I had not 'done' Monmouth. I will say too though, that it was well worth doing, on foot as from 11.30 am. It was a delightful ancient town – I had bacon sandwiches and coffee on a hotel patio, walked the main street, with many shops in it, and photographed the 13th century gatehouse on the bridge over the River Monnow and in a state of very good repair, and the only one of its kind in Britain.

I then proceeded up Watery Lane, which was fairly dry, into the open undulating Welsh countryside. Soon, I was climbing under the cover of King's Wood, and then descending from the summit to Hendre Farm. I varied slightly, at times, from the official Offa's Dyke Path – sometimes to see a village more closely, or to enjoy some scenic lanes etc. My route took me via Abbey Bridge, the remote little village of Llanvihangel-Ystern-Llewern – quite a gem, and to Onen, Tal-y-Coed and as far as Llantilio Crossenny – a larger village, also very attractive, with a fine, large 13th century church. (Time – 4.15 pm.)

But I needed to get back to Monmouth as soon as possible, to catch the last bus of the day to Newport. I reluctantly left the distant views of hills and mountains, and detoured back to inn/restaurant, Tal-y-Coed, which was very near, and the ideal place for help with transport arrangements. I was most impressed.

The proprietors and staff provided me with orange juice and chilled water straight away, and also quickly phoned for a local taxi. The lady arrived very soon, and speedily and safely transported me back to Monmouth bus station, which I reached 10 minutes before the bus departure time. These folk took significant interest in my walk, and talked quite a lot about the remarkable hot weather!

The bus ride was also a pleasant experience – incorporating tours of the scenic, historic towns of Raglan, Usk and Caerleon, en route to Newport railway station. I soon boarded a fast train – I calculated that it took four minutes travelling through the Severn Tunnel, so probably, it is about four miles long – and I changed trains as usual at Fareham, purchased and ate two chocolate ice creams at Cosham, and arrived home around 10.30 pm.

I think I should say I have had a delightful Indian summer walk.

Day 38
15/10/11

Llantilio Crossenny – Great Treadam – White Castle – Caggle Street – Llangattock Lingoed – Pandy
(9 miles approx)

I took the 'usual' train journey between Cosham and Newport, but then walked through the town centre to the bus station, whence I took the bus to Monmouth, via Caerleon, Usk and Raglan, as last time, but opposite direction. The helpful taxi driver, also referred to last time, drove me to Tal-y-Coed again, where the folk at the inn/restaurant again provided me with drink – and food. The prominent subject of conversation today however, with most people was the rugby match just played in New Zealand, in which Wales lost to France.

I walked on – the 'reverse' of the closing detour of last time, and recommenced the 'official' start at Llantilio Crossenny, about 12 o'clock. What a contrast in the weather – from record heat of 1st October, to an also very pleasant day, cool, breezy – even cold sometimes. The autumn colours are showing up very well.

So I continued via a number of cabbage fields and then numerous meadows and paths to Great Treadam, and climbed the gradient to the mainly 12th century, partly moated White Castle. It was somewhat ruined, but a fine sight and there were fine views from this hilltop. Walked down to Caggle Street, and then up and down, through many more meadows, past Old Court, and up to the quaint little village of Llangattock Lingoed. I followed another hilly section through to Great Park, and made the final descent of the day, via Llanteems, to today's destination, the village of Pandy (4.30 pm). I enjoyed a very good vanilla ice cream here plus coffee.

The views from this village were inspiring. As I approached, the vista across the valley grew ever clearer, and the foothills of the Black Mountains and the mountains themselves, ever closer, of course. I look forward, all being well, to entering this next section of the walk as soon as possible. It really beckons me.

The taxi driver returned punctually for me, and conveyed me via Abergavenny town, to the station, where I boarded a train, which sped me down the Usk Valley to Newport. Here I got a good connection right through to Fareham, and another to Cosham, and my good connecting car home.

Among the many enjoyments of the day, I would also say - and by no means at all the least – were delicious Welsh cakes, which I bought at White Castle, and ate in the train, in the evening.

Day 39
11/11/11

Pandy – Hatterrall Hill – Cwmyoy – Henllan – Llanthony Priory
(9 miles approx)

Again, I took the fast train from Cosham to Newport, and then changed to a fast Holyhead-bound service, up the Usk Valley to Abergavenny. The same helpful taxi driver as before transported me on to Pandy, so I was able to start today's walk as early as 10.45 am.

To begin with conditions were cloudy, but the views were clear. I walked the steep lanes and paths up to the top of the Black Mountains – quite an ascent. (Via Groes-lwyd to Hatterrall Hill.) However, quite thick mist took over, and the views to the valleys eventually disappeared!

I met two walkers, local folk, and told them I was heading for Llanthony Priory. I pronounced it 'Clanthony', but they pointed out that at this 'end' of

Wales, virtually on the English border, they say 'Llanthony'. Further in the heart of Wales, e.g. Llanelli it is 'Clanecli'. So I was grateful for this guidance. Perhaps I tend to exaggerate, but I could imagine the following:

Visitor: Can you direct me to Clanthony please?
Response from local: A look of 'Stop trying to show off', and later:
Visitor: Can you direct me to Llanelli please?
Response from local: A look of 'You silly, ignorant man.'

(*I emphasise – I really like Welsh people very much – the above is of course a joke.*)

At this point, I also had a rethink about my route. Would it be a good idea to go down into the valley, and see the beauty of it, rather than plod on and only see mist? I can still hope, later in the programme, to enjoy sun and views on this bleak, but most inspiring mountain-edge walk.

So yes, I followed less prominent paths than Offa's Dyke, steep and slippery, downwards and suddenly got a tremendous view of the Vale of Ewyas on the west. The golden autumn colours of the coniferous forests, and other foliage were really some sight – and mountains beyond too. After this, I looked at picturesque valleys, and cloud-covered mountains above me for the rest of the day.

I descended to the foot of the valley – I'm not entirely sure which route I took exactly, but I asked a few drivers on the remote lane ' below' if I was near Llanthony.

Again, when I can't recall all the detail of a conversation, I am prone, I think, to exaggerate but the following is interesting:

Initially, two helpful vehicle drivers seemed to be of the opinion that Llanthony was two or three miles away, roughly. Having walked a little further up the Vale of Ewyas, I asked some farmers – who were of the opinion it would be 'a good three mile'. Some way on from here, I passed a cyclist who was ably repairing a puncture. Having expressed my 'condolences' to him, he explained to me that he'd cycled all the way from London – and then 'this happens to me, only four miles from my destination, Llanthony!'

I wondered if I would see a road sign round the next bend: 'Llanthony, 5 miles', and at the bend after, 'Llanthony 6 miles', and so on!

But there were no mileage signs at all. And it was a very lovely trek – the winding lane, streams and rivers to watch, the autumn hues, the peace and quiet, and the towering cloud-clad mountains all around me. It rained a little. My route was via Cwmyoy and Henllan. Villages and hamlets as lovely as always in this part of Wales.

Llanthony (reached around 4.15 pm) was another small old 'stone' village, centred round the majestic but partly ruined priory, founded in 1103. I enjoyed eating crisps while waiting for my taxi, and before long was being driven in the dusk back to Abergavenny station, where the rain came on very heavily, and lasted all the way to Westbury!

Had good snacks en route home – a repeat journey of the morning trains, in opposite direction, plus a change at Fareham.

Day 40
23/11/11

Llanthony Priory – Loxidge Tump – The Black Mountains
(north-eastern edge) – Black Hill *(see below)
(9 miles approx)

*A*nd again, I took trains from Cosham to Newport, and from Newport to Abergavenny. Also again, I was driven on by the same taxi driver, this time of course to Llanthony Priory.

How fine to see the old priory again, not now in light rain and gathering dusk, but bright sunshine with clear views of the Black Mountains in the background. Autumn colours showed up well again, this morning too.

I started walking about 10.45 am. It was, needless to say, a very steep climb up to the mountain top and Offa's Dyke Path. I can't show off a knowledge of many Welsh words – I do know a very few – my progress was 'ARAF' - that is, slow. (You get to see that word painted on the roads a lot, so can't help learning it.)

*Another point to stress about the walks I'm doing in this phase of the programme is that the comparative shortness of the mileages is really due to having to allow for return journeys all the way back home in the same day – as far as I can tell, I'm not entering an era of inability to cope with distances! But there are great distances to cover by transport homeward in the evening.

Today's weather differed much from last time. All day the views 'from the top' were clear and impressive. England and Wales, particularly the latter, could be seen well far below. But I found the going distinctly cold and windy – but mainly dry. The quiet was sometimes interrupted by RAF activity – planes, even below me, roaring up the valleys – training exercises, I should think.

I met few walkers, but those I did were very friendly and conversational, giving me interesting information about Offa's Dyke Path further north. I had reached the path via Loxidge Tump – once I reached the top, the path was generally quite flat, following the (English/Welsh, Herefordshire/Monmouthshire-Powys) boundaries along the north-east edge of the Black Mountains. It was very open and wild scenery, and many peat bogs were crossed, generally by means of large rough stone slabs to form continuous path crossings. Plenty of mud everywhere, after recent rains. Immediate views down to the valleys below were impressive – Capel-y-Ffyn on the left, and Olchon Valley on the right. A fine, colourful panorama – and beyond, too.

Last walk, it was difficult to be sure of the correct route 'down', and I came down too soon - this walk was again difficult, and I came down too late! But it didn't matter, except I got a bit late.

I seemed to miss a path, but after a detour descended the 'ridge' of Black Hill – steep indeed. I continued on to Craswall, all this part being walking additional to the 'walk itself'. I had agreed to be picked up by the taxi from the village of Michaelchurch Escley about 4.45 pm and the time was already getting late for this. Very fortunately a lady driving her car out of her farm, from whom I asked directions, offered to drive me to the village. I accepted of course – this was not 'cheating', i.e. missing out the walking, as 'the walk' had been completed. She said that walking the Black Mountains this time of year sorted out the men from the boys. I hoped she thought I was a man to have attempted it – but perhaps she thought I was a boy, to have got in a muddle at the end.

My taxi soon arrived – and I was soon in the train at Abergavenny, and caught the Portsmouth train at Newport. Indulged in various snacks again – changed trains again at Fareham; car at Cosham 'as usual'.

Reached home reflecting on another glorious day; reminded myself that I now knew a Welsh word (Araf means slow); and wondered why I didn't know the Welsh for ice cream. How remiss of me.

DAY 41
5/12/11

BLACK HILL – HAY BLUFF EAST SLOPE – CADWGAN –
CUSOP DINGLE – HAY-ON-WYE
(8 miles approx)

I am wondering if I'll manage many more day trips to Wales – I expect soon, it will be necessary to stay overnight. But things went remarkably well again today, despite yet further road and rail mileages.

So – ditto from Day 40 to Abergavenny after which the 'same' taxi (as reliable as ever) conveyed me to Olchon Valley and I walked on to Black Hill (via Glandwr and Upper Blaen, through extremely winding, narrow, scenic lanes below the Black Mountains).

The climb up the side of Black Hill was of course extremely steep – and rough and rocky but the views as excellent as last time. I started the 'official' walk around 11.45. Weather – there was a very light sprinkling of snow high on the mountains. The sunshine was glorious (although cloudier, later) but the wind 'biting' cold. I was on the Black Mountains again!

In such lovely scenery and strong sunshine, as I climbed the mountainside I thought:

'This could be spring in Scotland and it is winter in Wales'
How similar some parts of highland Britain can be.

I eventually reached the summit. Offa's Dyke Path is 'quiet' today – I hardly met anyone. I was quite soon on a generally descending section toward the Wye Valley. The path followed below the summit of Hay Bluff, and descended the east side of it. Views of the River Wye, more of the Black Mountains and I think the Brecon Beacons, and the hills of South Radnorshire, were all really spectacular.

From rugged open mountainside, I progressed down to open heathland, fields and woods via Cadwgan, Upper Danyforest and Cusop Dingle. Suddenly Hay-on-Wye was right in front of me – a fine little old Welsh-English border town, which deserves more exploration, I hope soon. I like to think of it as a gateway to mid-Wales.

But I was just right for the 3.24 pm bus, so had to drag myself away. I was transported via the Peterchurch route to Hereford, which seemed to include quite a grand tour of the last-named – with excellent views of the cathedral and other fine buildings from many angles. There was a very good train connection on via Abergavenny to Newport, another good connection to Fareham and another to Cosham.

I was home remarkably early – between 9.05 and 9.10 pm. Plenty of pleasure 'crammed' in today!

Day 42
19/12/11

HAY-ON-WYE – BRONYDD – BETTWS DINGLE – NEWGATE – NEWCHURCH
(*7 miles approx*)

Well here is another day trip to Wales – this time, taking train from Cosham to Newport, and changing for train right through to Hereford, via Abergavenny. As there was some time before my bus was due to leave, I enjoyed seeing quite a lot of the City of Hereford on foot. It really was a grand old city – I had a meal at a café, saw the main shopping area and admired quaint old buildings.

Hereford was extremely busy, which caused the bus I boarded to get later and later, so I reached Hay-on-Wye eventually, at not much before 1 o'clock – but not a problem.

I had already enjoyed wonderful views from the train of the Black Mountains, covered in a significant layer of snow. The views were even more impressive at Hay, especially of nearby Hay Bluff. So the Black Mountains were white today – much more so than last time. At times today I was walking in several inches of snow, in the lower areas too. And rain fell quite heavily at times but views were still pretty good. Some of the roads I walked were completely flooded in places, though not to a very great depth. Also, it was a very cold windy day!

I had a very quick look round Hay, on foot. In Day 41 I said I would hope to 'explain' further. It seems to be pretty well entirely in Wales – boasting a castle, other impressive old buildings and it is of course famous for its many historic bookshops. I left around 1.15, today's walk taking me initially along the River Wye road bridge. The river was pretty full today, and flowing at speed. Indeed, there was a lot of water everywhere.

I think I was walking in the Welsh county of Powys all the time, this part probably being the former old county of Radnorshire. I followed along the Wye Valley, quite near the river to start with, but entered fairly hilly areas after. Offa's Dyke Path, which again I generally followed, took me along the edge of Bronydd into the very beautiful Bettws Dingle, i.e. a deep wooded valley, with a torrent of water cascading through the foot of it. A real gem of scenery.

After this, I followed hilly lanes via Penrhoel, Newgate and Tyn-y-Cwm, into the little old village of Newchurch – arrived, 5 pm. The last mile was not so 'seeable' in the gathering dusk, but there was a pleasant atmosphere with snow illuminating the scene. Indeed they were real 'Christmas card' scenes, especially at the end, with sheep dotted around the snowy fields, and the snow-clad mountains in the distance. Also a little light from the setting sun was a welcome contrast to the rain earlier.

This also reminded me – a good many years ago, I took my parents for a day-trip car drive from Hampshire to Chepstow, Wales – and back. My father studied the weather quite closely but I think tended to forecast the day more with pessimism than optimism. He anticipated rain all day! I, with no grounds for my viewpoint other than hopefulness, said as we started off in the morning deluge that it would probably clear in due course. It could be argued, with considerable difficulty, that I was right.

It rained pretty hard all day (but we still enjoyed ourselves), but at the very end (about seven miles from home) precipitation packed up and there was a very small gap in some cloud, revealing a tiny piece of blue sky!

I had another taxi driver to pick me up today – again I was very fortunate. The very helpful lady who had driven me around before was now 'replaced' in this different area by a very helpful chap, and he shared a lot of my interest in the countryside. He drove me back along the Wye Valley to Hereford station. I caught trains back on the same routes as my outward morning journey, changing at Newport – also Southampton.

Quite a late finish – bed around 1 o'clock in the morning – but a most satisfying day!

DAY 43
9/1/12

NEWCHURCH — HENGOED — GLADESTRY — HERGEST RIDGE — RIDGEBOURNE — KINGTON
(8 miles approx)

*T*he opening events of the day do not give me much credit! On arrival at Cosham, I looked, unsuccessfully in my car for my rucksack. I had left it at home. I drove back and returned to the station to see my train leaving before I could get anywhere near it, so had to wait for the 7.26 am instead of the usual 6.15 am. Travelled the usual route, i.e. changed at Newport and took a Manchester-bound express to Hereford. It was then necessary to take the 'same' taxi again, to get back to my original timetable – there was no bus to connect. He was most obliging again, and soon whisked along the scenic Wye Valley to Hay, where I continued in another taxi, which I had already pre-booked – this helpful driver took me on to Newchurch, where I was able to resume my walk at the planned time, 1.15 pm but with a little less money in pocket!

Today's walk was partly in Wales, partly in England – Powys (formerly Radnorshire), and Herefordshire respectively. The weather – cloudy with light showers, some sun too, and good clear views. I would describe the hilly countryside as somewhat rugged, somewhat rolling. The former gave a feel rather like the north of Scotland. At the same time, the latter made me feel I could be in the south of England.

En route I enjoyed a mobile phone conversation with my brother, so gave him a glowing description of the delightful surroundings. I followed the lane route via Hengoed to Gladestry, and then reverted to Offa's Dyke Path itself, with a steep climb to Hergest Ridge, which I followed along, and enjoyed the best views of the day. I passed the Whet Stone, said to be a large glacial boulder, and walked among sheep and ponies grazing on this high moorland area.

The descent from this 'top' was very pleasant – turfy slopes gradually leading into the very picturesque approaches (via Ridgebourne) to Kington – which itself was most picturesque – unspoilt, charming, old – all the usual stuff I really like. I had a good walk all round it – narrow streets, river, bridge etc. I concluded the walk at about 4.15 pm, celebrating with appropriate snacks.

The helpful taxi man arrived very punctually, and soon returned me to Hereford station. I took trains back on the same routes as this morning, changing at Newport and Southampton.

Great fun again – perhaps a bit too much when I forgot my rucksack.

I've already made up an elementary kind of little poem, to assist in future:

> I've got my glasses, and cap,
> I've got my case with my map,
> I've got stick, and anorak,
> and I'm sure I've got my rucksack.

If the weather was warmer, there might have been some more about remembering my ice creams as well, but thankfully I don't seem to have problems on that subject.

Day 44
23/1/12

KINGTON – BRADNOR, RUSHOCK AND HERROCK HILLS – LOWER HARPTON – EVENJOBB – BEGGAR'S BUSH – DOLLEY GREEN
(7 miles approx)

Well thankfully, I got things better organised than last time, and took the 6.15 am train from Cosham, complete with rucksack and all other relevant possessions. Had the usual change at Newport, and reached Hereford about 10.30 am. I took a quick walk in the city, and boarded the 11 o'clock bus for Kington. A lovely rural ride through a number of villages. I think Weobley (apparently pronounced 'wobbly') was particularly impressive – Tudor, largely I should judge; the only wobbly-looking areas were the slanting and leaning parts of the old buildings, but I would think they were actually quite secure – and most picturesque.

I started the walk out from Kington around 12.15 pm seeing a little more of the old town in the area of the square. Really lovely to explore. The day was quite sunny and bright, with some cloud and showers at times. I began with a steep climb, via Bradnor Green and golf course to the top of Bradnor Hill more or less – and a good viewpoint. Then on to Rushock Hill – an example where the ancient Offa's Dyke itself was very prominent, and to Herrock Hill – further excellent views all around of rugged and rolling hilly landscapes – this entire section was quite outstanding for the vistas. But then, a very steep descent to Lower Harpton and Ditchyeld Bridge – after which I continued along scenic lanes and roads. Plenty of snowdrops out too.

I walked through the beautiful little old village of Evenjobb, and then via Beggar's Bush and Maes-Treylow, before rejoining Offa's Dyke Path (in the River Lugg valley), which I followed into the hamlet of Dolley Green. (Arrived about 3.45 pm) I seem to have been rather more in Powys/Radnorshire than in Herefordshire today. Also, I walked on into the old town of Presteigne, near Dolley Green, in addition, as it was convenient for my 'usual', helpful taxi man to 'collect' me from there. I had an orange juice at the pub, and enjoyed seeing the rather historic main street. Also enjoyed the ride in the early dusk to Hereford station, and soon caught train to Newport; another to Southampton; and another to Cosham – and car, and home.

Yet another day of happy memories. I did have the added challenge of coping with two watches – one was, it seemed gaining time, the other, losing time. I was rather unnecessarily early, therefore at some points, but slightly alarmingly lacking in punctuality at others.

Which did remind me of someone I met many years ago. He was very exceptionally early for an appointment. He offered an explanation for this, which was remarkably short, and surprisingly lacking in detail.

He said: 'I came early, so that I wouldn't be late'!

Day 45
27/2/12

Dolley Green – Whitton – Rhôs-y-Meirch – Frydd Wood – Knighton
(7 miles approx)

I suspect this will be the last of the 'day trip' arrangements, as the walk mileages are really getting low now. I hope to stay away overnight next time, I think.

So – 6.15 am train from Cosham again today, with the usual change at Newport, and arrival in Hereford in time for the taxi around 10.45 am. A very scenic ride via Presteigne, to Dolley Green. The same taxi man took me on this drive – he really seemed to be enjoying the run as much as I was. Talked a lot about the increasing strawberry growing, and apple orchards, which we saw en route. Spring lambs were appearing too – I thought they looked rather cold although the weather was milder than last time – clear distant views but cloudy with light rain later. Trees were coming out in blossom, and daffodils were shooting up.

I started walking from Dolley Green around 11.30 am initially following rural roads, enabling me to see the village of Whitton en route – typically pleasant. I then followed a long climb by road again, past Cwm Whitton to Rhôs-y-Meirch, where I rejoined Offa's Dyke Path once again. I followed it along quite high hills, where there are well-preserved sections of the original dyke earthwork itself. Also, there were excellent views today, of hills well to the east of Ludlow – Titterstone Clee and Brown Clee.

Then the steep descent to Knighton, through beautiful Frydd Wood. Fine views of this charming, and very historic little town, nestling in the valley below. The Welsh name for it (Tref y Clawdd) means 'Town on the Dyke'. The clock tower stood impressively at the top of a hill, Broad Street. I enjoyed quite a full walking tour of Knighton, a browse round old shops, a snack in a café, and a visit to Offa's Dyke Centre – a very impressive exhibition and tourist centre, providing much information about the Dyke, and historical and tourist information generally. Books, maps, souvenirs etc on sale in abundance.

It was also significant that Knighton was approximately the halfway point of Offa's Dyke Path. A mileage signpost read, 'Sedbury Cliffs, 80 miles: Prestatyn, 97 miles'. So I hadn't actually quite done 50% of the Path yet. Although, because of taking alternative scenic routes at certain points, I had clocked up more than 80 miles already.

The railway was another interesting feature, Knighton station being on the highly scenic 'Heart of Wales' line running from Shrewsbury to Swansea. More about this in a little.

I should also mention that Knighton is right on the Welsh/ English border. So, having been walking in Powys, Wales and Herefordshire, England I can add that I have just walked into Shropshire, England as well today.

And, yes, the railway again. I was in very good time for the 4.19 pm train bound for Shrewsbury. The line really preserved the atmosphere, very much of a past era. Older signalling (little colour-light development); a one-coach diesel train (reminiscent of a tram); little old stone-built stations; most remote, unspoilt scenery – and a general air of all that was old-fashioned. I took the train to Craven Arms, the junction with the main line from Shrewsbury to Newport etc. Intermediate 'halts' were at Bucknell, Hopton Heath (did not stop) and Broome.

I caught a fast train from Craven Arms, calling at Ludlow, Leominster, Hereford, Abergavenny, Pontypool and Cwmbran, before my station, Newport. Then a wait for the Portsmouth Harbour train, a change at Southampton Central, then a train to Cosham. Bed was reached at 1.15 in the morning. Yes, all being well, I will stay in Wales overnight next time.

It was good to reflect on 'about' half of Offa's Dyke Path being 'done', and another county, Shropshire reached; but sleep soon overtook the thoughts.

Day 46
6/3/12

KNIGHTON — PANPUNTON HILL — CWM-SANAHAM HILL — LLANFAIR HILL —
SPOAD HILL — NEWCASTLE-ON-CLUN — MOUNT AND
KNUCK BANKS — CHURCHTOWN
(13 miles approx)

Yes — the opening paragraph of Day 45 was right — I am now staying away overnight, again. So firstly, the journey to Wales yesterday, 5th March: I took a taxi to Cosham station, and a later train than recently — the 9.39 am — but calling at most of the 'usual' stations to Newport — followed by an express (Manchester-bound) stopping at Cwmbran, Abergavenny, Hereford, Leominster, Ludlow and Craven Arms, where again changed, to the Heart of Wales diesel rail bus — as 27th February — but only calling at Hopton Heath before reaching Knighton, where I alighted about 3 pm. I much enjoyed the 'bygone' atmosphere, as last week, of this 'third' train ride.

Had a pleasant afternoon in Knighton — meal in a teashop and a stroll round the streets — talked to various locals, including the policeman, all of whom gave me useful information on walking route, and put up at a lovely B&B (views of the next section of Offa's Dyke Path from my bedroom window). A fine, clear, cold, sunny day.

But now for today — very good accommodation and breakfast; I then shopped in the town before commencing walking around 9.15 am. I started out by the riverside path, following beside River Teme, and then crossed the Heart of Wales railway — very pretty wooded areas. The weather is really glorious — it is spring! Warm in the sun, refreshing in the breeze. Blue skies, light clouds, no rain.

A very steep climb was next on the list, from Panpunton Farm to the top of Panpunton Hill. Views all round, so clear today, including Knighton and the 'Gothic' arches of the viaduct at Knucklas. (The section from Knighton to Churchtown and somewhat beyond, is known as the 'switchback' part of the Dyke Path — extremely steep ups and downs, and the steepest, toughest part of the whole route!) I continued 'along the top' to Cwm-Sanaham Hill — then down (it seemed almost vertical!) to a cottage, Brynorgan, where I talked to a shepherd, who was with his sheep there. He confirmed I really had the best weather today.

Then on past Garbett Hall — gradients then became more moderate for a while — and up Llanfair Hill, and over Spoad Hill; then I left the Dyke Path, taking a steep 'down' to visit the village of Newcastle-on-Clun — a pretty spot. I continued along beautiful winding and hilly lanes, via Wellfield, Bridge Farm, Mount Bank and Knuck Bank. From woodland, I progressed to moorland — good views across Clun Forest.

Eventually I reached Offa's Dyke Path again and took the very steep descent through the conifers of Churchtown Wood. (In this 'Dyke' section, as in certain other areas today, there were particularly impressive views of it.) Churchtown was at the foot. The fine church, St John's, was the one feature – also, I think, a farm but nothing else. (Arrived – 4.30 pm.) A taxi man who met me said he took some Americans to see Offa's Dyke in this area. He asked if they needed any shopping before entering the 'wilds'. 'Oh,' they said. 'That's not a problem – we'll buy all we want at Churchtown!' The name conveys a very different impression to what it is like. A church – yes: a town – no.

Had a good ride back to Knighton via the picturesque old town of Clun – and, so, back to B & B. I have now done over half the Dyke Path.

Again, I was reminded of the 'certain' lady. (Knighton, though officially the halfway point because of its size, importance and position, is actually south of midway.) The lady would generously say, when sharing food at mealtimes with another person: 'We'll have half each, but I'll give you the bigger half.' There is no such thing. A half is a half! (I could say I have very much enjoyed starting the bigger half of Offa's Dyke Path today!)

But now for 7th March – the return home a real bonus, though not a walk. I took the 9.50 Heart of Wales line diesel rail bus, the other direction to 5th March, a three-hour trip through most beautiful countryside – valleys, hills, mountains – through 28 stations serving remote and charming villages – see Day 45 – it is the same 'bygone' atmosphere on a really grand scale. Stations are:

Knighton, Knucklas, Llangynllo, Llanbister Road, Dolau, Pen-y-Bont, Llandrindod, Builth Road, Cilmeri, Garth, Llangammarch, Llanwrtyd, Sugar Loaf, Cynghordy, Llandovery, Llanwrda, Llangadog, Llandeilo, Ffairfach, Llandybie, Ammanford, Pantyffynnon, Pontarddulais, Llangennech, Bynie, Llanelli (train reverses here), Gowerton, Swansea (Stopped at most)

The high old 'Gothic' stone viaduct at Knucklas and views from it, and the huge height of mountainsides above the line at Sugarloaf, were two highly impressive sights – but there was so much more! Plenty of tunnels, embankments, river bridges . . .

Changed to train for Cardiff Central at Swansea, semi-fast, via Neath, Briton Ferry, Port Talbot Parkway, Bridgend, and other stations; changed again at the capital of Wales, Cardiff Central, for Cosham via Newport, and the rest of my 'usual' route.

An extremely enjoyable 'mini break', and there was more time for walking again – hence a higher route mileage on this heading than for some time.

CHURCHTOWN — CWM — MELLINGTON HALL — BROMPTON CROSS ROADS
— LYMORE PARK — MONTGOMERY — ROWNAL — FORDEN — CILCEWYDD —
WELSHPOOL
(16 miles approx)

A similar arrangement to last time. So – firstly the journey yesterday: in fact – I could say this was identical to 5th March recorded in Day 46, with trains: 9.39 am Cosham to Newport, followed by Newport to Craven Arms via Hereford etc, and 'Heart of Wales' rail bus on to Knighton but calling only at Bucknell.

Then another pleasant afternoon in Knighton – even the meal was in the same teashop. And another good look around the town before booking in at the same very good B&B. The weather was a little showery, but quite cold.

However, now for the day of the walk, 18th March. After a rest, and another good breakfast, the same taxi man as last time drove me via Clun etc again, to Churchtown. There was quite a shower of rain, but it seemed to be what is known as the clearing-up shower, as the rest of the day was gloriously sunny and clear – with a chilly breeze. So the views were excellent.

I began walking around 10 o'clock, the steepest climb of the whole of this 'switchback' area – up, up, up! Very soon it was nearly as steep down. And another very steep up, and another steep down after these. The views down into the Vale of Montgomery, and all around, were grand. I entered the Vale at Cwm, after which the Dyke Path was much flatter. Proceeded through the woods in the grounds of Mellington Hall, which I saw – a most imposing 1876 mansion in fine 'Gothic' style - and then on to Brompton Cross Roads.

Then followed a very straight stretch of the Dyke Path, and very flat again for some distance (past Ditches Farm), but I detoured off through Lymore Park to get to Montgomery, which is such a superb little old town, overlooked by the castle ruins on the high hill. Broad Street is like a town square, a quaint centrepiece to the quiet country medieval and Georgian jewel. Many delightful old buildings – also a delightful ice cream – I much enjoyed. Apricot and walnut in brandy sauce! The ice cream season is upon us again.

Continued on a minor road which led me to Offa's Dyke Path again, and which I followed via Rownal. There are also 'Montgomeryshire' signs in this area, although I assumed this old county was absorbed into the new county of Powys. I was, of course also walking in parts of English Shropshire as well as these 'old' and 'new' Welsh counties. The Dyke Path rose again at Hem, and descended to Forden, where a road led through the village. I continued on this road, to detour to Welshpool, although the Dyke Path 'takes' another route. On via Fron, Cilcewydd, and here I was again beside the River Severn. I suppose I was last beside it at the start of the Dyke Path at Sedbury Cliffs – it was very much wider there.

I crossed the Severn on the road bridge, and followed rather busy roads along the valley, past the 'Montgomeryshire Mid-Wales Airport' – a smallish, rural location – and past Sarn-y-Bryn-Caled, getting better and better views of Welshpool and the Severn Valley. I was soon in Welshpool, the road running alongside the railway, and I reached the main line station around 5.30 pm. (I hope to see the steam railway station, and 'do' the lovely Welshpool next time.)

A local taxi man soon conveyed me via Churchstoke, Clun and districts on this pleasant spring evening, back to Knighton for my B&B.

And the homeward journey, 19th March: I had the same 'bonus' journey as last time, 7th March, 2012. The wonderful long way round, changing trains at Swansea and Cardiff again. The Heart of Wales line never ceases to impress. On this route, I was served with coffee, part of one of my snacks. The waiter who brought this to where I was sitting said to my surprise: 'I'm afraid I've dropped your stick. But it doesn't matter – I'll go back and get another one for you.' (!)

I glanced down – my stick was still propped up against the seat, and looked OK. I couldn't see how he could have dropped it. What did it matter if he had dropped it? I often drop it. But how kind of him to go back and get another one for me – perhaps he would bring me another rucksack too – and another map-case, and hat . . . Then I looked down again – on the floor was a small wooden coffee-stirrer – the shape of a model stick. Truth dawned!

So, another most enjoyable 'holiday' – glorious weather again, today too. But they do say parts of the country may be in for a drought. However, I've been so fortunate with so much sun for walks.

DAY 48
3/4/12

WELSHPOOL – THE MONTGOMERY CANAL (WELSHPOOL WHARF – BUTTINGTON CROSS – POOL QUAY – BURGEDIN LOCKS – ARDDLEEN – FOUR CROSSES) – LLANYMYNECH – PANT – LLYNCLYS – MORDA – OSWESTRY
(19 miles approx)

*F*irstly, the 'prelude' journey, 2nd April. The train routes were: Cosham to Newport; Newport to Shrewsbury (via Hereford, Craven Arms, Church Stretton etc); Shrewsbury to Welshpool – starting about 9.30 am, finishing about 4 pm. Very clear views of the countryside in the spring sunshine. Shrewsbury retains its status as an important railway junction, with a large-scale old station. Five separate lines from all directions meet here. Welshpool is on the Aberystwyth and Pwllheli route.

On Day 47, I wrote that I hoped to 'do' Welshpool – so I 'did' it straight away. I booked in at a good hotel, central in the town, and explored its picturesque old streets, walked to see the Welshpool and Llanfair narrow-gauge steam railway (a train just leaving) at Raven Square station, Welshpool – a fine sight – and I walked up a long drive through parkland to see the grand old Powys Castle, set in fine gardens.

I think though, it's now time to describe today's events. Breakfast was self-service and I was not mean with myself. I began today's walk – as from 9.45 am. A bright, chilly start (and a less bright, but more chilly finish). I started out at Welshpool Wharf, on the Montgomery Canal, which I followed northwards on the tow-path for a long way. Parts of it were shared by Offa's Dyke Path. It was just so beautiful, so rural, so charming. There was some boating but the canal is not navigable further on – reeds have taken over, with swans nesting in them. Some sections were deeply wooded, some open with extensive views around. There were quite a lot of lock gates. The route passed through Buttington Cross, The Moors, Pool Quay, Bank, Wern, Burgedin Locks, Arddleen and Four Crosses. Primroses and daffodils abounding.

After this, I left the canal and Offa's Dyke Path, as I particularly wanted to see Oswestry (it has a silent 'w' but the town is pleasantly noisy). So I followed quite direct road routes – via another Wern, Llanymynech, Pant, Llynclys, Sweeney and Morda (I would not recommend some of these busier roads, especially where there are only very narrow grass verges to walk on.) But pavements reappeared just before Oswestry.

Oswestry seemed a very interesting town – a signboard advertised it as 'Border Market Town'. It seemed remarkable that although it is a good distance from the border (it is in England), culturally and historically it is very Welsh. Welsh is often spoken there. It is one of the larger border towns, with many old buildings. The town centre really had character. But I will hope to see more next time. My bus was coming. It was now 4 o'clock.

A jolly nice ride back, on routes similar to my walk, and good views of the canal from new angles. The canal is also used for fishing. There are a lot of signs up about where to fish, and where not, that did remind me again, of the 'certain lady'. So, another aside:

Enquirer: Do they fish in this river? (The Meon in Hampshire)
Certain Lady: Oh, yes, they do. I've seen the notices – so I know.
They say, 'No fishing'!

I think the point in her mind was that the notices actually read 'Private Fishing Only'. How easy it is to leave the audience baffled and confused if one omits the main point of the case.

And talking about the main points – I did visit a café in Welshpool in the evening, and among other things, much enjoyed a banana-split ice cream.

But just to conclude – the return journey home, 4th April. I pulled back the curtains at the window to reveal a significant, continuing fall of snow which was laying a little. The view from my room (first floor) overlooked the narrow main street in the old part of the town. A fine sight! By the time I left to walk to the station, everywhere looked very white, and there was a very cold wind.

I took the 11.01 train, combined of its two portions from Pwllheli and Aberystwyth (for Birmingham International) and alighted at Shrewsbury. Then travelled on an express from Manchester back to Newport. Good snowy views, especially of mountains and hills, but no snow falling, and none on low land. And then the usual (and non-snow) route back to Cosham, i.e. same route as 2nd April, in opposite direction.

Another excellent mini break – and the snow was very pretty. I thought it was pretty impressive, although some people, unfortunately may have found it pretty disruptive (!)

DAY 49
16/4/12

OSWESTRY – UPPER HENGOED – WESTON RHYN – BRONYGARTH – FRONCYSYLLTE
– THE LLANGOLLEN CANAL – TREVOR – LLANGOLLEN
(16 miles approx)

Yesterday's journey was a little more eventful than usual. I took 10.23 am train from Cosham, which terminated at Southampton Central. Due to railway engineering work, I then transferred to the upper deck of a very full bus, and we were whisked along fast roads and motorway to Salisbury – there, our connecting train conveyed us by 'usual' routes via Bristol etc. I alighted at Newport in excellent time for a meal, and the 3.36 pm Holyhead-bound express – via Hereford, Shrewsbury etc to Gobowen. I alighted at this delightful little country station, and reached Oswestry by taxi around 6 pm, (at B&B).

A little nostalgia – I well remember the name 'Gobowen'. My mother used to take my brother and I by train from Havant, Hampshire to Folkestone, Kent, for summer holidays with grandparents. The route from Guildford, Surrey onward (and corresponding return journey) was often by cross-country steam train. More clearly I remember the 'return': a two-coach steam train would arrive from Sandwich, via Dover, at Folkestone Central and take us at speed, with few stops. But at Ashford, coaches were attached from Margate, via Canterbury; and at Redhill, coaches were attached from Hastings, Eastbourne and Brighton. On alighting at

Guildford, we left a very impressive express of about 12 coaches, looking vastly different to the little train at Folkestone. Many stations were announced that it would be calling at – in my young mind I wondered wherever these places were – including Shrewsbury, Gobowen, Ruabon, Wrexham General, Chester General and Birkenhead Woodside. The other end of the world? We boys got so excited – talking constantly of how we were going on the Birkenhead train: that another passenger asked our mother if we came from Birkenhead. 'Your boys are saying so much about it!'

Gobowen of 15th April, 2012 has lived up to expectations! Countryside very scenic, weather bright and breezy, the whole journey delightful.

But now for today. B&B was very good, as I always seem to find. I did a quick walkabout of Oswestry, including shopping, admiration of older buildings, and a look at the fine old station building and tracks. This was once the hub of the Cambrian Railway system, but is closed. Restoration groups are trying to re-open lines here.

My walk commenced around 10.45, with weather as good as yesterday.

My route was via Upper Hengoed, Wern and Weston Rhyn. Here was a shop, and it sold ice creams. The description on one packet was irresistible. 'Classic vanilla ice cream enrobed with Belgian chocolate'. They know how to 'get' me. I need say no more.

The area was one of distant panoramic views, and nearby parkland. I continued to Pentre-Newydd and Bronygarth, where I rejoined Offa's Dyke Path and had good views of Chirk Castle, high on wooded hills. A steep 'down' and a steeper 'up' took me near the castle. A view near here was even more panoramic, including Cheshire ahead, and it could be further north too.

A long, steady descent followed, past Tyn-y-Groes and Caeaugwynion and down to the Llangollen Canal. I followed it on the tow-path, which I much enjoyed, and also much enjoyed not doing one section of it – the Pont Cysyllte Aqueduct, 1,000 feet long and 120 feet high. But (and see Day 29, and references to avoiding using a Severn Bridge) I did much enjoy walking below it, and looking up at it. After this, I resumed the attractive canal tow-path route. I had already come through Froncysyllte, before the aqueduct, and rejoined the canal at Trevor after it. I crossed the River Dee too, in between. So, on up the Vale of Llangollen, and below, it would appear Ruabon Mountain, I walked. The mountain was steep, craggy and towering above. Route ran past Plas-yn-pentre, Plas Ifa and Trevor Uchaf – then I entered Llangollen – I went into the town, saw the station with the restored steam railway, and crossed the River Dee on a fine old bridge (5.15 pm). A lovely old town, Llangollen – historic, bustling and, I think, unspoilt.

I caught a bus to Acrefair and another via Chirk, back to Oswestry, where I had a meal in a café, before returning to B&B.

Another particularly interesting day — I have well and truly reached North Wales, and crossed out of Shropshire, via the County of Wrexham, into Denbighshire.

DAY 50
17/4/12

LLANGOLLEN — PENTREFELIN — VALLE CRUCIS ABBEY — HORSESHOE PASS —
PENTRE-BWLCH — NANT-Y-GARTH PASS — LLANFAIR DYFFRYN CLWYD — RUTHIN
(16 miles approx)

*D*ay 50 sounds like a 'Day of Jubilee'! (Perhaps it is appropriate to celebrate the last paragraph of yesterday.)

And today proved to be another most interesting day. On studying the map, I felt inclined to continue a variation from Offa's Dyke Path, as I do at times when I feel there is a good reason. I had detoured off yesterday after the aqueduct area to enjoy the beauty of the canal and Llangollen. By continuing by the direct not-too-busy road to Ruthin, I could enjoy excellent scenery and follow both the Horseshoe and Nant-y-Garth Passes. These two passes provided interesting, contrasting features. The former was very steep and winding by the road, to a very high, open summit: the latter involved a quite steep, also winding road route through a 'Mini Cheddar Gorge'.

It certainly was well worth it. Though the day started wet, sunshine soon prevailed, with chilly winds, clear views and just a few short showers. I took buses from Oswestry to Acrefair, and Acrefair to Llangollen where I had a strawberries-and-cream ice cream, and set off for Ruthin around 11.45. The road followed the canal and the preserved steam railway for some distance. Past Pentrefelin, I had good views of the ruined, but attractive Valle Crucis Abbey (established 1201) and of mountains all around, as I started the ascent of Horseshoe Pass. I was soon high up on the Maesyrychen Mountain. As I rounded one sharp bend, thinking I must be near the top, I saw a much higher part of my road come into view — and a much higher part of the mountain. 'The half had not been told'. I passed Oernant and eventually reached the summit, marked by a sign confirming the height of 1,367 feet, and a café, which I did not fail to visit. Marvellous views all round. The downward, northward descent of the pass was not so long and steep, and there were clear views westward of high mountains, which I assumed to be Snowdonia.

I walked via Tai-Newyddion, Pentre-Bwlch and Ty'n-y-pwll, and down the second pass (all downhill), the Nant-y-Garth Pass, as I said best described as a 'Mini Cheddar Gorge'. The Horseshoe Pass was very wild and open; this further pass was set low between well-wooded crags and hills, winding beside a fast-flowing stream which meandered among rocky boulders. Yes, both passes had contrasting but significant attractions.

I emerged on to flatter landscapes but with the glorious Clwydian Hills to the east. I passed the Llysfasi College of Agriculture – plenty of sheep fields – and reached the village of Llanfair Dyffryn Clwyd. I stopped at an inn for crisps, biscuits and orange drink, where the proprietor gave me a copy of their village news magazine; he and other locals took quite an interest in my choice of route for today's walking – and the reasons – as too, they did at my B&B.

Then covered the remaining two miles to the lovely old town of Ruthin by 7 pm, the time when a taxi arrived for me as arranged at the entrance to the castle. Its medieval ruins were 'overbuilt' in the early 1800s to create a fine castle/house building in which impressive 'medieval banquets' are held still.

So I was driven back via Wrexham to Oswestry B&B again. Certainly a day well worth remembering.

And to conclude with my journey home, 18th April. After yet another excellent breakfast, I had my third ride of the holiday by taxi – back to Gobowen for a train around 11 am, a simpler journey than 'coming up' – no works on the line. Just the change of trains at Newport and train to Cosham by my 'usual' route.

Another wonderful holiday – the more so, as I had two days out walking, instead of one.

Day 51
13/05/12

Ruthin – Llanbedr-Dyffryn-Clwyd – Bwlch Penbarras – Moel Famau –
Moel Dywyll – Llangynhafal – Pentre'r Felin –
Waen – Brookhouse – Denbigh
(15 miles approx)

Yesterday's journey was as usual, interesting. As I get further and further north, the train ride from Newport (South Wales) becomes ever more of an event. (From Cosham to Newport is of course, always enjoyable too.) Stops after Newport have increased to: Cwmbran, Pontypool & New Inn, Abergavenny, Hereford, Ludlow, Craven Arms, Church Stretton, Shrewsbury, Gobowen, Chirk, Ruabon and Wrexham General – where I alighted from the Holyhead express. (See also Day 49, re some of these stations.)

With clear, sunny weather, views from the train showed up well, especially of Welsh hills and mountains and the area of the Dee Valley between Gobowen and Wrexham. I caught a bus from Wrexham to Ruthin – and a taxi from Ruthin to a lovely remote old farmhouse/cottage, right off the beaten track, for B&B. Reached my destination around 6.45 pm, all very unspoilt scenery around this part of Wales. Wrexham, is of course a large town – urban, residential, industrial, impressive.

So to today – yes, the B & B house (I have mentioned) had a great atmosphere with wooden beams, slightly sloping floors I think – all the really good old stuff – near Rhewl. After the excellent breakfast, I walked into Ruthin before commencing the 'real' walk. This pre-walk took me through scenic woodland and on to a main road to Ruthin, which I explored further, seeing much of the well–preserved old town centre, the character of which fitted in well with the castle and its history, already observed on Day 50. Of some considerable interest too was the rather foreboding old Ruthin Gaol – a grim old place, but fascinating indeed – although I did not go inside! It was closed as a prison but open to tourists. High stone walls, securely barred windows.

Save to say that Ruthin was officially described as 'Historic Market Town' on road signs, I think it is time to describe the walk itself now – I started at 11.45 approx in good clear sunny weather which lasted all day, but in wind which grew ever-stronger, to gale force I should think! I had a cold coming on before I reached Wales, so thought, 'Plenty of fresh air will be the best thing'. Maybe you can have too much of a good thing – I felt I was getting rather an overdose of this remedy! It was very cold, high on the hills later too.

I followed the Mold road via Pentre to Llanbedr-Dyffryn-Clwyd, a charming hillside village, where I turned off into a very steep, narrow winding lane, which led me up and up, high into the Clwydian Hills. Up on the open moorland at the top, the views were well and truly rewarding. I passed Halfway House and joined Offa's Dyke Path again at Bwlch Penbarras – I followed this through Moel Famau Country Park to Moel Famau, the highest of the summits in the Clwydian Range, the name meaning 'Mother Mountain'. The ruined 'Jubilee Tower' stood at the top. Here, the wind had reached terrific strength – and biting cold. Plenty of walkers there, sheltering in the non-windy side of the tower. I joined them and gained very interesting information from them and from my guide book on the areas we could see around us, much being very far below. In the clear atmosphere, Birkenhead, Liverpool and even Crosby were distinctly visible; much of the Wirral; and the River Dee, towards Chester; I think (possibly) the Pennine Hills; the Irish Sea, of course; and Snowdonia Range, including Snowdon and Cader Idris and other summits – also other surrounding areas – quite amazing I thought.

I continued on the path, which descended very steeply and then rose to a lesser peak, Moel Dywyll. Views into the Vale of Clwyd, including the towns of Ruthin and Denbigh were especially good. I then descended a steep track into the Vale, reaching Plas Isaf and lanes through villages and hamlets (Llangynhafal, Ffordd las, Pentre'r-felin, Groes Efa and Waen) to Pont Glan-y-Wern. This road was busier so I turned off on a riverside footpath, to Brookhouse. All very scenic still. Then followed a main road into Denbigh (town centre), arriving about 6.15

pm. Quite a spectacular town on a steep slope. I had time for a vanilla, chocolate and walnut ice cream, before catching a bus back up the Vale to Ruthin. There I liaised with the taxi driver again, who transported my luggage to tonight's B&B. I was now staying in Ruthin, in another very old house – I really felt I was entering a stately home (16th Century) – a fine spacious hall – and I was in a fine spacious room. More old wooden beams and sloping floors.

A very rewarding day – especially the views at Famau. I was certainly tired, with, yes, probably more cold air than I really needed for my cold!

DAY 52
14/05/12

DENBIGH – TREFNANT – ST. ASAPH – RHYLLON – DYSERTH – TY NEWYDD – BRYNIAU – TAN-YR-ALLT – PRESTATYN HILLSIDE NATURE RESERVE – PRESTATYN
(16 miles approx)

Note: 688 miles from Land's End: 236 Offa's Dyke or Dyke areas

*A*fter a very good breakfast in the splendid surroundings of the B&B, I set off by bus from Ruthin to Denbigh (town centre), and commenced today's walk about 11.15, having also explored the main areas of this fine old town, including a climb up to the old castle at the top of the hill – a partly ruined, but still impressive castle.

Weather is still cold and clear and sunny – and not so windy as yesterday. I followed a pleasant rural, non-main road down the Vale of Clwyd past Plâs Chambres and Green Ucha, to the north-west part of the village of Trefnant. The local postman here helpfully confirmed to me the names of places I could see in the distance (St Asaph, and further on Rhyl and Prestatyn on the North Wales coast). I continued on a slightly busier road, via Plas–coch, Eryl Hall and Cornel, to the very attractive small city of St Asaph. The fine cathedral is in fact the smallest in Wales or England; 'a miniature city' is a good description of what would strike you at first sight as being a charming, unspoilt little old town, with fine river bridge and steep main street. I also enjoyed a small ice cream/lolly (orange) – quite modest for once. (I do eat a lot of other things by the way – it's just that some things stick in my memory more.)

I continued to walk by quiet, scenic country lanes via Rhyllon and past Ty-Ucha and Ty-Isa farms and Plas Is Llan, getting steadily nearer to the northern 'end' of the steep Clwydian Hills – views of which were very good. On reaching the village of Dyserth, I followed the main road through the hills, past Ochr-y-foel and up to the point where Offa's Dyke Path crosses. I rejoined the path, which

I had left after the two 'moels' yesterday, and followed it again, all the way to its northern end.

This last section was especially impressive – via Ty Newydd, Bryniau and Tan-yr-allt on high hills and cliffs above an old quarry to Prestatyn Hillside Nature Reserve – here magnificent views emerged of the town and sea over 500 feet below, but also of the coast along to Llandudno; the Snowdonia mountains; and the Isle of Anglesey – all distinctly clear! The 30 giant turbines out to sea closer up of the North Hoyle wind farm, were also quite visible.

After steep ups and downs in this area, the path took its final (very steep) down into Prestatyn – and through the centre of the town (High Street, railway station and Bastion Road) to Nova Centre, Prestatyn Tourist Information Centre – at the promenade, sands and sea – the Irish Sea, which I reached about 6 pm. A pleasant, popular, busy town and resort; and for myself, a great sense of satisfaction to have completed the route of Offa's Dyke Path – at times, the exact route; at times, equivalent routes - to explore valleys, villages, towns etc of alternative particular interest.

My cold had not really improved, but it certainly did not spoil the enjoyment of today! However, I was also pleased to board a comfortable taxi driven by a helpful taxi man for the return journey via St Asaph, Denbigh etc to Ruthin, and to enter the warm, comfortable room at my B&B.

As regards counties, the walk finished in Denbighshire although at times recently, I may have crossed in and out of Flintshire – both Welsh counties. But as regards countries, I have yet to cross from Wales to England, apparently because of the significant difference in the boundary now, and in the days of Offa.

But I have already enjoyed clear views into the north of England.

With regard to my return journey home, 15th May – I had a good breakfast with an American couple who had just arrived at the B&B, who seemed to be enjoying 'doing' Britain, and a number of other countries – they told me about long walks in the States. I took a bus back to Wrexham and train from Wrexham General to Shrewsbury, then another onto Newport, and the third, thence onto Cosham. But routes were the same as on Day 51 and views were good. I still had the cold!

But of course, I felt very pleased to have walked to another landmark. As to Offa's Dyke – there was a real atmosphere about this ancient structure. If I was asked what most impressed me about it, I might however feel tempted to indulge in a little silliness. At times, it looks very much like an old railway embankment – here I go, again! Imagine if there would be 'ancient' horses and chariots running the equivalent to a modern railway service, and then consider some of the announcements:

'When you leave the Chariot, please mind the gap between it, and the edge of Offa's Dyke, and please ensure you have all your personal armour and weaponry with you.

'Any armour or weaponry left unattended is liable to be removed, disposed of and blown up.

'We are informed that the Sedbury Cliffs to Prestatyn service is running approximately two weeks late. This is due to a horse having bolted, leaving the Chariot stuck. We apologise for the late running of this service, and for any inconvenience this may cause. Various soldiers are running after the horse. Please listen for further announcements.

Day 53
10/06/12

Prestatyn — Presthaven Sands — Gronant — Tan Lan — Mostyn — Llannerch-y-Mor — Greenfield — Bagillt — Flint — Oakenholt — Rockcliffe — Connah's Quay — Shotton
(21 miles approx)

The journey 'up' on 9th June — rather different and very interesting I would say. Due, I think to railway engineering works, I was allocated a different route. I started at Cosham as 'usual' — train to Bristol Temple Meads, then changed to a Manchester express, calling at Bristol Parkway and Cheltenham Spa, and Birmingham New Street where I alighted. This last-named station, I think could be best described as an enormous underground station. All well covered over. Prior to this, well-worth mentioning, I enjoyed the experience of riding up the Lickey Incline — I think it is about two miles long, and the steepest main line gradient in Britain at 1 in 37 ¾, but modern trains these days seem to take it quite easily — from Bromsgrove up to Blackwell. After this, there was a gentler descent via Bournville, into Birmingham.

I again changed trains — used a Holyhead express, calling at Smethwick Galton Bridge, Wolverhampton, Telford Central, Wellington, Shrewsbury, Gobowen, Chirk, Ruabon, Wrexham General, Chester, Shotton, Flint and Prestatyn — my destination.

The weather was good and the views were clear. But on arriving in North Wales I found out that parts of west, mid and north of the country were only just recovering from severe flooding after exceptional rain. Caravans were swept along, homes and streets flooded, people were airlifted out — thankfully, apparently there were no fatalities and I think no serious injuries.

I was met at the station by the proprietor of the B&B, but as they were full, and they owned another house, he drove me there to spend the time on my own, where I made myself very comfortable after a full day's travelling, which included more of the old Birkenhead train route (see Day 49).

And so to today – I made myself some breakfast and had a walk around Prestatyn. Weather very pleasant today – no rain fell, despite the floods of yesterday. It was generally pretty wet and muddy underfoot, but sunny and cool. Starting around 11 o'clock, I walked to the promenade, sands and sea where I enjoyed clear views of the Welsh coast, westward as last time. This 'northward' walk does take some temporary changes of direction at times, and I had to proceed south-east to follow the coastline of the River Dee Estuary. Continued on the sands and in the dunes, and beside the golf course and past the caravan parks. Interestingly, through the whole walk I was following near the Holyhead to Chester main railway line, and the River Dee. Walked via Barkby Beach and Presthaven Sands. Stopped for ice cream and crisps, and crossed from Denbighshire into Flintshire. I joined the main 'coast' road here, and in the circumstances, it was sensible to follow beside it, or similar roads for all the walk – particularly because for most of the way there were very pleasant, very wide grass verges – or good pavements in towns. Also, the views of the railway and the River Dee, and across it, were excellent.

I walked on via Gronant, Tan Lan, Glasdir and Garth – here were fine views (from a railway bridge) across the estuary to West Kirby, on the Wirral Peninsula. Continued to Mostyn viewpoint for similar vistas, including Mostyn Bank and Quay areas. There has been a quay here since Norman times. I passed Mostyn village and the now–closed railway station, with its well–preserved ornate old building. On past the Port of Mostyn – now very industrial – and Glan-y-Don, to Llannerch-y-mor for a further ice cream, this time with chocolate sauce. Then on to Greenfield, Walwen, Whelston and Bagillt, where I paused for more good views of the estuary and the Wirral (Neston). And so I walked on via Bedol to Flint, for ice cream number three (preceded by Cheddar cheese ploughman's sandwiches, I think). Flint proved a delightful old town, with some charming buildings, and especially the old ruined, but impressive castle, beside the narrowing Dee.

The final part of the walk led me via Pentre Ffwrndan and Oakenholt into more industrial areas again – and then urban areas – Rockcliffe, Kelsterton, Golftyn, Connah's Quay and Shotton, with its interestingly combined high-level and low-level railway station. I arrived around 7.30 pm and caught a train back via Flint to Prestatyn, and walked back to the house. Certainly a very lovely day again, and rather different to the recent inland ones. 'Variety is the spice of life'.

Just one slightly amusing point. In the very comfortable house, one aspect needlessly disturbed me. At times I was aware of muffled or faint sounds. I seemed to hear distant creaks, clicks – and footsteps – but nothing else in the stillness (ghosts?). The following morning I suddenly thought to check the obvious. Going outside I realised this was a semi-detached house – I have lived, and stayed, often in 'semis'. I suppose when the neighbour is very quiet, and you don't hear talking or TV or music etc, the few remaining sounds can be interesting to the imagination. I hope I didn't shout out in my sleep and cause the neighbour alarm because of my unfounded fears!

Section 4

Chester, Lancashire, Lancaster & Morecambe Bay

117 miles

Day 54
11/06/12

SHOTTON – QUEENSFERRY – SANDYCROFT – HAWARDEN AIRPORT –
SALTNEY – CHESTER
(11 miles approx)

So, after an excellent night's sleep and the assurance I now had of the absence of ghosts (!), I commenced the day with a walk into Prestatyn centre for some breakfast and a general look around the town. Weather was ideal for walking again – just like yesterday. What was very remarkable was that having avoided the rain and floods in Wales, I now heard that intense rain and severe floods were starting to affect parts of Hampshire and West Sussex (Portsmouth, Chichester, Bognor Regis and Worthing areas) – i.e. my own 'home areas' – but not so seriously as in Wales. Roads and streets were deeply flooded, some main routes closed and homes, shops etc, flooded.

The most convenient train connection I was able to use took me via Flint to Shotton, where I was able to commence walking around 11.45 – a little late, but not a problem. A Bounty ice cream was a very early highlight of the walk. I continued to use quite direct roads and streets, as good grass verges were still usable for most of the way. My route was via Queensferry, Pentre, Sandycroft and past Hawarden Airport, and Beeches Farm and Cop House Farm – after this, the road ran parallel to the River Dee, a wide river, instead of, as yesterday, an enormous estuary. I then transferred on to the River Dee Path to the industrial, riverside part of Saltney, and back to a main road.

Here I reached a very significant landmark – not just the boundary of Flintshire and Cheshire but the boundary of Wales and England. I was back in my 'Home Country' again! But I supposed the north of England now, not the west of England as before, or the English/Welsh borders. The route was now resuming its northward direction again – in 'England's green and pleasant land'.

So at this point, I entered the City of Chester. It was highly impressive and a real historical 'gem' – interesting that it is set in an area which has become quite industrial since its ancient times. But there were very beautiful parts of England and Wales nearby, and I did not feel that recent developments spoilt impressions.

My approach to the city centre was through a fine, older, residential area of Chester, with spacious properties. I crossed the River Dee on a high-arched bridge and gained clear views of the castle, city walls, racecourse and the cathedral – and the really old part of the city. Chester has the most complete city walls compared with any other British city – I walked part of them – they were virtually entirely preserved. Its Roman history, and that of other eras were well in evidence. One very outstanding feature was The Rows. These black and white half-timbered buildings in the city centre form two-tier galleries of shops, so for the upper level, I walked up steps, to a kind of balcony frontage to the stores – excellent shops of all varieties they were too and the buildings themselves were medieval. I explored the Eastgate area, especially where the City Wall Walk ran above the grand old gate, with its fine clock. I indulged in very good refreshments – all-fruits lolly, two tub ices (vanilla and strawberries–and–cream), orange juice – and later, at the station, soup and cake.

I had originally intended to walk on beyond Chester, but the city so captivated me, I felt I should linger. How best can I describe? It must rank very high as one of Britain's best Roman cities. It was a gem of a place certainly, unique in many aspects – I would say magnificent, most charming and intriguing. I hope to come back and stay there soon.

I completed today's walking about 4 pm and returned by train via Flint etc to Prestatyn again, and made myself at home in the house – for the evening and night.

As to the return home, 12th June – the news informed me that flooding was continuing in the south in some areas. The 'house owner' kindly drove me back to where a good breakfast, at a very pleasant homely café (near to Prestatyn station) was served by someone known to him.

I took a train from Prestatyn right through to Newport, via Chester, Wrexham, Shrewsbury, Hereford etc, and changed to the 'usual' service via Bristol Temple Meads etc to Cosham for taxi home – and learned that our area was not now affected much by the flooding, although things were still 'not too good' in parts of West Sussex.

So – a very worthwhile mini break, again. Pastures new reached. The walking was a lot flatter this time and made for faster progress; I liked the challenges of the hills, but there was an 'up' side, speed-wise when you don't go 'up' so much – although also a 'down' side, when you don't go speeding 'down' so much – excuse the slightly confusing pun, please.

DAY 55
8/7/12

CHESTER – MICKLE & BRIDGE TRAFFORD – DUNHAM-ON-THE-HILL – HELSBY – FRODSHAM – SUTTON WEAVER – PRESTON BROOK – DARESBURY – HR. & LR. WALTON – MANCHESTER SHIP CANAL – WARRINGTON (BANK QUAY)
(21 miles approx)

Yesterday's journey was quite eventful. The recent weather has still been extremely wet, with more flooding in various parts of the country. This accounted for late running of trains – my train from Cosham was 20 minutes late (via Bristol Temple Meads to Newport, South Wales) and I missed the connection for Chester. A later Manchester-bound express, which I took, terminated at Crewe! En route, I noted that the River Wye at Hereford looked almost about to burst its banks, and many fields further on were completely flooded, with farm vehicles stranded as if out to sea – paths and lanes were flooded, too. On approaching Shrewsbury, we were informed that a freight train had derailed, closing all lines to the north of the station. Our train conductor dealt most efficiently with the rearrangements. We were advised to stay on the train, which was diverted on very circuitous routes via Wellington, Telford Central (and nearly back to Wolverhampton!), Penkridge and Stafford, to Crewe – which proved much better than taking a replacement bus service. Another train reached Crewe and took us to Chester – arrival time nearly two hours late! Crewe, incidentally, I found very interesting, with its miles of sidings and railways works buildings. A huge station on the London Euston to Glasgow Central main line, and fast Anglo-Scottish expresses (I assume) thundering through non-stop. After a quick meal at Chester station, I made my way to my B&B nearby.

Another weak pun – I must not allow myself to be carried away by trains, as this is a book about a walk. Time to get to 8th July itself. After an excellent breakfast in this pleasant old house near the city centre, I set off walking about 10 o'clock, enjoying fine and dry weather, despite recent heavy rains – indeed it was very warm in the sunshine most of the time. I followed a main road through a pleasant residential part of Chester – again, I followed not-too-busy main roads nearly all day, finding the wide grass verges ideal. I was particularly impressed with so much rural beauty all the way to Warrington in Merseyside. I had thought that proceeding north would lead me to more industrial localities. Progressively, I saw more factories, chimneys, pylons – toward the end of the day I think, too, refineries, and other evidence of chemical industry, but all these were generally in the distance.

I was soon out in the open country, and enjoyed the walk through the charming villages of Mickle Trafford and Bridge Trafford, with their picturesque houses, and gardens in bloom. Then on via Morley Bridge, and into Dunham-on-the-Hill, similarly lovely, with views from the Hill looking good. And so to Helsby, a pleasant little town with pleasant large ice creams, and via Netherton to Frodsham, a larger town, particularly lovely, with its wide tree-lined main street and old buildings. There were distant views of the Mersey Estuary in this area.

I walked on via Newtown, and crossed the bridges over the River Weaver and Weaver Navigation. I passed Marshgate Farm, and continued through Sutton Weaver to the border of Cheshire and 'Mersey', as the sign recorded it. Then on via more pleasant country, through Preston Brook village, and beside Preston on the Hill, to Daresbury, and past Hollyhedge Farm. I crossed the Cheshire Ring Canal at Higher Walton and, after Lower Walton, crossed the Manchester Ship

Canal by a bridge, which can be 'lifted' for shipping as required. Thus, I entered Warrington, proceeding to the town centre area and Bank Quay railway station (which I reached around 6 pm). At this point, Liverpool lay to the west of me, and Manchester to the east.

Bank Quay was, to me, an interesting station, being on the main 'West Coast' London Euston to Glasgow Central line, like Crewe, and I saw at least one more Anglo-Scottish express, among other trains. I returned by a more local service, calling at Runcorn East, Frodsham, Helsby and Chester, for my walk back to the B&B.

Certainly another memorable day. People I met were very helpful and friendly – indeed typical northern Britishers, too. I much enjoyed listening to the Lancashire accent (although I think it is tomorrow when I actually cross into Lancashire hopefully).

DAY 56
9/7/12

WARRINGTON (BANK QUAY) – LONGFORD – WINWICK – NEWTON-LE-WILLOWS – HAYDOCK PARK – ASHTON-IN-MAKERFIELD – BRYN – GOOSE GREEN – WIGAN
(*14 miles approx*)

*A*fter another good breakfast, I walked direct to Chester station, and took the train back up to Warrington Bank Quay, calling at all stations, as yesterday. I then resumed 'official' walking for the day, firstly seeing the town centre in more detail (about 11.45). There was a pleasant mix of old and new architecture. I visited shops – the Indoor Market, with its highly comprehensive range of stalls, was most impressive. At a postcard stall, a very jolly, helpful, Lancashire-type guy gave me very useful information on the best route to Wigan. Just to follow the A49 all the way – a direct and interesting route, including Newton-le-Willows (which I think he pronounced in his local dialect as 'NEWTLY WILLAS').

So I walked to Warrington Central station where I joined the A49. Weather was cloudier and cooler today, but the views were clear. I proceeded via Longford. This suburban area of Warrington was quite industrial, but in due course I reached the countryside, and the pleasant village of Winwick. It was again a day of good grass-verge walking, very much beside this relatively quiet 'A' road. I passed Cop Holt Farm before entering Newton-le-Willows. It was quite a small town, one of the few medieval towns of Merseyside, and, in fact, Saxon in origin. Parts of it looked quite old, and interesting, certainly.

My route then took me past Haydock Park, and into the busy little town of Ashton-in-Makerfield – a good ice cream stop. Stone and brick buildings and cobbled areas gave quite a fine feeling of a northern town.

Interestingly, I saw a lot of people in this area and in the next town, Bryn, but it was only just after that, I had occasion to want to ask for some information, but by then, there was hardly anyone to be seen! I saw some high distant hills to the east, and wondered if they might perhaps be the Pennines.

I saw one man, working by a van, but he said he was not from this area at all. I saw two people just ahead, but they crossed the road and disappeared. Then I did meet a chap, who assured me the hills were not the Pennines. I do also like to double-check information, to be quite sure, though. I then saw somebody ahead who suddenly disappeared down a cul-de-sac; then a couple with a baby in a pram, who were rushing somewhere (obviously in a great hurry); then a man parked in his van, but he was on his mobile phone; then a man who suddenly disappeared into business premises, but he came out again, and was then talking on his mobile phone – and then success: a chap just ahead, with earphones, but he willingly took them out. Answer, 'No – they are definitely not the Pennines'. He explained he was a 'local', who knew the area very well. Much ado about nothing!

So I continued downward via Goose Green and Newtown into Wigan, reaching the town centre around 5.15 pm. I passed some commercial and industrial suburbs – also residential – and the canal, and Wigan Pier; apparently some well-restored history here. Reached the two stations, North Western and Wallgate, and climbed the street up a short, steep hill at the town centre. Plenty of fine old buildings – and good shops here – I bought a few maps. Fine, interesting stations, too, I should say.

I took a London Euston bound express (probably from Scotland) from Wigan North Western to Warrington Bank Quay (particularly impressive), and changed to a stopping service, as yesterday, to Chester, and enjoyed a meal there, again, before returning to B&B. Another very enjoyable day.

And so for the return home, 10th July. Good breakfast and good trip. The return services were the exact opposite to 7th July! Everything went like clockwork. There was some heavy rain, but no flooding disruption apparently. I took the 10.20 from Chester, via Shrewsbury, Hereford etc to Newport, with an excellent connection for Cosham via Bristol Temple Meads, and I was home by about 5 pm.

Very pleasant to reflect on all the memories of the North of England. As they say there, and I like the accent immensely, I feel that I can say that I'm really getting 'OOP COUNTRY'.

DAY 57
29/7/12

WIGAN — WHITLEY — STANDISH — COPPULL MOOR — CHARNOCK RICHARD —
BOLTON GREEN — EUXTON — LEYLAND — FARINGTON — LOSTOCKHALL —
BAMBER BRIDGE — PENWORTHAM — PRESTON
(20 miles approx)

*D*ay 57 — I think of '57 Varieties'; perhaps appropriate as I now seem to be starting on a new variety of train routes. Firstly, Cosham to Southampton Central (fast) — then a Bournemouth-to-Manchester express (CrossCountry) calling at Southampton Airport (Parkway), Winchester, Basingstoke, Reading (and thence via scenic parts of the River Thames Valley), Oxford, Banbury, Leamington Spa, Coventry, Birmingham International, Birmingham New Street — to Wolverhampton, where I changed to a Virgin Voyager Edinburgh-bound express, calling at Crewe and Warrington Bank Quay, before Wigan North Western, where I alighted. Saw some fine countryside — pleasant rolling landscapes, tranquil rivers including the Thames itself. The day started hot in the south, but it was sunny, cold and windy in the north. Having recently enjoyed the Queen's Diamond Jubilee Celebrations, as a nation, the present theme to occupy everyone is London Olympics 2012, which are now proceeding!

Having booked in at a good hotel in Wigan, I had time in the evening to explore, to see a little more of the town than last time. The benefit of the lighter evenings in the north of England was noticeable. Interestingly, I see I referred to a 'short, steep hill' last time (Day 56). Honestly, it was not a steep hill — this shows the difference between climbing a hill at the end of a day's walking to at the start of a walk, now — it's 'all in the mind'! I also visited Wigan Pier (like a 'stump' jutting onto the canal). This was an area I only passed by last time — tonight I experienced the atmosphere of history, and saw well-preserved, old waterside buildings close-up — mills and warehouses I think. I feel I have 'done' Wigan properly now. And a good chicken roast at the hotel, too!

So for 29th July — after a good rest and a much enjoyed breakfast, starting at 10 am I walked northwards out of the town, through the pleasant residential area of Whitley, towards the country. It was one of those days of short, sharp showers, and plenty of them — like Day 32, but more so — coat off and on, non-stop! But later, sunshine prevailed.

I walked on grass or pavement beside the A49 again — and other roads later, also very interestingly, seeing a lot of the London to Glasgow West Coast main railway, at times — and fast expresses. Walked through the small town of Standish, and entered Lancashire at Langtree. On via Coppull Moor, Charnock Richard, Charnock Green, Bolton Green and Euxton, where I saw the station, 'Euxton Balshaw Lane'.

Then walked through the town of Leyland; and Farington, Cuerden Green and Lostock Hall, to a fine disused railway walk from Bamber Bridge to Preston. It followed rural cuttings and embankments for some distance, via Penwortham, eventually crossing the River Ribble on a high bridge, whereby I entered the City of Preston – impressive. After an excellent ice cream, quite chocolatey, I saw much of the city: the centre, a riverside walk and parts of docklands – now they seem to be more of a marina. A fine city and a fine large old station. Walk completed about 6 pm.

I took a fast train back to Wigan North Western. I've been enjoying hearing the Lancashire, and indeed the Scottish accents, especially on the trains now. I particularly like to hear the Scottish staff speaking on these trains. That country has always appealed to me immensely – they are, I think, very likeable people.

So I walked back to the hotel, Wigan, for a good meal, after another really good day. And so to bed.

And the homeward journey, in the morning: after breakfast duly enjoyed, I took trains on the same routes as coming 'up' and calling at the same stations, with an exception at the end. After Wigan/Wolverhampton/Southampton etc the last train terminated at Fareham, due to power supply problems. So I took a taxi home from there. A very short, but a very good holiday.

One interesting thought also crossed my mind. Some people walk all the way from Land's End to John O'Groats. I have walked almost half this trek. So if someone asked me if I had walked from L/E to J O'G, I could say 'Not half'! To avoid confusion, I should really say 'Not quite half'.

Day 58
19/8/12

Preston – Fulwood – Sharoe Green – Broughton – Barton – Bilsborrow – Brock – Catterall – Bowgreave – Bonds – Garstang – Cabus – Forton – Galgate – Scotforth – Lancaster
(23 miles approx)

Yesterday's journey 'up' followed a similar pattern to that recorded on Day 57. This 'new' pattern of travel gave an interesting insight into this 'new' area of England, of course. So trains were Cosham to Southampton Central, and thence to Wolverhampton, and thence to Preston (instead of Wigan as last time). Otherwise, routes and stops were as before. The weather was hot in the south, but refreshingly cooler in the north again.

I reached Preston around 4 pm, after a full six hours travelling. I walked to the very nice hotel, very near the station, but took a walk out in the evening and enjoyed a good meal, and of course a good ice cream. I met a guy who told me he had, fairly recently, cycled from John O'Groats to Land's End, in 13 days.

And now the walk, 19th August, 2012 – after the enjoyment of a good rest and breakfast, I set off on what I might call 'A Tale of Two Cities' insomuch as I walked from the City of Preston to the City of Lancaster. Leaving Preston at about 10 o'clock, and having enjoyed a quick look at the centre again (the grand old dark-stone North-England buildings), I looked out for the A6 main road (which I followed for most of the day) with the help of two very friendly, typical Lancashire local guys. I could summarise the weather:- very warm start, very, very wet midday, very pleasant evening – but it was all very pleasant really. Yes, the rain was very heavy and persistent at times, but there was compensation and distraction as I was following near the London-Glasgow main railway again – plenty of impressive expresses to see. Also, good views of canal at various points, and often good wide grass verges (or pavements if not) to use.

After the city centre, I entered a pleasant residential area, as often happens, passing attractive Moor Park, and also passed Fulwood, Sharoe Green and Hazelmere, before entering the countryside. Walked via the scenic villages of Broughton and Barton and Bilsborrow – where I enjoyed a snack, featuring particularly good ice creams, at a restaurant. There were more very good ice creams at places further on too, not surprisingly.

Walked on via further scenic areas, and gained good views to the east, of the significant peaks of the Forest of Bowland – an area of fells and moors, well-liked. So - via Brock, Catterall, Bowgreave and Bonds – I reached the very lovely old town of Garstang, which I browsed round; it was of the 'quaint, stone' category.

Then I walked via Cabus, Forton, Potters Brook, and past Ellel Grange to Galgate, and past the University of Lancaster, before descending via Scotforth into Lancaster itself. Walked via the city, a fine historic place (hopefully to be described in more detail tomorrow) and reached the station at about 7.15 pm.

I returned by train to Preston for food and a short walk to the B&B for the night. Yet another impressive day

DAY 59
20/8/12

LANCASTER — SLYNE — MORECAMBE BAY — PART OF EAST SHORE (HEST BANK —
RED BANK FARM — BOLTON-LE-SANDS — BOLTON HOLMES —
MARSH HOUSE FARM) — CARNFORTH
(12 miles approx)

*H*aving breakfasted well again, and travelled enjoyably on a Scottish express
train from Preston to Lancaster, I explored Lancaster on foot, particularly
appreciating the views of the fine old castle close-up — ornate, ancient, and as with
other old buildings of this city, grand and I might say slightly but very pleasantly
dark, even at times grim. But it was a 'grimness' that was appealing and attractive.
I in no way criticise. I walked the streets of the city centre area — a real feeling of
history preserved — North of England buildings many centuries old. Fine shops,
fine houses, it all felt fine.

My walk in fact began around 10.45. I continued to the River Lune, crossing
it on the north side of the city. Today's weather was sunny and bright, and ideal
for good views (after a little early rain). I walked via the east side of Skerton, up to
Slyne, and down to Hest Bank. At the level crossing over the London-to-Glasgow
West Coast main line superb views really did emerge (superb views of express
trains too!), for most of the rest of the day I was able to enjoy these views.

The huge extent of Morecambe Bay lay before me. I could clearly see the
coastline all the way to Barrow-in-Furness, to the north and west, with Grange-
over-Sands showing up very well. Southwards I could see round to nearby
Morecambe. The tide was coming in — nearly at its peak — to add to the beauty of the
scene. With the help of two knowledgeable local people, I was able to learn about
the Lake District summits, some of which were visible in the very far distance,
north of Grange-over-Sands and other points on that coast. The summits were
partly cloud-covered, and looked so small from so far off. I wasn't sure which they
were — but I think that on clear days, some of those seeable include the Langdale
Pikes and The Old Man of Coniston.

Most of the rest of my walk followed Morecambe Bay coastline. I saw how
fast the tide came in — really rushing at some parts of the sands. It is notorious. The
difference between high and low tides is extremely extensive and there is a public
right of way right across from Hest Bank to Kents Bank. I think it should only be
used with the leadership of an experienced guide (unless you are an experienced
guide yourself; and not on your own) and only in the right tidal, weather and other
conditions.

But I enjoyed exploring some of the water-filled channels, and flooded paths
and lanes. And then suddenly, the tide turned, and it was interesting to watch it

go out as fast as it came in. Water was now rushing back downs channels large and small, and across the various paths, in remarkable volume, and at remarkable speed! Soon the bay was beginning to look a bit empty. Vast extents of sand instead of vast extents of water.

The route I followed from Hest Bank took me along the coast, past Morecambe Lodge and Red Bank Farm, where I detoured inland to Bolton-le-Sands. This included crossing the busy railway again – long waits at the level crossing. The lane continued to the pleasant village where I much enjoyed an iced orange lolly, quickly followed by a cold orange drink. But my main reason for the detour was nostalgic. Years ago, on a number of occasions, I stayed with a couple, extremely good friends to me, very kind and most entertaining. They had both died fairly recently; I saw the house (now empty) and just stood and reflected on very happy memories. They had taken me, and others, on many good walks and country drives.

I returned to the coast where I had left it, and continued past Wild Duck Hall, Bolton Holmes, Marsh House Farm, and Galley Hall, detouring inland to Carnforth, with good views of Warton Crag to the north, to finish the walk about 4 pm. Had a snack at a hotel in Carnforth, and walked round the pleasant old town. Took train down the coast again to Lancaster, and another to Preston, where I had a good chicken roast, followed by the 'obvious' and returned to the good hotel for the night.

A most enjoyable day of course – also a rather different mileage to yesterday. That was more 'non-stop'; today more of 'stand-and-stare!' i.e, plenty to look at.

And lastly, 21st August, the journey home, the next day. Really, I can just say – repeat of the 'journey up', in the opposite direction. Same routes, as pleasant as ever, and good views and good weather. Very good memories to sleep on.

Day 60
9/9/12

CARNFORTH – YEALAND CONYERS & YEALAND REDMAYNE (EAST EDGES) –
BEETHAM – MILNTHORPE – WOODHOUSE – CROSSCRAKE –
NATLAND – OXENHOLME
(16 miles approx)

On 8th September, I again enjoyed the train trips, Cosham/Southampton Central/Wolverhampton – then, the Edinburgh express transported me on to Lancaster. It was a beautiful late summer's day, quite warm, with a kind of 'lazy hazy' feel. There were not the crowds of people much, harvesting of fields was in evidence quite a lot, and there was certainly an abundance of peaceful, rural views.

Apologies for the pun: as the rail journeys continue to get longer, I am doing more and more train-ing before my walks.

I enjoyed snacks, including one on Lancaster station, where I watched quite a lot of trains, before taking a taxi for about a mile, out on the Caton Road, for my very pleasant B&B.

I started out next morning, enjoying the walk back to Lancaster city centre, and onto the station, where I caught a train up to Carnforth, to commence today's 'official' walk, at 10.45. There was rain earlier, not much, and the weather became cooler and more breezy later. Views of the Lake District and the fells were rather hazy, but very impressive. I was taught, in geography at school, about how they resemble a 'basket of eggs' in their distant scenery, though I would prefer to say 'a basket of ice creams in cones'!

I followed the A6 main road for the early part of the route – enjoying the usual 'perks' of wide grass verges and sightings of express trains on the West Coast main line. I passed Pine Lake, Hyning Home Farm, and the edges of the villages of Yealand Conyers and Yealand Redmayne – then I crossed from Lancashire into Cumbria (formerly the counties of Westmorland and Cumberland). An iced lolly (orange flavour) and banana followed after this. Continued through Hale and Beetham, and beside the River Bela and Deer Park – particularly pretty – I saw deer on the slopes, among grazing sheep, and a heron.

And so into the little town of Milnthorpe – typically delightfully north English – all the right kind of stone buildings, narrow streets, unchanged for many many years, markets held there etc. Here I left the A6 and followed the lanes for the rest of the way. These are on-road cycle routes – also ideal for walkers, also very narrow, and with high hedges or stone walls often – and long sections with grass growing to lawn standard, mid-road. Very much like cart-tracks, or paths. I thus continued via Haverflatts and Woodhouse, and crossed under the London to Glasgow line where train-watching was advantageous. I ate cakes until an express thundered by – a good way to pass the time till you see a train!

Then walked on via Viver, and passed a canal, where some volunteers were doing restoration work, very impressively. On past Sellet Hall and Sellet Lodge, and through Crosscrake to Low Barrows Green and Natland, with its pleasant, spacious village green. Finally, I followed a bridleway across fields, to the railway station 'Oxenholme The Lake District' (the official title). So ended the walk, about 5.15 pm, at the village of Oxenholme.

And the fun was not all over. I spent a happy hour watching trains, fast and slow, at the station, till mine took me back via Carnforth to Lancaster, at great speed. I indulged in a good meal at a café, before walking back to my also good B&B. Certainly another glorious day, in such unspoilt, historic and beautiful parts of the north of England.

One other thought – a story came to mind. I feel I do rather indulge myself in the joys of luxuries. The Great Outdoors, with all its range of weather conditions – wild, rough sometimes – draws me constantly. But the comfortable cafés, and en-suite accommodation in, shall I say 'The Great Indoors' are also OK!

So, the story (true, but I will repeat it as best as I can recall). Friends of mine met some chaps, hardy walkers, who told it to them. They said they reached a road after a tough trek, tired, hungry, thirsty, hot, perspiring, much wanting a shower. In the lay-by an older lady had been escorted out of her car by a friend and was now seated comfortably in a well-cushioned chair before a tea-table (lace cloth, best china) for afternoon tea in the sun and gentle breeze. Best clothes on, hair neat and tidy. She conversed with these walkers a little, and sipping her tea and selecting her favourite cakes, said to them:- 'Now I'm going to tell you something about myself. The one thing I really do like – I just love to rough it'!

SECTION 5

The Lake District

65 miles

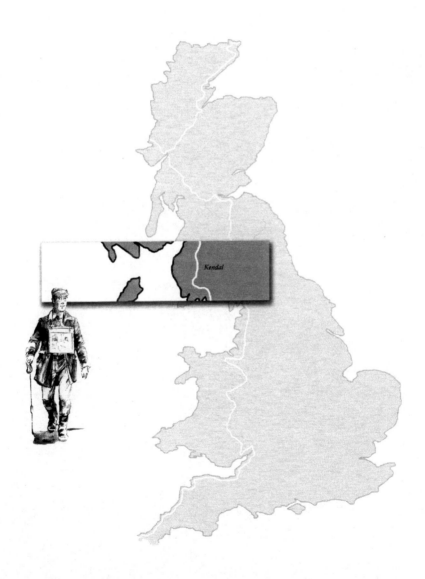

Day 61
10/9/12

OXENHOLME – KENDAL – PLUMGARTHS – BONNING GATE –
CROOK – FELL PLAIN – CLEABARROW TURNING – COCKSHOTT POINT –
BOWNESS-ON-WINDERMERE, LAKE WINDERMERE & WINDERMERE
(15 miles approx)

Sausages, mushrooms, egg, tomato, toast etc, duly and much enjoyed, I did a repeat of yesterday's walk back to Lancaster station, but then took a train which conveyed me very fast again, via Carnforth to Oxenholme, where I commenced the 'real' walk at 10.45. Taking a more north-westerly direction, to include 'lingering' in the English Lake District, I proceeded down the Kendal road, in which town I also 'lingered'. A very fine old town it was, the River Kent rushing through, the ruined castle dominating the hillside above, the maze of busy, narrow streets, fine old stone buildings overlooking them, and the peaks of the fells visible on the skyline. Plenty of shops and plenty for the tourist to enjoy.

At this point, the first of a series of heavy showers began. But there was fine weather in between. Interestingly, I had seen the fells in the sun from distant Morecambe Bay; in hazy sun yesterday, and nearer; and today, I didn't see them in the rain, but I did see them in the sun, close up, and fantastic to be right beside them.

I emerged from Kendal town centre, took the Windermere (main) road up above Lane Foot, and then diverted onto a more winding, rural road, from Plumgarths, where I entered the Lake District National Park itself, at which precise point, an extremely heavy shower welcomed me into this territory! Continued via Brundrigg, Bonning Gate and past Pound Farm, to the picturesque village of Crook, where I turned up a narrow lane which proved quite hilly, and up and down past Beckside and Waingap, to Fell Plain where I joined the Dales Way. More heavy rain, and the feeling it might be time to take a short break, led me to seek shelter under a tree, but it was a very small tree, and rather than keeping the rain off me, I wondered if it was more of a case of me keeping the rain off it! Here, the Dales Way led me off the lane, into most beautiful Lake District scenery – and sunshine again. Plenty more ups and downs, and twists and turns, following cart-tracks and paths, among sheep and cattle, crags and fells all around, near and distant peaks, lots of rocks and boulders waiting to be tripped over, and numerous roches moutonnées (types of small rock outcrops) too.

I left the Dales Way between Crag House and Outrun Nook. About this point, I met an interesting party of people – a family, very likely. One chap was walking at great speed with four dogs (huskies, I think) – he was holding them on four separate leads in one hand, and pushing a baby in a buggy with the other hand. The other folk, another man, a lady and a boy, were racing along behind, endeavouring to keep up. One of them asked me if it was very much further to the main road – in fact it wasn't a very great distance – they seemed anxious to get back to their vehicles which were parked there; I should think they had got a little late unintentionally. I stayed with them till they were back on four wheels again, and checked my route with them, too.

Having thus reached the 'main road' (I would say a rather narrow country route) near Cleabarrow (and having come down another steep, scenic lane), I continued downward, below Brant Fell on the said road, through more beautiful scenery – very wooded areas, to a more main road, which followed near the shores of Lake Windermere. Down in the valley now, I passed some fine residences, including country hotels, mellowed over time, among the scenic surroundings. Many such buildings, standing in their own grounds – Lake Windermere ahead, and the fells towering all around. All this was very awe-inspiring, and enough sunshine to enjoy it. Off the 'main road' too, now, I followed the shores of the lake, with excellent views of the thickly wooded fell-slopes opposite, nearby and afar. Windermere is the largest lake in England, and very long north-south. I walked past Cockshott Point, round to the delightful little old town of Bowness-on-Windermere, with its old stone buildings – houses, shops etc clustered round the quaint narrow streets, which wound down to the lake. Having seen the lakeside – the steamers and other boats at and around the jetties, I ascended the main street up through the town, still enjoying the views of the towering fells all around, and the lake below. The more distant fells appeared to be less wooded, or open entirely.

I continued on the main road up to the similarly delightful town of Windermere itself – less hilly perhaps, no lake there, but still the stone buildings, narrow streets, the 'olde-worlde' charm, the towering fells and the railway station (arrived at 5.45 pm).

'Magnificent' is what I say to it all. Too, I much enjoyed the train ride – calling at Staveley, Burneside, Kendal and Oxenholme – back to Lancaster – for meal at café again, and walk back to B&B again – all very good. It shows how impressive the scenery has been – I quite forgot to say I had an excellent blackcurrant and cream ice cream (Bowness)!

And, in closing, I had a good journey home the following day – basically a repeat of the journey 'up' again, but the 'other way round'. Weather was colder and drier. An abundance of very pleasant thoughts to reflect on for sure!

DAY 62
1/10/12

BOWNESS-ON-WINDERMERE, LAKE WINDERMERE & WINDERMERE — TROUTBECK
BRIDGE — WATERHEAD PIER — UNDER LOUGHRIGG — COTE HOW —
RYDAL WATER — LAKE GRASMERE — HUNTING STILE —
GRASMERE & RYDAL VILLAGES — AMBLESIDE
(18 miles approx)

There were just some minor differences on the preceding rail journeys 'up': I started out from Cosham on a train to Winchester (via Fareham and Eastleigh) and then joined the usual Bournemouth to Manchester express through to Wolverhampton. On this train I met a chap who I enjoyed talking to for a lot of the journey. He was interested in the Lake District, which he was also bound for, on other routes, and was knowledgeable on Wainwright and Wordsworth — and also on Jerome K Jerome — *Three Men in a Boat*, etc. He had an excellent sense of humour and much appreciated that of JKJ!

The next train, an express bound for Glasgow Central, took me at speed right up to Oxenholme (via Lancaster etc.) and I changed for the final train on to Windermere via Kendal. There had been plenty of rain in the north and as I entered the Lake District it was beginning to clear, but there seemed to be numerous additional mini lakes in the fields etc! Enjoyed liver, bacon, onions and mash in a good café in Windermere town, walked to another excellent B&B, and later did another walk in the picturesque old town (described 'last time'). So for 30th September, 2012.

The following morning, revitalised by a super breakfast, I commenced the walking around 10 o'clock, enjoying distinctly brighter weather than on Day 61 — glorious sunshine provided excellent viewing of fells, lakes etc, though there were heavy showers at times. There were a lot of walkers out everywhere today.

I re-explored Windermere and Bowness-on-Windermere in these ideal conditions (towns already referred to in detail 'last time'). The same goes for Lake Windermere, but today I saw much more of it. I followed close to its shores, taking the very scenic 'main' road past Rayrigg Hall and Millerground Landing, and partook of a delicious 'Yorkshire Dales' vanilla ice cream, before continuing to Troutbeck Bridge on another scenic 'main' road, and onward past Brockhole, and Wansfell Holme. I also detoured onto a lakeside footpath, getting even grander views of the glorious lake itself, extending far, and the many towering fells all around. I reached Wanlas Howe, and Waterhead Pier — a hub of tourist activity — steamer, smaller boats, cafés and shops of the smaller sort.

At this point, I embarked on a long detour (as opposed to last time, a short detour). It proved most rewarding. I followed a remote lane, basically 'access only', very narrow and winding, which was signposted 'Under Loughrigg'. I passed Miller Bridge House and Fox Ghyll, and closely followed a very full small river, also passing the 'Stepping Stones' crossing, on my right.

At Cote How, I reached the southern shore of Rydal Water, which I followed on a path, rising and falling on the hillside too; and I continued (below Loughrigg Terr) to the very similar Lake Grasmere southern shore, which I followed but also with hillside detours. I reached a lane at Hunting Stile, near which I saw a beautiful rainbow in the sun and showers, extending above the lake, and above an also-beautiful tree in its golden autumn colours. All the scenery was, needless to say, really magnificent – and so for the rest of the day. A very 'Lakes-and-Fells' day. I see I have repeated the word 'magnificent' from Day 61. No surprises if I repeat it again tomorrow. I reached Grasmere village (after passing The Wyke), an outstandingly attractive old village – very typical stone-built/Lake District in character. No wonder William Wordsworth, the poet, loved it so. I passed Dove Cottage where he lived, at the Town End part, and returned to following busier road routes again, but with summits above me, and water extending below, there was so much to see all around, that traffic did not really distract much.

So I followed the eastern shore of Lake Grasmere, then entered woodland around White Moss Common, and emerged on the northern shore of Rydal Water, at the end of which I reached Rydal village – as lovely as Grasmere, but smaller. Wordsworth also lived here. I continued past Crow How into Ambleside - the conclusion of the long detour, and of the walk – arrival about 5.15 pm. It was another fine old town, again so typical of the Lake District. Saw the tiny old 'House on the Bridge' (owned by the National Trust). It sat on the small river, in effect.

Travelled back to Windermere, upstairs on a semi-open-top bus, had a good meal in the same café as yesterday, and returned to B&B, where I reflected happily on valleys, peaks, lakes, rivers, open-fell slopes, wooded-fell slopes, and the Yorkshire Dales ice cream, which was also magnificent.

Day 63
2/10/12

Ambleside – Seathwaite Turning – Kirkstone Pass – Brothers Water – Hartsop – Beckstones – Rooking – Glenridding, Ullswater & Patterdale
(14 miles approx)

*T*oday, my walking was much more direct, after the significant detouring of yesterday. Again, there were plenty of other walkers about. The weather I will describe in due course – it was either sunny and clear, or very very wet!

After more excellent feeding at the B&B, I took a quick walk round

Windermere town and boarded a bus to Ambleside, which I also took a quick walk around. Began the walking for today's project at around 10.45. I was pleased that the route took me over the summit of Kirkstone Pass (1,490 feet above sea level) as I could then claim to have done some fairly significant climbing (as in walking climbing), and descending while in the Lake District. It proved to be a very enjoyable experience.

I ascended, past Seathwaite, by means of a very narrow, steep, winding lane, uphill most of the three miles to Kirkstone Pass summit. It was a gloriously remote, open area, wild moorland all around, and much like a cart-track walk. The rugged grandeur of the fells above, and clear views of Lake Windermere below, I drank in – only very near the summit, where the lane joined the more main sort of road over Kirkstone, did the sunshine turn to rain, which was extremely heavy. It reached 'stair-rod' standard just before I got to the inn door, followed by hailstones after I was inside! The precipitation lasted for the duration of my meal (very welcome vegetable broth, fruit crumble with ice cream and cup of tea) and I was very comfortable near a roaring log fire, and learned a little about the area from staff and customers I talked to. The inn is the highest in the Lake District, and the third highest in England, and over 500 years old. (The Kirk Stone stands nearby.) Views extended to Windermere, and across the Furness Fells to Morecambe Bay. The inn is a fine ancient building, its white walls conspicuous from miles away, and it stood out clearly at the pass summit.

By the time I was ready to leave, the rain was clearing, and I soon saw the towering peaks above the pass summit, and all around, in sunshine. Too, the torrential rain proved to be a bonus – waterfalls were very full, as were streams and rivers, and grass and woodland looked very fresh and green. I descended beside the Windermere-to-Penrith A592 road, which was not busy, soon getting very clear views of the smaller lake, Brothers Water. A very steep, very long, downward hill, with some very good grass verges in places, and torrents of water everywhere.

Further down I took a footpath (I was on paths for most of the rest of the walk) across the valley, to Hartsop Hall, and followed above the west shore of Brothers Water (good views of the lake from Low Wood through which I walked), and took the A592 for a very short distance south-east to Hartsop village – then footpaths and narrow tracks, northward, below Angletarn Pikes, and via Beckstones, Crookabeck and Rooking, to a lane which led me back to the A592 at Patterdale, another pleasant valley village, and I continued beside the A592 again for the short distance along the valley, past Grisedale Bridge to the south-west shore of the lake, Ullswater, which I followed into the delightful village of Glenridding, following the lakeside green to the pier and hotel and shops and centre. Excellent views across Ullswater, to Place Fell. I arrived about 5 pm.

Took a taxi back over the Kirkstone Pass to Ambleside (very obliging and helpful lady drove me), and I got a good bus connection back to Windermere.

Heavy rain now setting in again! Good meal too, at the 'same' café, and walk back to the good B&B. Yes, I can only repeat the word again for today – magnificent!

So for the return home, 3rd October, 2012 – a very wet start again, but it was drier in the south. The journey 'back' followed the same pattern as the journey 'up' of 30th September, except the change of trains in the north was at Preston, instead of Oxenholme. I enjoyed good meals on the journeys too. I seem to be collecting a lot of train travel and reservation tickets; and changing trains at more and more different stations. All very interesting, and of course a really great holiday!

I was reminded of the over-simplification of a rail journey (the opposite extreme) in a joke about railway travel, from many years ago:

Conversation at station ticket office:
Passenger: Can I have a return ticket?
Ticket Office Clerk: Where to?
Passenger: Back 'ere, of course!

Day 64
22/10/12

GLENRIDDING, ULLSWATER & PATTERDALE – SILVER CRAG/SILVER POINT – SANDWICK – HOWTOWN – RAVENCRAGG – SHARROW BAY – POOLEY BRIDGE – TIRRIL – YANWATH – EAMONT BRIDGE – PENRITH
(18 miles approx)

The northward train journeys of 'yesterday' were as follows: Cosham to Eastleigh (South West Trains), Eastleigh to Wolverhampton, via Winchester and then the 'usual' route (CrossCountry), Wolverhampton to Lancaster, as 'usual' (Virgin Trains), and Lancaster to Penrith (an Edinburgh-bound TransPeninne Express). The clear sunny weather gave ample opportunity to enjoy the attractive scenery, especially on the last-named route. Very good views toward the Lake District were followed by the scenic valley of the River Lune, and the ascent to the summit at Shap, and more good views on the descent to Penrith. Here, I boarded a local bus where I had a certain amount of preview of 'things to come', in the evening sunshine, travelling beside the glorious lake, Ullswater for some distance, to Glenridding nestling below the Lake District peaks. I enjoyed a feast of roast lamb, mint sauce, Yorkshire pudding, with plenty of potato, veg and gravy, plus pot of tea, and a climax of citrus tart with vanilla ice-cream, at a local café. Then walked to the B&B, a wonderful place, a good old stone house, and from my upstairs room I had superb views across an open green to Ullswater, trees in their golden autumn glory, and the towering fells beyond.

So today. I awoke to these superb views again, and enjoyed my very good fried breakfast in a room full of pictures of the Lake District. Then set forth from Glenridding (already described 2nd and 21st October, 2012) around 9.30, and although the weather was a little overcast, the peace and calm, and the beauty of golden trees and falling leaves were very inspiring. Today, again I met a lot of other walkers. My walk-route took me alongside Ullswater, and past Grisedale Bridge, into Patterdale (on the A592). I then took a path to Side Farm, and followed the very lengthy south-east shore of Ullswater (beside or above the lake) – a particularly delightful experience, and on rough and rugged ascents and descents, by footpaths in and out of woods – fantastic views across the lake, to Glenridding etc, including yesterday evening's bus ride route. Thus I proceeded below Place Fell, past Blowick and Silver Crag and Silver Point, and below Birk Fell and on to Long Crag, Sandwick and below Hallin Fell and past Waternook, to Howtown, a beautiful remote hamlet. I watched a pleasure-steamer arrive, and leave, the pier.

Still near the shores of Ullswater, I took a very narrow lane on via Swarthfield, Ravencragg, Sharrow Bay, and past Cross Dormont and Park Foot, to Pooley Bridge – a very typical Lake District village, at the north-east end of Ullswater, quaint and charming. Here, I reluctantly said goodbye to Ullswater.

On that section, there were a number of walking parties much enjoying themselves, although I did overhear one small boy say, with a mixture of weariness and hopefulness to his father, 'I say Dad. Have we got half way round the walk yet?'

I followed a non-main road route for the last section of my walk, past Cracoe and Barton, and through Tirril and Yanwath, and then diverted back to footpaths, across fields, and beside the River Eamont. In this area, the interesting subject of whether or not I could see the Pennine Hills cropped up again (see Day 56!) This time however, on enquiring from two 'locals', the answer was a very definite 'Yes'. I was too eagerly anticipative before. Now, the line of (as they called the range, in my school day lessons) 'The Backbone of England' was clearly evident to me, to the east, and continued to be so, for the rest of this holiday. (In fact, the Pennine Way goes on into Scotland.)

I crossed Eamont Bridge, and entered Penrith via Pategill. Penrith is another fine, typical, North of England town – grand old stone buildings abound, and I also saw the ruined castle. Visited shops too, and bought postcards. (Arrival 16.30.)

I caught a bus, as last evening, to Glenridding again, and indulged in a repeat performance of yesterday's meal at the local café! Then back to B&B, where I reflected on the joys of the English Lake District. During my sojourn here, I have walked significant lengths of the shores of 5 lakes (Windermere, Rydal Water, Grasmere, Brothers Water and Ullswater) and done the climb up to (plus the down from) 1 summit (Kirkstone Pass summit). But I think today sees the last of the walking in this – I use the word again – magnificent – National Park. Tomorrow, I hope to be plodding further north.

SECTION 6

Carlisle & towns of the Scottish Borders

III miles

DAY 65
23/10/12

PENRITH — FAIR HILL — KITCHENHILL — CALTHWAITE —
BURTHWAITE — CURROCK — CARLISLE
(18 mile approx).

*A*fter the very good experiences of a comfortable night, an excellent breakfast, and the superb views from my room window again, I took a taxi from Glenridding to Penrith and was thus able to make an earlier start on the walk. Commencing around 10.15, with good weather conditions again (foggy earlier, followed by sunshine, then some cloud later — and still the autumnal colours to enjoy of course), I set off through the fine old town, northward, soon entering the Cumbrian countryside — a remote, narrow lane led me over a moderate hill and down to flatter countryside. I then followed similar lanes, many with good grass banks or verges, ideal for walking along.

Initially, I was following close to the West Coast main railway again, so enjoyed seeing express trains pretty near to me. I was now following a very direct route, having completed my Lake District 'wanderings'! In fact, for a very long distance I was walking on an old Roman road, now a very straight byway, but about as straight as it always had been, when it presumably led right into Carlisle. I was quite close to the M6 motorway a lot of the time, but this did not distract me from the beauty of the undulating countryside, fields, woods, villages ... I also continued to enjoy views of the Pennine Range still, not so far from me.

The route took me via Fair Hill (it was a fair hill), Greengill, Kitchenhill, and past Lowstreet House to Calthwaite, and just a little further on, I thought it would be a good idea to enquire of 'locals' if it would be possible to see the hills of Scotland soon. I met a lady on a farm, and later a lady on a bike, both of whom were clearly 'sound' on local information, and they were very interested to hear I was walking from Land's End to Wherever (?). Yes, they said, I should soon see the hills, and they told me where to look out for them!

So having passed close to Southwaite Motorway Services, somewhere on the higher land I was on, a few miles south of Carlisle, these Scottish hills most certainly and clearly appeared. Miles and miles of them, on the horizon, about 12 miles distant, the hills of Dumfries and Galloway. A thrilling feeling it was, indeed — I have seen SCOTLAND! It was very fortunate that the weather was so clear.

I also had views of the border City of Carlisle (as it is called, though in England), below. Having walked through the areas of Monkcastle and Foulbridge, and through the village of Burthwaite, I descended to the valley of the Solway Firth and past Oakland House, and into the south of Carlisle, by the remote lane I was using. Walked through the suburbs of Blackwell and Currock, and was quite soon in the main streets and city centre. I appreciated the ornate, historic architecture of the grand old stone buildings – very impressive – but the time was now 5.15 pm, and I could not stop to see too much. Bought some more Ordnance Survey maps, and made for the station, for my train. An express soon whisked me back to Penrith, where the taxi man met me and 'returned' me to Glenridding.

I enjoyed a meal at the same good café. Having had snacks earlier, I opted for a leek and potato soup, a pot of tea, and ginger-beer jelly with raspberry pavlova ice cream, tonight. And so I returned to the good B&B, after an extremely interesting day!

And my journey home, 24th October. After some more good lookings-out at the views from my room window, and another good breakfast to set me up for the day, I took the bus again – to Penrith station – views and weather and autumn colours still very favourable on my journeys homeward.

The train arrangements were: Penrith to Wolverhampton (calling only at Preston, Wigan North Western, Warrington Bank Quay and Crewe – very fast Virgin express): Wolverhampton to Winchester (the 'usual' route): Winchester to Cosham (another 'usual' route). Yes, once more, another truly wonderful holiday!

And, contemplating the view from my room again, led me to think of the sister of the 'certain lady'. A situation came to mind concerning her. (I had been emphasising the perks and luxuries associated with my accommodation rather!) She could excel at this.

She had been to lunch at a very nice restaurant in the Isle of Wight, and a friend asked her how she enjoyed it. Oh (she said), it was absolutely marvellous – such a beautiful old building – an extremely pretty village – were very well looked after by the staff – so kind to us – when you opened the door your feet sank right down into the carpet – it was a lovely shade of red – the curtains matched it perfectly – the tablecloths were beautiful – one of the loveliest chairs I've ever sat in. At this point her friend felt it was time he said something, 'Yes', he said, 'It all makes the food taste nicer, doesn't it?' If he hadn't interposed, I don't know how much longer it would have been before we found out what she had eaten (!)

(Apologies if I may have inadvertently exaggerated at all in this last paragraph.)

DAY 66
11/11/12

CARLISLE — WHITECLOSEGATE — TARRABY — HADRIAN'S WALL (COURSE OF) —
HOUGHTON — HARKER — HEATHLANDS — FLORISTONRIGG —
GRETNA — SPRINGFIELD — GRETNA GREEN
(13 miles approx)

Note: 922 miles since leaving Land's End — crossed from England to Scotland today

Yesterday's long northward journey took from about 9 am to 4 pm, using train services Cosham to Southampton Central, changing for connection to Wolverhampton, and again changing for, this time, a Glasgow Central express, as far as Carlisle — all very interesting of course — good weather and good views — especially between Oxenholme and Penrith, via Shap etc.

I enjoyed cream of chicken soup, 'Christmas lunch' sandwiches, lemon drizzle cake and a cup of tea, at the station café at Carlisle — but no ice cream — don't worry, I am not unwell at all, but the dosage does get adjusted in the colder seasons. Saw a little more of the impressive historic architecture of Carlisle city centre as I walked to my good B&B nearby, itself a typical fine older north-country house, blending in well.

And now, for the following morning — after good rest and breakfast, I set forth to explore the city more fully. It was Remembrance Sunday, and I tarried for a while to witness the commemorations, from 11 am. There was an enormous crowd gathered in the city centre for a very good open outdoor service and wreath-laying, and the march past by the military. The bands and music were very impressive — and I enjoyed the singing (including the National Anthem, and *'O God, Our Help in Ages Past'*.) There was of course, a very solemn side to the occasion, but a rousing aspect — including watching the procession of many servicemen up into Carlisle Castle, a fine ancient fortress. I also saw the impressive cathedral and visited the Lanes shops and other, older areas — fine buildings, fine shops etc, a continuation of 23rd October and 10th November already described. I saw more of the Citadel and Botchergate areas, and crossed the River Eden bridge — good views of scenic park areas around here.

It was more like midday before I was actually walking out from Carlisle. Weather was sunny, but it became cloudy later. I felt it would be good to proceed, which I did, via Whiteclosegate to Tarraby, to identify the old course of Hadrian's Wall. Here was the site of an ancient Roman 'milecastle' — I presumed that meant an old fort. There was little there now, except banks, bushes and trees, to connect with the past, but it was clearly where the Wall used to be, as per the Ordnance Survey map.

I continued walking via Houghton, past Harker Grange, through Harker, and into Low Harker — then followed a quiet road quite close to the M6 and the main London Euston to Glasgow Central railway again. Some good grass banks and verges for walking on again, too, and I now enjoyed very clear views of the Scottish hills and coast. Walked via Heathlands, near Todhills, and Floristonrigg, and crossed the River Esk (which leads out to the Solway Firth) on a bridge between the motorway and railway. Then passed Mossband Hall in the flat coastal area of the Esk Valley and then — I really became ecstatic — I rounded a bend on a small downward hill to see the sign — 'SCOTLAND' — with welcoming message; also signs — 'Dumfries and Galloway', and 'Gretna'. So, I have 'completed' Cumbria and England, and have entered this magical, enchanting land, for which I have always had great affection — Bonnie Scotland indeed!

Yes, I have really crossed the Border! I walked on through the pleasant town of Gretna, with its extensive tourist shopping areas, and the 'Old Marriage Room' where many weddings had been conducted over the years. I then entered the very scenic area of the village of Gretna Green, with the hillside and woodland adjacent, quaint old cottages, particularly quaint the Old Blacksmith's Shop where too, many marriages have been conducted. The village of Springfield was immediately adjacent. Too, there were a number of tourist shops (I bought postcards) and quite large hotels, and a museum. A Scottish piper plays the bagpipes at certain times outside it.

Having completed the walk around 4.45 pm, I continued to the nearby Gretna Green station and caught the train back to Carlisle. I had a chicken roast at a nearby restaurant, and walked back to the B&B.

I hardly need to say that this has been a very wonderful and memorable day!

Day 67
12/11/12

Gretna Green — Quintinshill — Chapelknowe — Solwaybank — Barnglleshead — Bloch Farm Turning — Langholm
(15 miles approx)

So, today was the first day of walking entirely in Scotland. Duly reinforced with another good breakfast, I took a bus from Carlisle to Gretna, and proceeded to Gretna Green where I had another walkabout. Today's weather was misty with light rain falling at times, but the views were still pretty good.

I set off from Gretna Green around 11.45, following delightful, remote Scottish lanes nearly all the way. Very soon, I crossed over the main London to Glasgow railway, and to my surprise, I saw a plaque, commemorating of all things, what I think was the worst railway accident in British history. I was at Quintinshill, I felt very solemnised – a huge number of Scottish soldiers died in, I think, 1915, when a major train collision took place and a serious fire broke out. It was indeed a terrible disaster.

The peace and beauty of the countryside through which I continued, contrasted so much with that event. I passed through the hamlets of Beechwood and Milligansbush to the village of Chapelknowe. The scenery was of typical undulating Scottish lowlands, with farms and other settlements scattered here and there. All very unspoilt and 'far from the madding crowd'. Picturesque old cottages and houses, and a mixture of fields and woods as far as the eye can see. Plenty of grass paths to enjoy beside the lanes, and a good number of bridges over Scottish burns.

So I continued past the farms of Cadgillside and Cadgillhead, and later of Solwaybank and Barnglleshead. After this there was a descent and rise past a very scenic piece of coniferous forest – the golden autumn colours were impressive. I seemed to subsequently enter an area of quite high open Scottish moorland (between cattle grids), wild and marshy at times, but the mist was thicker now, so visibility was restricted a bit, but I enjoyed the atmosphere of Scotch mist of course!

The lane then descended past Bloch Farm to the B7068 road, which I followed along a valley, beside the fast-flowing Wauchope Water, into the fine old Scottish border town of Langholm. It did impress me, although I couldn't see it too well, as it was now starting to get dark, and the rain was falling more heavily. I had a sense of being surrounded by old stone buildings, large and small, of crossing quite a long bridge (over the River Esk) and entering the narrow old street at the centre of the town (in fact, the main A7 Carlisle to Edinburgh road).

The time was about 4.45 pm – I had a look around the shops, and then took a bus back via Canonbie to Carlisle. Did it seem rather strange to be back in England?

Enjoyed a repeat of the restaurant meal of yesterday (chicken roast), and the walk back to the B&B.

Yes, I have certainly enjoyed the Scottish flavour of things today! Aye! Indeed, I think I may need to improve Scottish pronunciations myself. At breakfast in the morning, I was talking to a North Country fellow-guest about the routes I hoped I might follow.

I said I was hoping to walk to Langholm, which I thought I pronounced quite reasonably. He looked puzzled, and paused. Then 'Oh', he said, 'Langum'! I wanted to tell him I might go on to Hawick, but I thought I had better be more careful this time. I pondered. Probably to call it 'Howick' – 'o', instead of 'a' would be just right – so I said it thus. This time, however, he looked more puzzled, and paused longer. Then he suddenly realised what I was trying to say, 'Oh', he answered, 'HOYKE'!

I think if I had felt so bold as to suggest to him that I might also eventually reach Edinburgh, I would have said it something like EDINBUR-R-R-R!

Well, just the comments on the journey home, 13th November, 2012. After breakfast and a little shopping in Carlisle, I took trains back on the same routes as 10th November, i.e., changing at Wolverhampton and Southampton Central – to Cosham. There was some rain, but views were pretty good.

Back home, I felt it was appropriate to celebrate this Scottish mini break with a supper of lemon iced cakes, bought in Scotland (Langholm), and I really felt they tasted delightfully different – of Scotland!

DAY 68
9/12/12

LANGHOLM – EWES WATER – EWES (KIRKSTILE) – BUSH – MOSSPAUL – LINHOPE – TEVIOTHEAD – TEINDSIDE – NEWMILL – BRANXHOLME – HAWICK
(24 miles approx)

I can now write about my journey yesterday as 'from England to Scotland'. I was travelling from about 9 am till 6 pm. Quite cold, and sunny, (although more cloudy in the north, and light rain was falling). There had been quite a lot of snow – some remained – as I noticed from the train, specifically at Shap summit, Cumbria.

Train routes were: Cosham to Winchester; then a Southampton to Newcastle express, which I took as far as Birmingham New Street by 'usual' routes – except that Coventry and also Birmingham International were omitted – the train travelled through Tyseley, and other stations; then a Manchester express to Wolverhampton; then a Glasgow Central express, following routes as last time, to Carlisle; and finally the bus to Langholm, Scotland, via Canonbie. Various snacks enjoyed en route, and a quick walkabout at my destination, and I settled in comfortably at another very good B&B in the centre of this lovely old Scottish town.

So today, rest and breakfast indulged in happily, I set forth on one of the 'long mileage' expeditions, at about 10 am. I was again impressed by the town of Langholm, and my impressions of it as described, Day 67, were fully justified in the morning light. Today, the walking conditions could be described as cold, sunny and for about the last hour, dark – again! I had received very helpful advice from the B&B 'owners' – particularly the points on the road where care should be taken rather more – bends, traffic etc.

It was most practicable to walk on the verges and banks of the main Carlisle to Edinburgh (A7) road throughout. Other routes would have involved enormous detours, and it appeared to me that so much of the beauty of the scenery could be clearly observed from the A7 that diverting was not justified. The route gave excellent views of the valleys, rivers and high rugged hills – open views far around; a predominantly sheep-farming part of Scotland with few villages and scattered farms.

To start with, the road ran near the River Esk where it was joined by Ewes Water, a river which the A7 continued to follow for a long distance. I thus followed a gradual ascent up the valley, through or past very small settlements and hamlets - Wrae, Ewes, Kirkstile, Briery Bank, Bush and Fiddleton – then followed a steep, winding ascent beside Mosspaul Burn and an attractive coniferous forest on the immediate right – for some length – after which I crossed high open moorland. At Mosspaul Hotel, I passed from 'Dumfries & Galloway' into 'Scottish Borders'. These regions of Scotland presumably replace earlier county names.

I reached the summit of the road soon after and continued on a fairly steep descent past Braehead, Linhope and through the village of Teviothead – after which the road levelled and continued close to the River Teviot for some distance. I passed Gledsnest and Teindside, and entered the village of Newmill as dusk was falling. Then continued through Branxholme and past Martinshouse – and so into Hawick, arriving around 5.45 pm. In the darkness, I did gain an impression of the size of this grand old Scottish Borders' town – with some views of the River Teviot, and of the old streets.

I found a bus stop, and was able to confirm with locals that I could get a bus back to Langholm from this point. I do enjoy their Scottish dialect. I could listen to it for hours. To my inexperienced English ears, they seemed to say: (something like) 'Jistikootchand and Bossllstoopfya'. I replied with two rather English 'pardons', to question the meaning, and then realised they were advising 'Just stick out your hand and bus'll stop for you'. They did not seem to be put off by my Englishness and I was grateful to them.

So I had a dark bus ride back to Langholm. I much enjoyed roast duck, chips and a variety of vegetables at a very good old hotel, before 'retiring' to bed at B&B.

A very rewarding day – and a long walk. I did also see a distant layer of snow on one of the higher hills. Winter, on days like this, is also a very enjoyable time of year for a good hike.

DAY 69
10/12/12

HAWICK — STIRCHES — DRINKSTONE HILL — ASHKIRK HILL —
ASHKIRK VILLAGE — BIG WOOD (SIDE OF) - SELKIRK
(12 miles approx)

Once again, a very appetising cooked breakfast set me up well for the day and I took a bus about 10 o'clock from Langholm to Hawick, following, of course, the route of yesterday's walk, and in daylight I enjoyed seeing views which had only been strange, dark shapes yesterday, toward the end of the journey.

Today's weather was certainly cold – and fine – sunny generally – just a few showers. But Hawick deserved a little exploration before the walk 'proper'; I felt the town centre main street, with its abundance of shops and some impressive architecture, to be quite grand and imposing. The town was a good size – and a sense of history, good old Scottish stone and character, of the attractive River Teviot rushing under the bridges and beside parkland, of steep hillside streets – all remained pleasantly jumbled up in my mind.

I exited Hawick around 11.30, following the 'Borders Abbeys Way' up a narrow street, on to high open hillside giving a good view of the town spread in the valley below. Although I didn't notice any abbeys (I might have missed some very ruined ones), I found this Borders Abbeys Way very good for views and scenery, and I followed it for a good distance. I proceeded by steep ups and downs over unspoilt rugged, open hill country, by lanes or paths, via Stirches and past Tandlaw and Sunnybank, and up Drinkstone Hill, into a section of beautiful coniferous forest, very undulating as far as Ashkirk Hill. I had good views of young deer. I then followed a different forest track, which was just about an ice-rink. I was slipping and sliding all over the place!

I thus reached the main Carlisle-Edinburgh road again at Ashkirktown Farm and followed this (good grass borders on this, the A7 again) via Ashkirk, past Dryden and Big Wood, and right into Selkirk. There were lovely views of distant hills, northward, the Southern Uplands of Scotland. The road route was very pleasant, rising and dipping between hilly and valley areas.

Selkirk was yet another very impressive, typical Borders' town – again, fine old stone architecture – I followed the winding street, down into the town centre. A good selection of shops and quaint old buildings. I completed the walk at about 4 pm.

I made one rather amusing mistake in a bookshop in Selkirk – entirely my fault. I had one map with me of course, and intended to buy another, but it was not in stock. I entered the shop, therefore with one map, expected to come out with two, but actually came out with none!

In trying to compare other maps in the shop with mine, I had laid them all out together, and then piled them all up together, and (generously) handed them all back to the assistant. I only realised what I had done, after boarding the bus back to Langholm, and I had never even noted the shop name. All was well 'tomorrow' – I purchased the two needed maps at Carlisle.

I had quite a long – and dark - bus ride back via Hawick to Langholm, enjoyed a repeat performance of roast duck, chips and various vegetables at the same hotel as yesterday, and 'retired' to B & B to reflect on more of the joys of Scotland.

And now, of course, the observations on the following day's journey home. It was particularly interesting to me to join the queue at the bus stop at Langholm, and hear quite a number of Scottish ladies talking together, apparently most were travelling down to Carlisle for a day's outing – shopping etc. I experienced further enjoyment of the local dialect, which of course, continued throughout the bus journey.

Trains southward were as follows: Carlisle to Birmingham New Street – then I changed to a service down to Basingstoke, I think following the same route as two days before on the way up – and then a train to Cosham. In fact, the 'usual' routes were generally followed.

It was very cold, with excellent views of snow-capped Lake District peaks in the distance, and freezing fog abounded, especially in the Midlands.

Once again, a very happy holiday. And in closing, and further to my earlier comments, I recalled travelling to Dumfries with my parents many years ago and eating at a café, and we much enjoyed listening to the local accents of the staff at the counter – these ladies were talking among themselves. But we did notice that some of them seemed to be looking across at us. Then we overheard one of them say, 'I do so enjoy listening to them!' So I suppose the enjoyment was reciprocal.

Day 70
6/1/13

SELKIRK — ABBOTSFORD — TWEEDBANK — DARNICK — MELROSE —
GATTONSIDE — LANGLEE — GALASHIELS
(15 miles approx)

Once again, a long northward journey undertaken, 5th January, 2013 the summary of which is as follows:

Basically very similar to last time. Train from Cosham to Winchester; followed by taking the Newcastle express again, on the Tyseley route (not Coventry), to Birmingham New Street; then I was most fortunate to get an earlier train, an Edinburgh-bound express (with about one minute to spare!), to Carlisle, where I paused for a light meal at the station café before taking the Edinburgh 'limited stop' bus, via Langholm to Hawick, arriving about 5.30 pm.

Weather was mainly dry, but there was a lot of flooding still to be seen from earlier rain. In the Thames Valley and around Oxford, and also fairly generally, many fields and paths – and some roads – were under flood water – rivers having burst their banks.

The end of the journey was quite dark and cold. I found my way to the B&B – a very short walk in the old town centre. The couple running it are most hospitable – and I had a very good evening and night.

Duly refreshed, after excellent breakfast, I accordingly proceeded with the programme for the day. Firstly, the bus ride from Hawick to Selkirk and then the walk began about 10.45. Today there was some sun, also some cloud and mist on some hills. I started with a tour in Selkirk itself. I have already described it, in Day 69 – it impressed me. I followed another steep downhill winding road to the river, Ettrick Water, and followed the footpaths along its bank – attractive views including a nearby mill, and rejoined the main A7 road. Good banks and verges made walking easy again.

After a while I turned off, slightly eastward, embarking on a significant but well-worthwhile detour. I started on this pleasant 'secondary' road, gaining fine views of the River Tweed some way below. I passed Faldonside House before reaching Abbotsford and Abbotsford House. This fine old house on the hillside commanded fine vistas of the river and the valley. It was of course, the home of Sir Walter Scott, who lived 1771-1832. A romantic historical novelist, his works gave Scotland that enchanting image which is so treasured still today. Writings include Waverley, The Heart of Midlothian, Ivanhoe and Rob Roy. The house was of ancient style, an extensive, inspiring and imposing, partly castle-style stone building, and most beautiful gardens adjacent. It was not open to view today but I could see it clearly from the nearby Visitor Centre, which I enjoyed calling at.

I then rejoined the Borders Abbeys Way, following a path down to the River Tweed, and I walked its banks past Tweedbank and Darnick. The relatively wide river was flowing fast and full, and the route led me to one of the most attractive of all the Scottish Borders' towns, Melrose. Dominated by impressive high hills above it, the River Tweed flowing beside it, and the beautiful and ancient, although ruined abbey within it, this historic residential town of spacious and also less spacious old houses, shops and other buildings of old stone, mellowed over time, blending into gardens, parks and woodland quite magically and majestically, left me with a very deep sense of satisfaction.

I crossed the River Tweed by Chain Bridge – a footbridge – and followed a short section of the Southern Upland Way. Part of it overlapped with the Borders Abbeys Way – it seemed like a good Scottish bargain of 'two for the price of one'!

I was now following the return section of the detour, on the banks on the opposite side of the River Tweed. I thus reached Gattonside and then followed another 'secondary' road, above the Tweed, past Pavilion Farm into Langlee and on to Galashiels, a very sizeable Borders' town, and also very impressive – I can only repeat – history, stone … etc (Arrived about 4 pm).

Just as I entered the bus station, a bus did too – I was thus transported back, via Selkirk to Hawick, most promptly. I enjoyed a vegetarian roast, very good though not my usual custom, at a restaurant before returning to B&B. My very hospitable hosts invited me to tea and biscuits downstairs – also with a Polish guest – we talked for about an hour, largely about our monarchy in Britain! A very enjoyable conclusion to a very enjoyable day.

'Final conclusion' – I have noticed a number of boards conveying information at various points, on historical events – battles etc - while on the walks. I have been humbled by my lack of knowledge! But it did remind me of the 'certain lady' I write about. I must give her credit. Like we can all be, she obviously wasn't thinking at all when she said once to someone that I was going on a trip to Hastings – 'apparently it's something to do with some battle that was fought in the past, somewhere there. I'm not sure what'!

Day 71
7/1/13

Galashiels – Buckholm – Bowland – Ferniehirst – Stow – Watherston – Symington – Fountainhall
(14 miles approx)

After a further very good breakfast, and interesting conversations with hosts and guests, I proceeded to the bus stop for the journey via Selkirk to Galashiels, and alighted at the bus station in quite heavy rain. This soon cleared, although rain returned later in the day – generally lighter, but sometimes rather persistent. But the views were certainly sufficiently seeable to enjoy.

I started the walk with a tour of the town centre and shop-visiting, around 11.15. There were good views all around as I ascended the hillside on the main A7 road. Galashiels showed up well around me and below in the valley as I walked through Halliburton. I continued, following above the river (Gala Water – I followed this river all day) via Buckholm – around here the road descended lower into the river valley. Indeed, the whole day was one of very attractive, significantly high hills all around, and unspoilt countryside, as I approached the Southern Uplands of Scotland.

So, on via Whitelee to Bowland. Here I left the main road. There were not such wide grass verges and banks as on other parts of the A7 I had walked, and I was able to follow most pleasant winding lanes, running roughly parallel to the main road, for the remainder of the day. Proceeding up the valley, there were four 'items' following along together – 'my' narrow lanes, the river, the A7 on the far side, and – weaving in between – the disused 'Waverley' main Edinburgh to Carlisle railway course. This last-named, I think, may be getting a new lease of life – I think there are plans to reopen it, from Edinburgh to Tweedbank.

I continued via Dryburn, Ferniehirst and Stagehall, but then diverted across to the other side of the valley, where the A7 passed through the beautiful old village of Stow – well worth seeing. Then, returning by the same route back to the initial point of diversion, I resumed the lane, which took me via Watherston and past Bankhouse and Symington to Plenploth, and into the village of Fountainhall – a pleasant, peaceful spot – and walked a short connecting lane over to the bus stop on the main road at 4 pm.

It was tempting to consider walking on further, but both darkness and rain were falling – indeed, this time of year and this far north, one has to expect early dusk, of course. I was reminded of another 'certain lady'. She had an ingenious knack of turning statements into the complete opposite. I remembered, as I decided to terminate today's walk, of the wisdom in taking precautions. She would misquote this, saying 'you should never take precautions'!

Two other examples, incidentally. She rendered 'to kill two birds with one stone' as 'to kill a bird with two stones'; and 'you could have knocked me down with a feather' as 'you could have knocked me down with a hammer'!

I really must be careful, all these things I say about certain ladies – I'm sure certain men are quite as amusing.

I returned via Stow, Galashiels and Selkirk to Hawick on an appropriate bus, indulged this time in a chicken roast at the same restaurant as yesterday, and returned to B&B with shop purchases in the form of iced pineapple tarts for immediate consumption – a very suitable substitute, at this season of the year, for the more traditional ice creams. And a very good conclusion to a very good day!

Also, of course, the journey home, 8th January, 2013. After the excellent hospitality at the B&B (as already stated), I found my very nearby bus stop and returned on the 'limited stop' again via Langholm to Carlisle. Then trains: Carlisle to Wolverhampton; Wolverhampton to Winchester (the Coventry route on this Manchester to Bournemouth express); Winchester to Cosham. So the route was very similar to 5th January. Weather was rather wet today, but the flooding seemed to have receded somewhat in the last few days.

Another very memorable mini break.

SECTION 7

Edinburgh, Firth of Forth & Stirling

109 miles

Day 72
3/2/13

FOUNTAINHALL – HALTREE – HERIOT – MIDDLETON – GOREBRIDGE –
NEWTONGRANGE – LOTHIANBRIDGE – ESKBANK – DANDERHALL – PENTECOX –
CRAIGMILLAR – NEWINGTON – EDINBURGH (NICOLSON STREET)
(22 miles approx)

The 'usual' journey of yesterday was indeed, basically the same as last time, Day 70 – i.e. Cosham to Winchester thence to Birmingham New Street (via Tyseley etc), thence again by the 'skin of my teeth' to Carlisle. But the bus ride onward was, of course, longer (via Langholm, Hawick and Selkirk, to Galashiels, where I stayed in another good guest house, most conveniently literally opposite the bus station).

It was a bright, dry day for travelling but noticeably colder in Scotland. Flooding was even more evident than last time, again mainly in the Thames Valley and Oxford areas. Also I saw snow on some Lake District peaks.

I followed my practice of a light meal at Carlisle station café, which set me up well for the long bus ride. I think I reached B&B about 6.15 pm.

So, now to today – good rest, good breakfast and good walk. Also had a pleasant bus ride from Galashiels to the bus stop on the main road, for Fountainhall. The weather sticks clearly in my mind – a very cold, and strong wind, head on for much of the walk! Patches of snow were scattered on the ground – remnants of drifts – one was about one foot deep – and more to be seen on more distant higher hills. But it was a bright, dry day, with good clear views of the Southern Uplands and all around.

I began walking about 10.15, following the short connecting lane from the main road, back to Fountainhall village, and then continued up the valley using quiet lanes, with the river, the main A7 road, and the disused railway running roughly parallel to the east of me, as last time. The route took me via Brockhouse, Haltree and Sandyknowe, to the village of Heriot – very attractive byways – but I then rejoined the main A7 road again, following its grassy verges and banks past Falahill and up over higher, open landscapes, crossing from Scottish Borders into Midlothian. In some paperwork I had been reading, there was reference to Selkirkshire, an old Scottish county, which I had presumably been through too.

The vistas were wonderful – so extensive with distant high hills – a fine unspoilt panorama. I descended from these viewpoints via Middleton to Eastwood and Harvieston, and then detoured into the town of Gorebridge and through Arniston. I also stopped for a banana and a cake. In this area, there seemed to be some restoration of the track-bed of the closed Waverley railway (see Day 71). Work appeared to be going on.

Again I rejoined the main A7 road, passing Newtonloan and Newtongrange, and in between, the National Mining Museum – a most interesting combination of old buildings, wheels and machinery. Walked on through rather more urban areas – Lothianbridge and past Eskbank, South Melville and Sheriffhall, where I crossed the Edinburgh city bypass, and after which I entered the City of Edinburgh itself! I continued on the A7 via the Danderhall area.

I also gained some very good views around. The high Pentland Hills, snow-covered, showed up very clearly. And ahead of me, as I descended from a summit of the A7, there I beheld the thrilling sight in the distance of Edinburgh Castle and other nearby historic buildings!

My arrival in Edinburgh was, I think, the most enjoyable experience so far, of the whole walk – but more about that 'tomorrow', hopefully!

I continued the descent into the city – the route took me past Moredun, Pentecox, Little France and the huge Edinburgh Royal Infirmary. Dusk was now falling, but I was able to pick out the character of the following areas, in the street lights; Inch, Cameron Toll, Craigmillar and Newington. I passed through some typical fine residential areas – large, stone-built residences, mellowed over time, set in attractive gardens. (Earlier, and later, there were shopping areas.)

I thus reached the southern approaches to the city centre – Nicolson Street and Surgeons' Hall (a museum), where at 6 pm I found a bus stop and soon caught a bus back to Galashiels via the Newtongrange and Fountainhall areas, and settled in comfortably again at the guest house, where I enjoyed eating 'goodies'.

This has been a particularly memorable day, including the very satisfying climax – arrival in Edinburgh!

DAY 73
4/2/13

EDINBURGH CITY WALK: NICOLSON STREET – WAVERLEY – PRINCES STREET –
CASTLE – ROYAL MILE – OLD TOWN – PALACE OF HOLYROODHOUSE – SLOPES
ARTHUR'S SEAT/BELOW SALISBURY CRAGS – CALTON HILL – NEW TOWN –
NICOLSON STREET
(10 miles approx)

It seemed appropriate to me to set the whole of today aside to 'do' Edinburgh on foot. So, after useful discussions over a good breakfast with my host, I took the bus again – from Galashiels right through to Nicolson Street bus stop, Edinburgh and commenced the walkabout around 11.15. The weather was a great subject again – very much like yesterday. There was sunshine, cloud, very gusty wind, rain, sleet, snow, and later, darkness and quite a lot more snow! It really was good fun – an exhilarating experience getting blown round the city.

Edinburgh is a most inspiring city – the capital of Scotland, of course. Perched on the edge of an extinct volcanic landscape, and near the sea, it is regarded by many as Britain's most beautiful city. It has been called the 'Athens of the North'. Its history, with the architecture so well preserved, is reflected in the Medieval character of the Old Town, and the Georgian character of the New Town. There is an atmosphere of both romance and grandeur. The charm too is reflected in the skyline – tall, ancient spires and towers; and massive rugged hills and crags; and in the windswept coastline; and in the very nearby rolling countryside.

So – I started out over the streets of South Bridge and North Bridge (the latter ran above the roof of Edinburgh (Waverley) railway station – this huge, busy, grand old station I also visited). Then I proceeded along Princes Street – quite a 'gem' of the city, with its splendid large shops and imposing buildings on one side; and Princes Street Gardens, the main railway, and of course Edinburgh Castle (I visited the castle ramparts and entrance – splendid views over the city, and beyond) on the other side. Princes Street was jammed well with traffic, especially buses, and tramlines had been laid, but the trams were not running yet.

Also walked in the gardens, saw trains, visited the shops, admired from below too, the views of the castle (perched on its 'cliff top',) and enjoyed lunch at Debenhams, and later afternoon tea there. I might just mention strawberries and cream tart, among quite a lot of other delightful items.

Then continued to the Royal Mile, the ancient cobbled hill/street (Medieval), which runs down through the Old Town, from the castle to the Palace of Holyroodhouse, the Queen's official residence in Scotland. Cobbled streets and historic buildings abounded in this area. Having now walked down to the palace, I stood to admire its magnificence. It is a very old abbey, a very grand building (but dwarfed by the towering slopes of Arthur's Seat and Salisbury Crags) and converted into a palace in 1460, by King James IV.

My walk continued on past the very different, very much more modern, imposing Scottish Parliament building, and on to the lower slopes of Arthur's Seat, and below Salisbury Crags, and the area of Holyrood Park, gradually ascending this huge, wild, rural retreat – I did the complete circuit round. I followed near the narrow road routes high up, but still below the higher peaks, and enjoyed excellent clear views over parts of Edinburgh, including too, the snow-covered Pentland Hills and the sea at the Firth of Forth coast – interestingly, I had walked over 1,000 miles since I left Land's End, and this was my first sighting of the East Coast of Britain! I also passed Dunsapie Loch, very small but attractive, before the descent back to the Palace of Holyroodhouse.

I also 'climbed' the streets up to Calton Hill, to see the grandeur of the architecture of the New Town, of the Georgian era, with its wide roads – crescents and circuses – spacious old stone-built residences, in attractive gardens, abounding.

I thus completed the walkabout around 5.30 pm, back at the Nicolson Street bus stop. On reflection, I suppose one spot – the castle ramparts and entrance – was particularly nostalgic. As a young boy, I was given View-Master pictures of Scotland. One, I think, was of that very place, and I had wondered, at that early age, what this magical place in this faraway land of Scotland must be like! To summarise, I say Edinburgh is unique – it is, I think Britain's most beautiful city in this most beautiful country of Scotland. I certainly stress how much I enjoyed today!

The bus ride back to Galashiels took place in quite heavily falling snow, with about four inches lying in the whole area – exciting! And so, back to my B & B.

And the journey back, 5th February. I woke to this four-inch layer of snow, which 'lasted' nearly to Carlisle – the bus route back looked so scenic. Driver did very well, especially on one steep hill, where he controlled some wheel-spin. Hills, valleys, towns, villages – all snow-covered! In my enthusiasm, I slipped off the bus seat, trying to see more – also, the seat sprang up behind me and knocked the back of my head. No damage – maybe it knocked some sense into me! Trains – Carlisle to Birmingham New Street; thence, via Coventry route to Winchester; thence to Cosham. Cold, but no snow, generally in England, except Cumbria. My hosts, I also stress, were so helpful, ensuring travel was OK in the snow.

What a superb holiday!

Day 74
3/3/13

EDINBURGH (NICOLSON STREET) – BROUGHTON – WARRISTON – GRANTON & HARBOUR & POINT – SILVERKNOWES – BARNTON – CRAMOND BRIDGE – DALMENY
(13 miles approx)

And a wonderful trip to friends at Fochabers, Moray (Train/car)

This section looks like being an extremely interesting account – although less walking, a great deal of pleasure 'crammed in'. Especially, very good friends visited.

On 2nd March, I took trains: Cosham to Winchester; thence to Birmingham New Street; thence to Manchester Piccadilly (calling at Wolverhampton, Stafford, Stoke-on-Trent, Stockport – the last two stations seemed to be of very historic, quite ornate character) – also passed through stations at Stone, Macclesfield, and other places with good views of rugged hills – I think, the edge of the Pennines - and good views of the City of Manchester too, the fine architecture in the centre and very noticeable on the next section. Train on from the impressive Manchester Piccadilly, calling at also impressive Manchester Oxford Road, Bolton, Chorley and Preston – some more historic, ornate stations, as were most of the major stations too. At Preston, the train divided – for Barrow-in-Furness, and (for me) Edinburgh Waverley. Called at Lancaster, Oxenholme, Penrith, Carlisle, and over the border for some fine Scottish views. Fine, unspoilt country for miles and miles. The crossing of Shap summit was impressive, in England; crossing Beattock summit, in Scotland certainly was. Called at Lockerbie (station names were in both English and Scottish Gaelic on the signboards, as at other Scottish stations too.) Then on to the high fells areas of Beattock. Followed the River Clyde much of the way down to Carstairs Junction and so on to the beautiful City of Edinburgh again, calling at Haymarket and Waverley stations. After a meal, I travelled by taxi from Waverley to my hotel in the Newington area, Edinburgh – very good accommodation. A good length day for travelling – and good weather, fine and cold.

And so to today's walk: after excellent rest and breakfast, weather less cold, but rather cloudier, I proceeded straight into the city centre, commencing the 'official' resumption at Nicolson Street bus stop, again about 10 am. Saw more of glorious Edinburgh, again – Princes Street, Waverley station and district – and followed streets through Broughton to Warriston, where I passed the entrance to the Royal Botanic Garden. Architecturally, all these areas were as impressive as ever – typical of the city – spacious old stone residences, sometimes crescents of terraced stone residences, buildings of character, the atmosphere of history. I soon reached Granton and Harbour, on the Firth of Forth sea coast estuary. A quaint old fishing port, typical Scotland, I should say, the Fife coast visible distantly. Followed coastal roads and paths westward, beside rocks and sands, past Granton Point to Muirhouse, Silverknowes, and past Lauriston Castle (hidden in woodland), Davidson's Mains and Barnton, for a happy café stop (cake included). Then on via Cramond Bridge, Lowood and Burnshot, following the main A90 road for a little, but using good footpaths/cycle-tracks. I soon took minor roads via Easter Dalmeny (views of Dalmeny Park) and reached the beautiful little village of Dalmeny – small stone cottages and church, clustered round a tranquil village green. So to Dalmeny station – close, impressive views of the Firth of Forth railway and separately too, the road bridge. (I say the railway bridge is by far the better of the two!) Walk ended about 3.45 pm – then train from Dalmeny via Haymarket to Edinburgh Waverley; snacks; and walk via city to the good B&B!

Another well worth walk, certainly.

And a most enjoyable 4th March. Early walk to Edinburgh Waverley station – took fast train calling at Haymarket, Kirkcaldy, Leuchars for St Andrews, Dundee, Arbroath, Montrose, Stonehaven and Aberdeen (fine views of rugged coasts and cliffs; fine views from Firths of Forth and Tay Bridges). Then train calling Dyce (Airport), Inverurie, Insch, Huntly, Keith and Elgin (through glorious country – high hills (snow-clad), river valleys, very scenic).

Friends met me and we had a good lunch out. Also had a good car drive through the beautiful River Spey Valley area, and walks at Spey Bay on Moray Firth coast, and at a very picturesque, steeply wooded cliffside to the river inland. All spent a while at their home, a lovely cottage at Fochabers – a very rural setting, snowdrops blooming in the garden. So much to talk about over cups of tea, biscuits etc – catching up on the past – families, friends, Scotland, farming, fishing, cottages, churches. I saw interesting pictures in photo albums, and they took a great interest in this Walk, and this book – and my photos of the Walk etc! And drive back to Elgin; saw the ancient cathedral there and continued to the station, where I had to leave on the train for Inverness (calling at Forres and Nairn). I had a wait at Inverness station as darkness fell. So I didn't really see the Grampians and other mountains and scenery on the fast train back, (calling at Carrbridge, Aviemore, Kingussie, Newtonmore, Dalwhinnie, Blair Atholl, Pitlochry, Dunkeld, Perth, Markinch, Kirkcaldy, Inverkeithing, Haymarket and Edinburgh Waverley). Cold, clear and dry day. Taxi to B & B – late finish. There has been so much to enjoy – and see.

And – return home, 5th March – taxi, after very good rest and breakfast, to Waverley again, for train, express, calling Alnmouth for Alnwick, to Newcastle Central. Good views of rugged coasts and cliffs, and the border town of Berwick-upon-Tweed. Then fast train calling Durham, Darlington, York, Doncaster, Sheffield, Derby, Birmingham New Street; and to Winchester on 2nd March route, thence to Cosham. As yesterday I travelled through numbers of imposing stations and other impressive places – one springs to mind – Chesterfield – where I clearly saw the 'leaning' church spire! Early fine, clear weather was replaced by fog later. Interestingly, a great amount of the rail travel this holiday seems to form a figure of eight, with that, is nearly all of Britain covered? A most enjoyable, rewarding time!

DAY 75
24/3/13

DALMENY – FIRTH OF FORTH BRIDGE, RAILWAY, SOUTH SIDE – SOUTH
QUEENSFERRY – NEWTON – UNION CANAL (CRAIGTON – PHILPSTOUN –
LINLITHGOW) – L'GOW (PALACE AND LOCH) – LINLITHGOW BRIDGE –
UNION CANAL (WHITECROSS – POLMONT)
(16 miles approx)

The northward journey of yesterday followed the same very interesting routes as last time – trains: Cosham to Winchester, thence to Birmingham New

Street, thence to Manchester Piccadilly, and thence to Edinburgh Waverley. Called at all the same stations as last time too. I was again, much impressed by the beauty of the countryside, and of the villages, towns and cities – and their stations – as already described (Day 74).

And, too – the weather! It was certainly cold, but views were clear and bright. There was evidence of earlier flooding in some areas, but the snow had taken over a lot. It was officially spring now, and in a week the clocks were due to change to British Summer time, Easter weekend. Snow was falling steadily, and laying a few inches as far south as the Winchester to Basingstoke section of the line. We ran in and out of it all the way to Edinburgh, but it was particularly deeper in the Birmingham area and parts of southern Scotland. Peaks in the north were well covered. Newly born lambs looked as if they were having a rather rough time unfortunately. Some parts of Britain had been cut off (drifting).

I had good hot snacks, including one at Waverley station, after which I took a taxi to the same hotel as last time, Newington area, where I again enjoyed warm, comfortable accommodation.

Now to 24th March, 'the walk'. Duly refreshed, including the enjoyment of the good cooked breakfast, I started of course by train from Edinburgh Waverley (having done the 'pre-walk' from the hotel, through the city to the station) and reached Dalmeny via Haymarket about 10.30. It was still very cold weather, but I set off straight away on the hike and had the benefit of the 'biting' east wind behind me most of the day – and 'pushing' me on. I had a cough and cold, but it didn't seem troublesome, really. Weather was dry too, and quite bright, with clear views all around. There was little snow lying, although later in the day, I walked into drifts about 18 inches deep. Clearly, strong winds had whipped across open areas, and deposited the snow against banks and hedges and across paths.

The first views to enjoy at Dalmeny were of the Firth of Forth, the railway bridge (a tremendous engineering feat for its time (1889), of steel construction), and the road bridge – each appeared to be at least 1½ miles long. Beyond, the snow-capped mountains (?) of Fife (?) showed up very well, as did the Fife coast. I assumed they were mountains, not hills – and they might have been beyond Fife – but whatever, the point was that they looked very white, very beautiful, and I saw them for much of the day!

I descended by lanes to the Forth Estuary sea coast at South Queensferry. The wind and waves created a very wild atmosphere, in which I enjoyed admiring the railway bridge close up. Then walked along the shore to the very quaint little old town of South Queensferry, central part, with 'olde-worlde' buildings, cobbled streets, steep steps ... most charming. And so, under the road bridge, and up out of the town and beside a fairly busy road for a while, and I crossed near the construction site of the new Forth Road Crossing project, as yet in very early stages. Continued via Newton past Hopetoun Wood and down a lane past

Craigton, to another very interesting, scenic experience – followed the tow-path of the Union Canal right through to Linlithgow – past Fawnspark and Philpstoun and some long open stretches – also deep cuttings, and well-wooded sections. It was a very peaceful, unspoilt canal route. I met a few fellow-walkers from time to time. Linlithgow was another lovely old town – the great attraction is, of course, the ruined palace, beside the 'large' and beautiful loch. 'Large' that is, for it is so extensive within the town – a fine feature, surrounded by parkland slopes. (It is about a mile long.)

I discovered there were plans to restore the ruined palace, the birthplace of Mary Queen of Scots. I saw parts of the magnificent old building – huge, very high old stone walls and towers, and saw the waters of the loch below. The palace dates from the 1400s.

I explored the historic town, too with its fine old buildings and enjoyed 'tattie' soup (Scottish for potato soup) with vegetables, and cup of tea at a café. Then walked on via the 'suburb' of Linlithgow Bridge; around here I crossed into (I think it is called) the county of Falkirk, having been in the Lothians for a good while. Took a lane through Whitecross to the lovely Union Canal again and followed the tow-path, near Brightons (scenery as good as the earlier section) to Polmont (station), arriving 5.30 pm, where buses were replacing trains, so I travelled by road via Linlithgow to Edinburgh Waverley station (stop for meal at station) and walked back through the city to my warm and comfortable hotel room.

The bus driver told me about the new Forth Road Bridge, already referred to. The present bridge is about forty or fifty years old, apparently. It did also occur to me: the railway crosses on the first Forth Bridge; the road, on the second Forth Bridge; they hope to build another road on a third Forth Bridge; might there ever be a fourth Forth Bridge?

Another very enjoyable day, including a lot of 'items' of interest.

Day 76
25/3/13

UNION CANAL (POLMONT – REDDING – HALLGLEN TUNNEL) – FALKIRK – GRAHAMSTON – STENHOUSEMUIR – PLEAN – BANNOCKBURN – STIRLING
(18 miles approx)

*A*fter further good bed and breakfast, I undertook my walk through the south of the city again, to Edinburgh Waverley station, and took train calling at Haymarket, Edinburgh Park and Linlithgow, en route to Polmont, where I alighted, re-commencing yesterday's walk at about 11 am. Weather was as yesterday – cold east wind, snow on higher slopes, and drifts in some areas.

I did a third, very pleasant hike along the next section of the Union Canal, from Polmont, past Redding, out into the countryside – scenic views from the tow-path – open country, woodland, deep wooded cuttings again. The thrill culminated at the last part – proceeding through Hallglen Tunnel (620 metres long), which was dimly but satisfactorily lit – carved through rock – and with water dripping in considerable quantities from the roof!

At the end of the tunnel, my route took me from the canal down into the sizeable, attractive old town of Falkirk – fine stone buildings in abundance again – at a café, I selected my soup of the day; this time it was carrot and coriander (and other items). Due to the prolonged cold weather, my 'soup season' seems to be extending into what should normally now be the 'ice cream season'! Also did some shopping, and I then walked on via Grahamston, Bainsford, Carron, Stenhousemuir and Antonshill (all urban areas) before reaching some extensive new housing development in a more rural setting of country lanes and open fields. I crossed the M876 and M9 motorways, and also crossed from (I assumed) the county of Falkirk to Stirlingshire.

And so, well out in the open undulating countryside now, via Bogend and Gallamuir, I reached the main A9 road at the edge of Plean and followed it up and then down. At Gartclush or thereabouts, I gained an inspiring view, in the gathering dusk of the City of Stirling ahead, the old castle dominating it and beyond that the huge Wallace Monument on the hillside. At Greenyards, I followed part of a ring road system round the city, on the edge of Bannockburn, and I passed the site, according to the map, of the Battle of Bannockburn (1314). In the area of Loanhead, I took a direct route into Stirling city centre, but it was too dark to see the glory of it all (next time, I hope!). I reached the railway station around 6.45 pm – just beside a much narrower River Forth than at S Queensferry.

After a short conversation with a local guy about historic Scottish/English battles, including Bannockburn (we were quite amicable!), a train arrived which I took back to Edinburgh Waverley (calling at Larbert, Camelon, Falkirk Grahamston, Polmont, Linlithgow, Edinburgh Park and Haymarket). After a light meal at the station, as it was quite late and dark, I took a taxi back to the comfortable hotel.

Oh dear – one more pun. I like to think of today as a sterling/Stirling effort! But did the strain of it tell? When I entered my hotel room, I forgot there was a long mirror in front. I saw someone – not an intruder, I hoped – possibly a domestic worker? I said 'Hello' to them quietly and politely – then I realised it was me (!)

And the homeward journey, 26th March: I left the comfortable hotel by taxi for Edinburgh Waverley station again. Interestingly – just as the 'up' route to the north, on Day 75 followed the same as Day 74 - so today's 'down' route from the north (again, including the stations stopped at) followed the same as Day 74.

That is to say: Edinburgh Waverley to Newcastle Central; thence to Winchester, via Birmingham New Street; Winchester to Cosham – and of course, most enjoyable again. But the weather was different to 5th March. This time, snow fell from time to time, especially in southern Scotland and northern England, where there was a covering of a patchy sort. The continuous, heavier snow layers were evident mainly in the Sheffield, Derby and Birmingham areas. It was as cold as ever, but (except for some fog further north) visibility was very clear, so the views, as referred to last time, were generally ideal again. I also enjoyed, particularly, this time views of architecture at the ancient cities of Durham and York, and the beauty of countryside in the Derby area. After Birmingham, the route was, of course, well known to me anyway with its attractions

Yes, another very well worthwhile mini break.

And, to close – I have referred a great deal to the Firth of Forth. The 'certain lady' to whom I have referred, quite a lot, in connection with her 'uncertain' statements, when visiting Scotland once, passed a message to her family that she had just crossed the 'Forth of Firth Bridge'! On a similar note, on other occasions, she referred to a limousine car, as a 'limonnise', and to a soda siphon as a 'cider soephon'!

Day 77
21/4/13

Stirling – St Ninians – Foot O'Green – Easter Buckieburn – Carron Bridge – Kilsyth – Wellshot – Twechar – Kirkintilloch
(21 miles approx)

*A*ccording to the normal custom – firstly, the account of the day before: this time, the first train (route), Cosham to Winchester, was followed by Winchester to York. I had only done this journey in the opposite direction before. It called at the 'usual' stations (via Birmingham New Street, etc). I noticed, more so this time the beauty of scenery between Derby and Sheffield, on the borders of the Peak District, in limestone areas – attractive hills, rivers and woodland; somewhat rugged, and quite steep slopes.

At York I changed to an Edinburgh train calling at Darlington, Newcastle Central and Berwick-upon-Tweed. Finally, I took a stopping service from Edinburgh Waverley to Stirling, calling at Haymarket, Edinburgh Park, Linlithgow, Polmont, Falkirk Grahamston, Camelon and Larbert. On entering this train, I asked two passengers if it was going to Stirling, both of whom replied, 'Hope so'! I also enjoyed talking to a gentleman and a lady on the journey who showed much interest in my walking routes thus far, and gave helpful information about hoped-for future walking. The lady kindly gave me a lift in her car to my B & B – once again, very comfortable accommodation.

A long and interesting journey – I see in my rough notes that I recorded weather as spring-like, fine, warmer and coldish, compared to last time. Does that make sense?

I started 21st April very refreshed from B & B, with a walkabout in Stirling, commencing about 10.00 am. I certainly found the historic city inspiring. Climbed the steep, sometimes narrow and cobbled streets past high old stone buildings of various shapes and sizes, through shopping centre and beside ancient residences to Castle Wynd, and then the castle itself, dominating the summit of the hill on which Stirling is built. The castle could be described as the centrepiece of Stirling – a grand collection of ancient buildings perched at the top of the rocky crags. The views from the entrance were very good. Apart from few heavy showers today, it was sunny, windy, clear and cold.

Indeed, it really felt like spring was in the air, albeit rather late – daffodils, lambs and ice creams were plentiful! A little snow could still be seen on hills. But – back to the castle – I could see the city below clearly, the valley of the Forth, high hills and maybe mountains. Stirling Old Bridge, over the River Forth was visible, a fine old gem from about 1500, and the William Wallace Monument, a huge old tower on the more distant wooded hillside, stood out well. On the fields below it, Wallace had led his troops to victory at the Battle of Stirling Bridge.

However, I thought, time to move on. I walked back, similar route to 'lower' Stirling. My direction now took a rather south-of-west turn. I walked via St Ninians and out into the countryside, past Foot O'Green on a most pleasant lane, up and down quite significant hills, vistas far and clear, following near Loch Coulter Burn, up to Loch Coulter Reservoir – an attractive lake. Then past Easter Buckieburn and down to Carron Bridge, crossing a second-class road (at the hotel) and the River Carron, and fording a flooded lane, along which I continued southwards, and crossed from Stirlingshire into North Lanarkshire. This lane, which runs across the east summits of the Kilsyth Hills, was therefore very hilly, very picturesque too, partly in coniferous forest areas, and also open scenery, eventually with quite spectacular views to Kilsyth and beyond. I passed Berryhill and descended a very steep hill near Colzium House, so arriving in the town of Kilsyth itself. It seemed a pleasant Scottish place, but I was most impressed by the rain – a real cloudburst of a shower!

I was fortunate to be in an attractive park where I took solitary refuge in a bandstand! I thought – I could have sung there – 'The clouds ye so much dread/ Are big with mercy, and shall break/ In blessings on your head'. (!) There was, of course, no musical accompaniment for me; and not spectators either. Everyone else seemed to be indoors.

Bright skies soon appeared – I continued to the wide Forth and Clyde Canal, and walked the peaceful, pleasant tow-path from Wellshot, crossing now into East Dunbartonshire, and past Twechar and Shirva Farm, so reaching the impressive sizeable town of Kirkintilloch.

It was about 6.30 pm (walk finished), but I had to get to Lenzie station and there was not long before the train was due, and too far on foot. I ran after a bus and just missed it. I saw taxis parked but there was no one in them. I ran after one moving taxi but was not noticed, and I saw a pedestrian to whom I called out, but he didn't hear me. Then I found a taxi office open, and all was well. I was soon sorted out.

So – taxi to Lenzie, train (via Croy and Larbert) to Stirling, cup of tea and ice cream (dairy milk with fondant sauce and chocolate pieces) at café, and walk to B&B. Yes, the ice cream season is upon us again, and quite right too.

Certainly, another rewarding, eventful and very pleasant walk.

Day 78
22/4/13

Kirkintilloch – Glasgow Bridge – Torrance – Bardowie – Milngavie
(9 miles approx)

*H*aving enjoyed another very good night and breakfast in this comfortable accommodation, I walked to Stirling station and took train back to Lenzie, same route as last evening and taxi again to Kirkintilloch.

After another quick look at the town, I located the Forth and Clyde Canal again, and at about 11.00 am resumed 'the walk' from yesterday, on the tow-path, which was as lovely as before, although a little more urban to start with. What was really different, though, was the weather. Rain was rather persistent – but the wind! That was, it seemed, head on and gale force. Although gusts came and went, they came again, quite a lot!

But I enjoyed the experience all right. I was resuming a more westerly direction again. Two boatloads of passengers passed, enjoying a cruise on the opposite easterly course, therefore aided by the wind and well protected behind windows and beneath a good roof to their cosy lounge. I managed not to feel at all jealous – indeed, I passed several walkers and a cyclist, so was in good company myself, and had sympathetic and humorous conversations.

I walked beneath Glasgow Bridge (a road bridge) and to – I feel sure it was called – Hungryside Bridge – how appropriate at midday. Thoughts of soup and roll, and other thoughts leading inevitably to ice creams . . . I didn't want to get 'carried away'. There were not even any crumbs to be seen at this bridge. It was another road bridge, and I joined this road route from here – rather busy, but good paths and grass banks for the walker.

I continued via the villages of Torrance, Balmore and Bardowie and passed Langbank – here, a remarkable change in the weather – both gale and rain creased! All was calm and bright, and views were much clearer too. So I entered Milngavie (pronounced 'Mulguy'), enjoying good views of distant hills or mountains, and seeing this very pleasant town to advantage.

Arrival time was about 2.30 pm. (After having had a good walk round – shops, station etc.) It was quite an early finish to today's hike but seemed logical, as I hoped to commence the next phase – 'the 'wilds' of the West Highland Way – tomorrow from here.

For the moment thoughts of still being on the 'hungry side' prevailed and I sighted an excellent café and indulged in cream of cauliflower soup with toasted turkey and cranberry sandwiches, followed by pot of tea, and apple pie with vanilla ice cream. There was also the pleasant experience, as often now, of listening to the Scottish accent, particularly here – the café was quite full.

I retraced my steps to the station, realising for now, I must get back to Stirling – a slightly circuitous train journey was involved.

Took train stopping at all stations to Partick, then changed to train from which I gained good views of parts of Glasgow and the River Clyde – after which we seemed to go underground to Charing Cross (Glasgow), and Glasgow Queen Street (Low Level). I transferred up the elevator to my next train from the impressive main line terminus, Glasgow Queen Street (High Level), and from this grand old station, took this further train calling Bishopbriggs, Lenzie, Croy, Larbert – and Stirling.

So, one further walk, to B&B (with shopping en route) for another comfortable night, after another excellent day.

The West Highland Way, including Loch Lomond
& the Head of Glen Coe
96 miles

DAY 79
23/4/13

MILNGAVIE – CRAIGALLIAN LOCH – CARBETH – DUMGOYNE – KILLEARN (SOUTH SIDE) – GARTNESS – EASTER DRUMQUHASSLE – DRYMEN – BUCHANAN SMITHY – MILTON OF BUCHANAN – BALMAHA (INCLUDING LOCH LOMOND AND THE TROSSACHS NATIONAL PARK)
(17 miles approx)

*D*uly refreshed, again at the comfortable B&B (beneficial rest and breakfast), and very helpfully advised by my hosts about travel and transport etc, I set forth to Stirling station, again on foot and took a train through to Glasgow Queen Street (High Level), then transferring to Low Level, after which a train straight through to Milngavie via Partick – i.e. – the same rail routes as yesterday.

I began walking about midday. Weather wise, today was excellent – sunshine, blue skies, cool breezes, clear views. Ideal for the commencement of the popular long-distance footpath, the West Highland Way, which is 95½ miles, extending from here through to Fort William. I met someone en route who said the distance was 96 miles. I had thought it was 95. We very amicably agreed to differ. But it seemed we were both wrong. Probably later, I will be told it is 94 or 97, or 100 or 101!

A quick look again at Milngavie, and I identified the granite obelisk in the town, the official start of the walk. I did indeed meet a lot of walkers, a cyclist and local residents. Daffodils were even more abundant today. Sheep grazed contentedly, their lambs never far from them. And I was resuming a generally northward direction again.

This 'end' of the Way was comparatively easy going. Gradients were more moderate, or virtually nil. I crossed back into Stirlingshire (from East Dunbartonshire) quite soon, en route. Initially, I was soon pursuing the Way through very beautiful deciduous woodland, through undulating countryside, which progressively opened out, leaving thicker woods behind completely. Hills and perhaps mountains became more and more visible, some quite near. Having left Mugdock Wood behind, and followed close to Allander Water, I continued close to Craigallian Loch and passed Carbeth, Carbeth Loch and Easter Carbeth. Then a very open, downhill section, moorland and hillside scenery, past Arlehaven, to valley scenery in which I picked up the route of the one-time Aberfoyle to Glasgow railway; so easy, flat, or nearly-flat walking – and for a good while. It was a well-maintained section of the Way via Dumgoyne and to the south of Killearn, but at Gartness, I transferred to country lanes. At Upper Gartness, I officially entered 'Loch Lomond and the Trossachs National Park'. This quite hilly section took me to higher viewpoints and just after Easter Drumquhassle I enjoyed the first view of

Loch Lomond. Very inspiring! The peaceful, extensive waters, islands within, and high slopes and peaks surrounding the loch – absolutely glorious, the grandeur of the scene!

But I had to press on. Soon after, at Gateside, I left the official route, wanting to see the beauty of some small villages. So I continued by lanes into Drymen, where I paused – firstly for a strawberry ice cream. It was a delightful little place – village green, fine church, hotel, inn, old stone cottages – all the best ingredients. People were very helpful too and having worked out that I would be too late for the last bus from my destination, I booked a taxi from a local firm.

And so for the last 'leg', and I didn't feel quite on my last legs! I followed beside the country road, munching shortbread as I walked. A very scenic route, with a good path or verge beside it; Buchanan Smithy (a very pleasant hamlet) and Milton of Buchanan (also very pleasant, 'olde-worlde' village) were the two intermediate settlements, well worth seeing; and so I reached beautiful Balmaha, rejoining the West Highland Way. But this road route, on this also beautiful evening, had enabled me to enjoy the ever-growing closeness of Loch Lomond and walk on its 'bonnie bonnie banks'! A very real thrill. And here I was, the meadows and woods around me, the grand slopes and peaks above me, mountains getting nearer and higher, and the extensive waters of the loch before me – so calm, so quiet, so tranquil. Balmaha, which I didn't have time to see in detail (6.30 pm now, and taxi was due) – pub, cottages, shore etc. I will hope to describe 'next time', properly. For now, I'll say, 'another superb holiday'!

The very helpful taxi driver transported me back via Drymen to Stirling, giving me plenty of interesting information en route. Pointed out interesting views too, Stirling Castle from a distance etc. After eating at café (including a second, very acceptable ice cream (chocolate)), I returned, very well satisfied, to the B&B, and also reflected happily (see also Day 73) about other Scottish View-Master pictures I was given as a boy, which also filled me with wonderment – of 'Loch Lomond and the Trossachs'! More nostalgia for me – I had walked today in what once seemed so far away a land.

But, again to return home (24th April, 2013). My kind hosts continued to show much interest in my walk, and gave me a lift back to the station. An express, calling at Falkirk Grahamston, Haymarket, Edinburgh Waverley, Newcastle Central and Darlington, (before I alighted at York), transported me at high speed, after which, fast trains on same routes as 20th April, whisked me, York to Basingstoke and Basingstoke to Cosham. Weather and views were good, except for sea mists on northern coasts, which reminded me of the following:

First party said (they were in fog): I've been in worse fog
Second party: Where?
First party: I don't know where it was, because it was too foggy to see!

Day 80
21/5/13

Balmaha - Milarrochy — Sallochy — Rowardennan — Rowchoish —
Cailness — Inversnaid (including Loch Lomond and
the Trossachs National Park)
(14 miles approx)

*A*n interesting variation on the journey 'up' this time. Yesterday, trains were: Cosham to Winchester; Winchester to Birmingham New Street; then, things rather different — on to Glasgow Central, following known route to start with, calling Wolverhampton, Crewe, Warrington, Wigan, Preston, Lancaster, Oxenholme and Carlisle, and continuing non-stop to Glasgow, via Lockerbie, Carstairs Junction and Motherwell and other stations. Views at Shap and Beattock summits, and of the Lake District and River Clyde (referred to Days 74 and 75) were rewarding, among other vistas.

I took a 'shuttle bus' from the impressive, 'old' Glasgow Central terminus, via the city centre area, Sauchiehall Street — fine shops, high historic-looking buildings etc, also impressive, of course - to the already described Glasgow Queen Street terminus (see Day 78), and descended from High to Low Level, taking a stopping service via Charing Cross, Partick, Anniesland, Drumchapel, Drumry, Singer, Dalmuir, Kilpatrick, Dumbarton East and Central, Renton, Alexandria (and other stations), before terminating at Balloch. More good views of River Clyde too.

Had a snack in Balloch, before boarding a bus for the scenic route via Drymen to Balmaha, where I enjoyed later afternoon tea at the bed and breakfast at the Bay, very comfortable, my room being in a novel and secure summerhouse-type building in a lovely garden. A very helpful and hospitable host, again here, made me feel most welcome. Weather very good today, sunny and cool.

And so, today — again, I must stress how helpful the lady, who runs this B&B was — after a jolly good breakfast, we discussed my walk. She used her knowledge of the West Highland Way (she had walked it) to advise on best transport links to and from, and the best location for further accommodation. In a nutshell, it was going to be easier to use ferries across Loch Lomond, than taxis a long way round it.

Therefore, around 10.15, in glorious spring sunshine, and slightly chilly breezes, with glorious clear views of Loch Lomond and the towering bens all around (throughout the day, all this lasted), I experienced one of the best, if not the best, days of the walk so far! A comment too, on wildlife. Very tame ducks surrounded me on the shore of Balmaha Bay (quite entertaining, and no doubt, hungry). And wild mountain goats were a feature on much of the route, and they seemed very friendly. As to walkers, they abounded! On this very popular West Highland Way, it was very pleasant to meet, and re-meet these enthusiastic people at different points and on different days, and sometimes at B&Bs and sometimes in cafés or the like, and catch up on each others' news.

Initially, I enjoyed the utterly unspoilt beauty of Balmaha Bay, the waterside, the cottages, the slopes above … nestled so attractively in such a glorious setting. But the fantastic views of Loch Lomond and the huge bens go on and on all the way up this eastern shore – and equally good views across to and on the 'other side'. And so I continued up 'East Loch Lomondside'. Bluebells and primroses abounding, too!

I walked on, sometimes on lanes, sometimes tracks, sometimes rough, rocky paths. I soon left the first lane, climbing steeply to the superb viewpoint near Craigie Fort, and descended equally steeply to a shore path and past Arrochymore Point, following sandy or pebbly beaches to and at Milarrochy. Then followed the lane via Blair into areas of coniferous and deciduous woodland – and forest. A path detour later led me to the lane again at Cashel: on past Anchorage Cottage and a very steep, rocky path 'detour' at Sallochy, after which I took the lane route through Rowardennan Forest and past Dubh Lochan (an attractive small loch), to Rowardennan, with its picturesque hotel and other attractive buildings. Here, the lane ended – I followed a good wide forest track, climbing higher and higher up the slopes of Ben Lomond – but nowhere near the summit. I was walking 'near' the shore but far above it. I passed above Ptarmigan Lodge, and through Rowchoish and Cailness, but progressively the track had been 'downgrading' to a path, and then a rough, rock-strewn path, undulating and descending to Inversnaid. I had had fine views of boats cruising far below, on the loch. I had one to catch myself at Inversnaid, but a very helpful couple I met up with kept a lookout for it with me as time was getting on. Reached Inversnaid 4.45 pm, much enjoyed ice cream (Cornetto) and orange juice at attractive, impressive hotel at this small settlement. It also boasted a splendid waterfall, high cliffs and pier/ jetty. A fascinating spot. I enjoyed the excellent views on the boat trip back to Inveruglas on the west side very much; a very kind guy (a munro-bagger) gave me a lift back to Crianlarich, where I indulged in potato and leek soup and orange juice (pub); and so to another excellent B&B!

The rugged grandeur of this superb scenery today had made me feel that I should be bursting forth in song, from the lines of 'The Bluebells of Scotland' and 'The Bonnie, Bonnie Banks of Loch Lomond'. It really had been an outstanding experience. Too, to put it in a comic way; ducks, mountain goats and walkers, (mentioned earlier) all very friendly!

Day 81
22/5/13

INVERSNAID — POLLOCHRO — DOUNE — ARDLEISH — INVERARNAN — BEINGLAS FARM — FALLS OF FALLOCH — DERRYDAROCH — CRIANLARICH (INCLUDING LOCH LOMOND AND THE TROSSACHS NATIONAL PARK)
(14 miles approx)

*W*ell, I would say the outstanding experience of yesterday certainly continued through today, undiminished. The spring sunshine, cool breezes, clear views, the glory and grandeur of Loch Lomond and district, the lofty mountains or bens, the 'olde-worlde' charm of the small settlements, the bluebells and primroses, sheep and lambs, the sound of the cuckoo, huge waterfalls ...!

True, there was a hail shower very near the end of the walk, but also snow has been falling at times on the high peaks above me, creating beautiful white caps on summits all around. The West Highland Way runs, it is said, where the Scottish Highlands meet the Scottish Lowlands — I seemed to be entering the former, leaving the latter way back now.

Having enjoyed the facilities and comfort and hospitality of this 'second' B&B, and enjoyed conversations, and received more helpful advice from my host, too; I certainly say I'm impressed with the accommodation at each B&B — both are excellent. Also, my luggage had been moved on, in advance, for me yesterday.

So, well-breakfasted, again, I walked along to Crianlarich station, noting with interest that - this far north - not only station name-boards but also road route signs, with place names, largely seem to be 'bi-lingual', in English and Scottish Gaelic. I took a train on the very scenic line, via Ardlui to 'Arrochar and Tarbet'. A train from Oban was joined to a train from Fort William (possibly from Mallaig too), to continue to Glasgow Queen Street. All the three stations I saw this morning are good examples of a sort of alpine-style chalet architecture, very appropriate for Highland mountain scenery. So, in this 'doubled' train, I travelled over high viaducts and other fine viewpoints, to pick out much of paragraph 1 above. On alighting, I enjoyed the short walk into Tarbet, a typically beautiful little village, and enjoyed beautiful strawberry tart and orange juice at a café. A quick look at Tarbet, its charming cottages, hotel and the green, and the pier — and then, from the pier, I took a cruise ferry boat (like yesterday's), across Loch Lomond to Inversnaid, of course much enjoying the extensive views as before. Plenty of walkers again today, so interesting to meet, talk, re-meet and talk again. We exulted over the weather, discussed our progress and never ceased to express our delight at the scenery.

Do I hear you say 'Whenever are we going to hear about today's walk?' Point taken! At about 12.15, I ascended the path at Inversnaid from the pier and jetty, passed the impressive hotel again, and descended to the shore path, the West Highland Way. This section rose and fell on the well-wooded slopes but not so much as yesterday. What must be emphasised however, was the tough nature of the walk, probably the hardest going of the whole Way. Plenty of rock hopping, boulders and tree roots everywhere, endless ups and downs, and one section up a bank but using a wooden ladder of some length. Progress was therefore slower, but it was well worthwhile. And the views of the loch and all around, and to the 'other side of the water', were as good as ever. (Oh dear – a pun again – sorry – it's about the views of the terrains/t-rains (!)The rough terrain; and I saw train after train, on the west side of the loch, the line I had just used.) So, past Sroin Uaidh, Pollochro and Doune and around the last-named the going was generally easier again. The Way went 'inland' from the shore at times, finally so at Ardleish, the northern end of Loch Lomond. I then continued on up and down gradients, often on open hillside; and the high mountains, as always, never far away. Via Ardleish and Blarstainge, and onwards, the gradients and course of the Way were back to 'average', rather than 'tough' – and so, down to Inverarnan, by the River Falloch where I saw the Drovers' Inn, interesting as it had been built in 1705, and stood well-preserved in its ancient glory, an extensive Scottish three-storey stone landmark.

At Beinglas Farm nearby, I enjoyed ice cream etc, at a café here and it was a particularly busy meeting-up point of a lot of us walkers. Then continued the Way on an undulating track, mainly on the east side of Glen Falloch, in open countryside, above the River Falloch and with excellent views of the rapids and waterfalls, including the Falls of Falloch – most spectacular! The track diminished to a path; the mountains 'continued' around, as high as ever; via Derrydaroch I reached the railway and the main A82 road. I left the Way, and continued on the main road grass verge, also seeing, I think, one more train and soon reached Crianlarich at 8 pm. Had a quick look round this pleasant little village, enjoyed soup etc at a restaurant, and settled in for the night at the excellent B&B.

What a rewarding day – again!

DAY 82
23/5/13

CRIANLARICH – ST. FILLAN'S PRIORY – AUCHTERTYRE – DALRIGH –
TYNDRUM – CLIFTON – AUCH – BRIDGE OF ORCHY
(15 miles approx)

After further useful advice, a good night and a good breakfast again, I set forth from Crianlarich, seeing it in some more detail and admiring its

Land's End

Trebarwith Strand, Cornwall

Clovelly, Devon

Lynmouth, Devon

Glenthorne, Devon

Bridgwater, Somerset

Canal, Frampton-on-Severn, Gloucestershire

Historic Docks, Cathedral Tower, Gloucester

Bristol Temple Meads Station

Black Mountains, Wales

Lymore, Powys

Valle Crucis Abbey, Denbighshire

Eastgate, Chester

Lancaster Castle

Lake Windermere, Bowness, Cumbria

Howtown Pier, Ullswater, Cumbria

Carlisle Castle, Cumbria

Gretna Green, Dumfries and Galloway, Scotland

Gretna Green, Dumfries and Galloway, Scotland

Royal Mile, Edinburgh

Princes Street, Edinburgh

Firth of Forth Bridge, from south side (Edinburgh)

Stirling, Scotland

Balmaha Bay, Loch Lomond

West Highland Way, north-west of Crianlarich

Loch Lomond, from Rowardennan

Waterfall near Loch Eilt, Road to the Isles, Scotland

Summit, Devil's Staircase, West Highland Way   At Morar, Road to the Isles

At Fort Augustus, south-west end of Loch Ness, Scottish Highlands

River Ness, Inverness

Wick Harbour, Caithness

Thurso, Caithness is the northernmost town on mainland Scotland

surroundings – it lies far below the towering snow-capped bens – on which more snow was falling and laying today. Weather was really cold for the time of year and today a strong wind was blowing, with rain showers and sunny intervals 'punctuating' my walk.

So, around 10.15, I left the village by a steep, winding path through a coniferous forest – after a fair climb I rejoined the West Highland Way near Kirk Craig, then through more of this forest, twists and turns, and ups and downs, eventually descending to valley floor level, where I crossed railway, A82 and the River Fillan, so reaching Kirkton Farm and passing the ruins of St Fillan's Priory. A little further, at Auchtertyre, I enjoyed chocolate ice cream and orange juice very much – these last two words refer to the amount of enjoyment as much as to the amount consumed too!

The path crossed back to south of the A82, past Dalrigh, in which area I passed a carved stone seat. Legend has it that it contains Robert the Bruce's sword. He was defeated here in 1306 at the Battle of Dal Righ – hence the name already quoted above, and meaning 'King's field'. I followed through areas of heather, then into pine woods, and so reached Tyndrum, seeing a fair amount of this pleasant village. Passed Tyndrum Lower station (on Oban line). The Upper station is on the Mallaig line. Daffodils were still in bloom, as well as primroses and bluebells.

The Way crosses the A82 again and follows close to the Mallaig/ Fort William railway for the rest of today. The scenery seemed even more captivating – quite out in the wilds. The route led onto lower slopes of dramatic mountains (after Clifton), through a high mountain pass, and then, among grazing sheep and lambs, quite steeply downhill to Auch in a low valley, with excellent views of the railway on its Horseshoe Curve on viaducts that followed the contours of the mountainside. I also saw trains. The Way used an old military road for a while as at certain other areas and was much flatter now in this valley route, a stony track. I have now crossed over from Stirlingshire into 'Argyll and Bute' and left 'Loch Lomond and the Trossachs National Park' way behind.

And so to Bridge of Orchy. First I reached the station – another of these fine alpine-chalet style stations, so appropriate to Scottish Highland scenery. Around this point there was another of these general meetings-up of groups of 'Way' walkers. Quite a mini 'Piccadilly Circus' again! This continued to apply at hotel at Bridge of Orchy, which we soon reached down a steep lane, and across the A82. I finished the walk at this fine, wee Scottish village around 5.45 pm. Much enjoyed soup, sandwiches and a pot of tea at hotel, before returning to the station for a very beautiful evening train ride through the country I'd walked today – calling at Tyndrum (Upper) and Crianlarich, where I alighted. The crossings of viaducts on the Horseshoe Curve were particularly impressive. So back to B&B, a chat with my host about accommodation, travel etc and to bed – with many happy reflections on another very fine section of the West Highland Way. These last three days really have made just the right sort of holiday!

But, to conclude the record with details of the also-enjoyable journey back south, 24th May. My host kindly arranged early breakfast for me so I could catch a convenient coach, 8.28 am, my best connection for the train. It was, of course, a very scenic ride. Weather was very bright and clear – only at the end of the day did I reach cloudier, wetter climes. Yes, the coach transported me down Glen Falloch and beside the west shore of Loch Lomond, through Ardlui, Tarbet and Luss – high, steep slopes above; extensive blue waters beside; and beyond, the beautiful east shore and peaks. Then via Alexandria, Dumbarton and Clydebank to Glasgow Buchanan bus station, where I transferred to the shuttle bus, as 20th May, for the Glasgow Central railway station, via the imposing city centre.

I took fast train, calling at Carlisle, Oxenholme and Lancaster again, 20th May route, so I enjoyed re-seeing the sights, before alighting at Preston. Had enjoyed conversations with friendly fellow travellers (Scottish) – a Prestwick lady bound for Oxenholme, and a Perth gent bound for Chester. Discussed areas of Scotland we knew from past and present.

I then took trains, using more or less the same routes and calling more or less at the same stations – as the journey 'up' – I also changed trains at Wolverhampton and Winchester, and so to Cosham and home.

Certainly, the clear, fine weather helped 'make' this holiday. I was reminded of the 'certain lady' again. After a motoring holiday together in Scotland, she said how much she had enjoyed it, concluding 'and we managed to see Mr W.' It rather sounded like he was one of the sights of Scotland that no-one should miss, such as a statue at the end of Princes Street, and the weather was clear enough to get a good view. He was of course a friend, but an Englishman, much-liked indeed, so not 'even' a Scotsman!

DAY 83
21/6/13

BRIDGE OF ORCHY – MÀM CARRAIGH – INVERORAN – BLACK MOUNT SIDE OF
RANNOCH MOOR – BA BRIDGE – KINGS HOUSE (THE HEAD OF GLEN COE)
(12 miles approx)

Certainly, the journey 'up' has lengthened again, somewhat! It lasted from about 9 am till 9 pm and fine weather and clear views provided much pleasure. The same pattern followed from Cosham to Glasgow Central as last time, with train changes at Winchester and Birmingham New Street, and calling I think at the same station stops. Shap, Beattock etc as good as ever to look at.

The 'shuttle bus' connection worked well again, from Central to Queen St stations via Glasgow city centre. And the 'Jewel in the Crown' of today (20th June) was the highly scenic, final, railway ride on to Bridge of Orchy. Train called at Dalmuir, Dumbarton Central, Helensburgh Upper, Garelochhead, Arrochar and Tarbet, Ardlui, Crianlarich (where the Oban portion of the train was detached from 'my' Fort William/ Mallaig portion), Upper Tyndrum and Bridge of Orchy. The highlights were: views of River Clyde, developing to the Firth of Clyde, as far as Helensburgh; the views down to Gare Loch, as far as Garelochhead; even more impressive views down to Loch Long, culminating with lofty views down to Arrochar and district; and then as already described in Days 81 and 82, the fine scenery above and around Loch Lomond; in the area of the Horseshoe Curve; and the mountain scenery of the Scottish Highlands generally.

I had a short walk to hotel, Bridge of Orchy, to complete my day, enjoyed good food and felt very welcome.

And now today, 21st June, 2013. Excellent accommodation at hotel, including a 'West Highlander' fried breakfast of high quality, and I set forth around 10 o'clock, on the longest day of the year, so plenty of daylight, especially so far north in Scotland! Fine weather continued, although there was Scotch mist and light rain a little of the time. Some delightful lines came to mind:

'And when, in purple hue, The Highland hills we view.'

I was certainly viewing such hills, and there was heather in bloom - just a little pink to be seen. The poetry was very appealing, and very evocative of this part of Scotland. I walked through the tiny village of Bridge of Orchy, and crossed the narrow, arched stone bridge itself, over the burn. (A 'military' bridge, built around 1750.) The West Highland Way took me on, up a steep, winding path through a pine forest, up on to moorland, to a summit at Màm Carraigh, where I enjoyed fine views down to Loch Tulla and of mountains surrounding. Then followed a steep, open descent to the lane at Inveroran. At hotel, I enjoyed shortcakes and a cup of tea. An attractive and welcoming place to visit.

I continued on the Way (which I stuck to, throughout) along the lane, over Victoria Bridge and past Forest Lodge. Then, interestingly, I joined a well-maintained, cobbled narrow track (but it deteriorated later on), one of Telford's (Drover's) old parliamentary roads. I followed long, steady climbs and some descents, adjacent to Rannoch Moor – plenty of bog and bog-cotton around me. Crossed the county border near Black Mount, from Argyll and Bute into officially 'Highland Region'.

So I progressed to Ba Bridge, under which the River Ba runs through a small gorge of red granite slabs; then on to the summit of the path, near which a Royal Naval helicopter was patrolling – some walkers told me 'to keep watch on everyone's safety'! A steep descent followed, with grand views emerging below of the 'top' of the Pass of Glen Coe (and the A82 road), mountains all around, and especially impressive, huge Buachaille Etive Mor and slopes and summit, between Glen Etive and Glen Coe.

I passed Glencoe Mountain Resort and Ski Centre, on the left of the downward slope, and Blackrock Cottage, at the 'foot' and crossed the A82 for Kings House, where I saw a few deer close up. I thus reached the 'Head' of Glen Coe (3.30 pm), and the fine old inn (17th century in origin), and I enjoyed 'generous' vanilla ice cream in chocolate sauce, and orange juice, there.

Returned by coach to Bridge of Orchy, gaining fine views of Rannoch Moor en route, and completed the day with excellent soup at hotel.

I mentioned Day 80, how friendly the ducks, mountain goats and walkers were – a 'comical' combination! Indeed, I met a lot more walkers today, who I enjoyed talking to about the route of the Way etc. I had expected too, to meet a further variety of friends today. People had said that they might abound, this time of year. In fact, there were only a few this holiday, surprisingly – just as well, as it is not a reciprocal friendship – I refer to midges!

Yes, another very happy day, with so much to enjoy and as just explained, it's sometimes what doesn't abound as well as all that does.

Day 84
22/6/13

Kings House (The head of Glen Coe) – Altnafeadh – Devil's Staircase – Kinlochleven
(9 miles approx)

*A*fter another very good night and breakfast ('West Highlander', fried, again!) I emerged from hotel well pleased, and boarded a coach for the trip across Rannoch Moor to Kings House, from whence I started walking again, about 11.30.

The weather forecast predicted rain so I was pleased that, after a wet start (with the good old Scotch mist!), the skies cleared and I had very good views of the very spectacular scenery on this part of the West Highland Way, which I continued to follow throughout today.

I met a lot of walkers again, particularly one group who started out about the same time as I did, and I re-met them later and joined up with them for the last few miles – they were doing a variety of interesting walks in the area, so we mutually discussed information about our hiking experiences. They were Scots, mainly from the Glasgow area. We certainly all shared a love of the Highlands.

Initially, I followed the Way, near to the high mountains on the north of the A82 road. My route was the Old Military Road again, now. At Altnafeadh, the Way met the A82 again – then the real fun began! Having descended the start of the Glen Coe Pass, the Way/ Old Military Road now turned sharply northward, and steeply upward. It was a well-preserved track, although quite rough and rocky.

I commenced the ascent of the Devil's Staircase. I hoped the experience would be one of a Staircase, not a Scarecase (not that I've ever heard of the latter)! In fact it was extremely enjoyable: starting as a fairly straight track, toward the mountain pass summit it went into a series of sharp zigzags. The views that unfolded were superb. The summit was 1800 feet, the highest point on the West Highland Way. The dramatic drop down to Glen Coe below and the vistas of the surrounding mountains, were outstanding.

And after the tough ascent, there followed the somewhat-tough descent – very worthwhile, but very rough and rocky. Two cyclists had just wheeled their bikes up it! They asked if I would take their photos, so I did – and they took mine. I proceeded down, down, down – with a few ups in between. It was a less steep but longer section than the climb I had just done, but it took a slightly circuitous route, to ease the gradient, and the descent did not finally conclude until Kinlochleven. There were, of course, marvellous views all round – many mountains, and below, the very extensive waters of the Blackwater Reservoir. Further on and further below, glimpses of Kinlochleven, and Loch Leven began to appear.

Eventually, the Way ran downward beside the pipelines that carry water steeply down into Kinlochleven. Interestingly, at some point today, apparently, I had entered the old county of Inverness-shire.

And so I entered the pleasant town of Kinlochleven. I walked on the scenic banks of the River Leven, and gazed up at the towering mountain peaks all around. Walk was completed about 3.30 pm. I visited the shops, bought an ice cream, and only one 'hiccup' (not literally) – due to luggage (shopping etc), I had to drop part of the ice cream down a drain, as my bus was coming and I couldn't hold everything very easily! I still think about that ice cream!

The bus transported me via further scenic routes, beside Loch Leven, through the villages of Glencoe and Ballachulish, over Ballachulish Bridge (across Loch Leven), and beside the shores of Loch Linnhe and through Fort William. Here I caught a train onto another very scenic route – it called at Spean Bridge, Roy Bridge, Tulloch, Corrour and Rannoch – some were very fascinating, remote stations – before Bridge of Orchy, where I alighted. Deer were roaming on the moorland, beneath the towering bens and beside the extensive lochs. I was really out in the wild Scottish Highlands. Hardly a road encroached for many, many miles. Scenic waterfalls in a gorge in the Braes O' Lochaber, and the gradual ascent beside Loch Treig for miles and miles, to a significant height, were particular highlights. I talked to a couple from Chicago, in the train – they had completed a holiday walking the West Highland Way, and were returning to their airport. He had, unfortunately, injured his foot while walking so he was moving around with considerable caution, but they were both highly impressed with the Scottish experiences.

And I duly returned to the hotel at Bridge of Orchy, where, in addition to snacks of the day (orange juice, shortbread, unfinished ice cream (!) ...) I also refreshed myself with excellent vegetable soup and roll, and cups of tea.

It had certainly been another of those wonderful days!

DAY 85
23/6/13

KINLOCHLEVEN — TIGH-NA-SLEUBHAICH — BLAR A CHAORAINN — NEVIS FOREST — GLEN NEVIS, WEST SLOPE — FORT WILLIAM
(15 miles approx)

Note: 1,207 miles since leaving Land's End: 96 of these are the West Highland Way

Good rest and West Highlander fried breakfast duly enjoyed again. I took coach as yesterday but via Rannoch Moor and further – via the very beautiful Glen Coe Pass into Glencoe village and, as yesterday, over Ballachulish Bridge etc to Fort William. Then further fine scenery enjoyed – I travelled by taxi, partly retracing route and taking the shore-side road on the north side of Loch Leven from North Ballachulish to Kinlochleven. A helpful taxi driver again – plenty of interesting conversation, especially about the immediate locality.

I started the West Highland Way about 11.30 and followed it for the whole of the walk again today, having had another quick look around Kinlochleven. The one very particular feature of today's walk was the weather. I think it was the wettest day I have experienced on this project since I left Land's End! I started out of the town, up a very attractive, steep, well-wooded mountainside, using a winding path. I didn't notice the rain coming on while sheltered under trees, but as I emerged onto open mountainside (with excellent views to Kinlochleven and Loch Leven far below, and mountains all around), the precipitation certainly seemed more persistent. I was entering a very bleak but beautiful mountain pass track (the Old Military Road again) and it soon dawned on me that I was going to be in for a good drenching. Hail too fell; the wind grew stronger and there was no shelter for miles. And so it remained very, very wet for about two hours.

I eventually did reach a ruined cottage during this time, probably the one marked on the map as Tigh-na-sleubhaich. It afforded very little shelter, but I was able to put on better waterproofs and re-line my rucksack with a rainproof dustbin bag. A lot of my possessions were in danger of blowing away in the wind during these proceedings! Also, fortunately, I met other walkers. We were all concerned not to get too cold and continued together, avoiding further stops until the rain and gale stopped. But there were not many walkers about today.

Continued past Lairigmor to an area that was coniferous woodland but had been cleared. By now the rain and gale had ceased and the rest of the day continued fine and clear. There was plenty of deep water to cross though – paths had quite disappeared under mini rivers. At Blar a Chaorainn, I enjoyed good views across to a loch in the Lundavra area. Now, the Way became a narrow path across moorland before entering the very lovely Nevis Forest – the route was very steep and undulating here – the coniferous trees, and beyond them, a highly (in two senses) impressive view of the massive Ben Nevis (highest point in Britain) were unforgettable sights for sure! I have walked to the top of the Ben several times, some years ago incidentally. (Admittedly, the higher part of the Ben was shrouded in mist – not unusual of course.)

The narrow path developed into a broad, winding track, forest all around and mountains all around too. I thus descended the west side of Glen Nevis with pleasant views of it. And I heard the bagpipes playing – now, this really was Scotland 'proper'! I joined the Glen Nevis road which I followed – and so reached the Nevis Bridge roundabout and Fort William. I walked through the town, particularly enjoying the High Street and the fine Scottish architecture around me, and glimpses of Loch Linnhe and beyond. Thus, at about 6 pm, I reached Gordon Square, the official terminus of the West Highland Way! The excitement made me forget something, I think. I enjoyed soup and bread at a café, but no ice cream!

Took a Caledonian sleeper train (but not bed), back to Bridge of Orchy, same delightful route as yesterday evening of course. I 'let' the train continue on to London Euston. It was very comfortable but then my hotel was very comfortable. I reflected, there, on the wonderful West Highland Way walk – it had been outstandingly enjoyable. Referring back to the start, Day 79, and controversy about its length; I estimated I had done 96 miles – half a mile up on the agreed compromise. And my official guidebook said 'allow between 5 and 8 days (inclusive) for it'. I did it in seven, so I'm not 'bottom of the class'! Of course, as recorded, I have done minor variations for various reasons but the overall distance result was that small amount 'up' anyway.

And so to conclude with my homeward journey, 24th June. Really, it was 'just' 20th June in the opposite direction – and just as lovely. Excepting that I took taxi between the two Glasgow stations, getting a good view of impressive George Square; and that I changed trains at Wolverhampton instead of Birmingham; all else with, I think, the same station stops was 'ditto'. I mustn't forget to mention the excellent West Highlander fried breakfast, so appetising at hotel. Weather was fine (some cloud admittedly), snacks were good, I just got my connections all right, and the scenery looked as splendid as when I travelled 'up'. A long day again.

At home, I much enjoyed reflecting again on a completed West Highland Way!

The Road to the Isles (Fort William to Mallaig)

51 miles

DAY 86
17/8/13

FORT WILLIAM – LOCH LINNHE (NORTH-EAST) – BANAVIE – CORPACH – LOCH EIL
(OUTWARD BOUND – LOCHEILSIDE – KINLOCHEIL) – GLENFINNAN (LOCH SHIEL)
(THE ROAD TO THE ISLES)
(18 miles approx)

I think I've been continually emphasising the length of the journeys 'up' – it's well and truly 'ditto' for this holiday. I was travelling by rail from 9.17 am till 10.06 pm! And so interesting too. Cosham to Fort William with changes of train at Winchester, Birmingham New Street and Glasgow Central and Queen Street (using taxi between these last-named two stations). (16th August, 2013.)

Weather was fine, if a little wet at times; and darkness fell on the last stretch, after Corrour. The whole route was as scenic as ever and most particularly, the more latter stages. Station stops were similar to before.

After about Lancaster, I got into conversation about my Land's End to ? project, with three fellow passengers sitting adjacently, and this lasted for much of the rest of 'that journey' and was very enjoyable. They showed great interest and fed me with Belgian chocolate toffee popcorns! On looking around the coach, I saw that a number of other passengers were listening as well so I included them in my 'informal speeches' too. I found I had a mixed Scottish and English audience.

The scenery, so impressive, Glasgow to Fort William I have already described, Day 83; also Day 84 (but reverse the direction). It was as good as ever. Quite an atmosphere at remote Rannoch station, where our train passed the Caledonian sleeper express (London-bound), and many passengers crowded the platforms.

At Fort William, I took taxi to another excellent guest house/ hotel (overlooking Loch Linnhe), where I settled in most comfortably for the night.

But it is time to speak of other things – the walking today. Also, of a full Scottish breakfast – fried, including haggis – very yummy! And too, of Fort William itself – I walked from the guest house, beside Loch Linnhe, a tidal sea-loch and past a pier, so enjoying the waterfront setting of this fine old Scottish town, grand old stone buildings, high mountains towering all around – this really had the feel of the heart of the Highlands. Visited the ruins of the old fort itself, and walked the High Street as last time (Day 85), and shopped – in pouring rain. But views were good today, and heavy squally showers lessened progressively, and sunshine eventually prevailed.

I commenced the walk 'proper' about 12.45 – The Road to the Isles. In a sense, this was a 'Walk within a Walk' as it was a detour from Fort William, in the one direction, with a planned return to the town 'on wheels' only. There was, I felt, not a sufficiently direct alternative walkable route back and I wouldn't be 'cheating' if I resumed walking from Fort William (after completion of this tempting diversion) - in another direction.

The Road to the Isles was road-walking (obvious!), using good verges, grassy banks and footpaths – the scenery was magnificent, huge mountains, extensive lochs – so the road was not at all boring. And it 'followed' the railway much of the time. A westward walk across old Inverness-shire.

Soon out of the town, with misty views of Ben Nevis, I walked close to Inverlochy and had a good view of Neptune's Staircase (series of locks on Caledonian Canal). Over the canal I passed Banavie village and industrial Corpach, and was soon following beside tidal Loch Eil – for some miles. Passed Loch Eil Outward Bound station, Fassfern, Locheilside station and then on through Kinlocheil village. On this stretch, I was delighted to hear a loud whistle and see clouds of smoke. The Jacobite steam trains were running between Fort William and Mallaig – fine locomotive, hauling about seven well-preserved maroon coaches, packed with passengers – I had a good close-up view.

In a 'foresty' area, I had a cake and water snack before reaching Glenfinnan. A scenic village, as other places en route are too. Glenfinnan's great attractions are, of course, the Monument (a tower – of Bonnie Prince Charlie fame), beside the shores of Loch Shiel (tidal possibly); and the majestic high, curving stone railway viaduct. But where was the station? I arrived about 6.45 pm, just right for the train, but made the fundamental error of thinking I knew, without checking the map. I turned off up lanes, tracks and paths to the wrong part of the railway – where I saw the last train of the day go by.

I walked back to a car park, where I was fortunate enough to meet two very kind girls, who said they could give me a lift back to Fort William, as they were staying at Glen Nevis camp-site. But their car was stuck in mud in a nearby waterlogged field! They thought they would need some help to get it out. I offered to assist, so a number of us went down into the mud to help. But the girl who was driving did a brilliant job, and reversed the vehicle out of quite deep mud, with no wheel-spin and virtually no help from the rest of us! I was therefore transported very comfortably back, direct to Fort William, on the Road to the Isles and sincerely expressed my gratitude.

A marvellous day! Snack at my B&B. But with all the fun, like Day 85, I forgot – ice cream.

Day 87
18/8/13

GLENFINNAN (LOCH SHIEL) – RANOCHAN – LOCH EILT – ARIENISKILL –
LOCHAILORT (THE ROAD TO THE ISLES)
(10 miles approx)

*H*ad a very good night and rest in this very impressive guest house – an imposing, older building with excellent service and again, the full Scottish fried breakfast including, I also have to stress, the haggis. These things are so worth mentioning, and repeating – I really am particularly well looked after here.

I had a later start again today and saw more of Fort William as I walked through the old town centre. Enjoyed the particularly scenic railway journey by diesel rail bus (not steam – that is more rare!) but the several-coach unit afforded all the facilities for viewing the Highlands in comfort of course. Train called at Banavie, Corpach, Loch Eil (Outward Bound) and Locheilside (unless no passengers to alight or board at the latter two – I've forgotten now). I thus basically followed the route of my walk of yesterday, enjoying the scenery all over again. And too of course, on to Glenfinnan, preceded by its famous viaduct (described yesterday), on which the train made a special stop for passengers to take photos.

So today I found out where Glenfinnan station actually was! On alighting, I toured the village again, including the shores of Loch Shiel, near the Monument most particularly.

My walking began around 1 o'clock. Today's weather was a less wet version of yesterday's but still very heavy showers, mainly early. Strong winds and bright sunshine featured well, later especially. All road walking again today, i.e. Road to the Isles walking, again too, in close proximity to the railway throughout, using the good grass verges and banks very much. Perhaps I should say that views of mountains, lochs, rivers and waterfalls were always excellent on the walk, unless otherwise stated – and you won't find any 'otherwise stated'!

The start of the walk was quite hilly, amid very open, rugged scenery with no settlements. After a while came the descent to Loch Eilt. Part way down – yes, I was not disappointed – as yesterday, the treat I had hoped for was coming. Very loud chug, chug, chug – and masses of smoke – a steam train was pounding up the gradient; again, I had a rewarding view of the fine locomotive with its maroon rake of coaches!

I continued down the gradient to Loch Eilt, where the road followed beside this freshwater expanse, on the north shore for some distance via a very small settlement, Ranochan. The purple heather was becoming more noticeable, presumably more impressive due to the rain, as indeed the waterfalls and burns most certainly were.

After the west extremity of the loch, the road followed close to River Ailort – and I thus continued past Arieniskill to the riverbanks, soon reaching Lochailort where hotel was open. At about 5 pm, the conclusion of the walk, I began feasting on ample potato and leek soup with roll, strawberry ice cream and orange juice. People there, mainly Scots, showed a very friendly interest in my walk. I continued of course, to enjoy listening to the Scottish accent, very much and this far north, it sounded more and more Scottish.

Had a very enjoyable train ride back from the nearby station at this pleasant, tiny village and again much enjoyed the stunning views back to Glenfinnan (the next station) and indeed, all the way back to Fort William (route and stations already described of course). A stopping train service again.

And so of course, walk back through Fort William to the comforts of the guest house again and happy reflections on today. I thought too, an advantage in walking the Road to the Isles was the additional pleasure of re-seeing the scenery of the day(s), on the return journey on wheels, by the Road, or the nearby railway – in the reverse direction.

Here again, I was reminded of a 'certain lady', once more, who so enjoyed a motoring trip we went on that she commented that it would also be nice to do it in reverse! (Meaning of course, in the reverse direction.) But one was left with a mental vision of a car speeding backwards in reverse gear as a means of re-experiencing the delights, but in a rather more dangerous way for the driver, the passengers and the travelling public in general!

Day 88
19/8/13

Lochailort – Polnish – Loch Nan Uamh (The Prince's Cairn) – Beasdale – Borrodale – Arisaig (Loch Nan Ceal) – Toigal & Kinsadel areas, River Morar & Morar (White Sands) (The Road to the Isles)
(15 miles approx)

Once more refreshed after a good night's rest and the Scottish fried breakfast, haggis, plus, plus ... all so worthy of note again of course, I had the further pleasure of a taxi ride (to ensure an earlier start to the walk), all the way to Lochailort on the Road to the Isles (of course) – the same driver who took me to Kinlochleven, Day 85 – helpful, friendly, and had more interesting conversations including aspects of Scottish history and geography.

I was able to start the walk around 11.15. Over these three days of walking, there seemed to be rather less rain each day. A few quite heavy showers today but also welcome sunshine and clear views to enjoy. Scenery as grand and rugged as ever. Despite my comments yesterday, I feel compelled to reiterate as to the beauty of the glorious mountains, lochs, rivers, waterfalls etc.

I started with some quite steep uphill on the good old Road to the Isles – convenient verges and banks to follow again – and something else very convenient – the steam train experience. I saw a steam train no less than three times today – thus a total of five sightings throughout the holiday. Where the Road followed quite high above and a little away from the sea loch Ailort – on the inland side - the train trundled past in all its smoky glory again, as good as ever.

Up and down, the Road continued – alternating gradients as expected. I walked via Polnish and then right down to the sea coast at Loch Nan Uamh. Very small rocky islands off the coast added to the charm of the rugged scene. Interestingly, near Cuildarrach, I saw and stood by The Prince's Cairn, the spot where tradition has it that Bonnie Prince Charlie sailed into exile in France in 1746.

I followed the winding road, up, down, up, down ... away from the coast via Beasdale and Borrodale, and near Carnach enjoyed today's second sighting of steam train. I've found I'm never far from the railway. This view was particularly interesting. I seemed to hear the engine chugging away in the distance for ages – and shrill whistling. Louder and louder chugging, then suddenly it appeared – I think it had been battling on some steep gradients – again, the train looked as good as ever.

Continued walking the road, downhill now and I turned off into the particularly delightful village of Arisaig. It really was a gem. Unspoilt isn't a good enough word for it. Truly excellent Scottish stuff! With the advantage of the main road re-routed to bypass it, its 'olde-worlde' charm hovered over it. The lane led down to the sea coast at Loch Nan Ceal. Picture-postcard cottages faced the shore of sands and rocks. A large collection of uninhabited small rocky islands scattered the sea loch estuary. Boats sail from this peaceful haven to other larger islands.

But I had to press on. I walked the lane, uphill again out of the other side of the village, back to the main road, a much straighter, less hilly section, with country views extending far and wide – all very open inland – and I saw the third steam train of the day! It was a long way distant – the railway is far from the Road here – it looked like a model engine and coaches. Heard all the sounds again. Yet again, 'as good as ever'.

I followed the Road to the River Morar Estuary. Passed Toigal on my left and Kinsadel on my right, and turned off what is now the Morar bypass, onto old roads and lanes, leading me into the village of Morar itself. Like Arisaig, it was particularly charming.

I was especially impressed by the White Sands of Morar. They were so beautiful. But I hope to write more about Morar next time. Train-watching today made me a little late. I had a train to catch myself, I could not linger. I found the station – relief – I was just in time. Amusingly, train didn't come – a bus did! (Bus replacement service, due to signalling problems.)

So, walk completed about 6.15 pm. I then 'rode by road' through all the glorious scenery again, all the way back to Fort William, calling at all the stations en route, in case passengers were waiting there. Then walked to my guest house, stopping en route in Fort William for 'ice cream of the day' – white chocolate! A fine complement to other snacks.

Another glorious day – but should I re-name the 'Road to the Isles', the 'Road to the Trains'?

And so, just the summary of the journey home – the following day. Arrangements were very helpfully made for me to have early breakfast (cereals etc). Well reinforced for the long journey, I started out by taxi through the town to the station – the same kind driver as before. Fine weather – cloudier in the north, warmer in the south. The routes, of course, were as scenic as ever, the same as 16th August, and the same stops – or more or less. I had taxi 'across' Glasgow again. Changed at Wolverhampton not Birmingham and had good meals on the trains. The travelling lasted from about 7.30 am to about 7.30 pm!

I have certainly had a wonderful time on the Road to the Isles of course, including steam train watching, if it hadn't been for which, I would probably have completed the 'Road' all the way to Mallaig this holiday.

DAY 89
21/9/13

MORAR (WHITE SANDS), RIVER MORAR & TOIGAL & KINSADEL AREAS — LOCH MORAR (NORTH-WEST) — BEORAIDBEG — GLASNACARDOCH — MALLAIG & COURTEACHAN (THE ROAD TO THE ISLES)
(8 miles approx)

Note: Total Road to the Isles including detours = 51 miles

One way of describing yesterday's journey 'up' could be 'unparalleled and uneventful', but this sounds ambiguous. Much of it was outstandingly scenic, also it followed basically the same route as on the last visit. I could say 'marvellous and much the same'! But you certainly don't get tired of these lovely trips. So this long day was again a great thrill – Cosham to Fort William, changing at the same stations as Day 86 and following a route in the English Midlands via Coventry, Hampton in Arden and Birmingham International. Weather was fine, but foggy, drizzly and dark after Garelochhead on the 'final' section. Passed the London-bound Caledonian sleeper express after this at Rannoch again and I took a taxi again at Fort William to the same very good guest house overlooking Loch Linnhe.

And now on to the next day – the walk. But I do stress the full Scottish fried breakfast again too – as good as ever – after which, I walked into Fort William to visit shops etc. and enjoy the town as before. I had two steam train experiences today but without seeing the train! Firstly, from the town I saw distant clouds of white smoke in the Banavie area. Later, walking near Morar I heard a shrill whistle, and loud 'chug, chug, chug'. Well that was better than nothing.

Took the diesel rail bus about midday from Fort William to Morar – it called at most of the stations as before – after Lochailort, these are Beasdale and Arisaig (which is the most westerly station in Britain) before the stop at Morar for resumption of walking. Needless to say, train window views as good as ever.

I began this final section of the Road to the Isles walk, about 1.30 pm; the weather was fine but cloudy; but rain fell by the latter part of the walk. As on the train, so on the walk, the glorious views of lochs, mountains, heather coming increasingly into bloom and golden autumnal tints were captivating. Also the sea coast and islands further out were a great attraction.

Morar was indeed a pleasant village. This time, I not only saw the White Sands of Morar – I walked on them. They were apparently formed from sea-waves grinding down pebbles into fine sand – fine in two senses! I remembered reading a fictional book as a boy about a young schoolgirl (whose parents had died in World War II) – she had been found wandering in London streets in the Blitz and her family could not be traced. At boarding school she learned about Scotland 'where the sands are white' and it triggered something in her memory. She (unwisely!) managed to run away northwards (from Rugby) to, presumably, the Morar area. Not only did she find the White Sands, which she recognised from earlier years, but she was re-united with other members of her family – all Scots, as she then realised she also was herself! The story did impress me very much.

Also, View-Master pictures (I referred in Days 73 and 79 to these), which I remember enjoying as a boy did include this part of the Road to the Isles too – which also filled me with wonderment at that time. This then – unknown Scotland – how I would love to see it!

Morar – I resume – was indeed tranquil and unspoilt and rather similar to Arisaig, but hillier and with small cliffs. I re-enjoyed walking around the areas of the River Morar Estuary with its impressive waterfalls and again, its white sands, the areas of Toigal and Kinsadel, and followed a lane to the north-west 'corner' of huge Loch Morar and continued to the scenic Road again, at Beoraidbeg and beside the railway uphill, then downhill to Glasnacardoch, where I climbed a lane, which afforded excellent views of Mallaig below; the sea beyond; and the Isles of Skye, Rum and Eigg – and possibly others. Mountains or hills all around on mainland and islands.

Explored the busy, yet remote fishing port, Mallaig quite fully – town, shops, harbour – a very Scottish atmosphere, and a sense of history in its fine old narrow streets and stone buildings. Quite an outpost and the end of the Road to the Isles! I also climbed lanes up the cliff areas along the coast to Courteachan. Saw a car ferry come in from, I think, Skye and concluded the walk around 5 pm, celebrating at café with vanilla ice cream and other more solid items.

Returned by train from Mallaig to Fort William, Morar being the next stop and I have really already described the glories of the route. It is said to be one of the most scenic in the world. And walked to the very good guest house again.

And so I have completed the Road to the Isles walk, in a sense a 'Walk within a Walk' as I wrote, Day 86, as it is a kind of 'extra' in one direction only. And a very well worthwhile extra indeed.

The Great Glen Way (Fort William to Inverness), including Loch Ness
74 miles

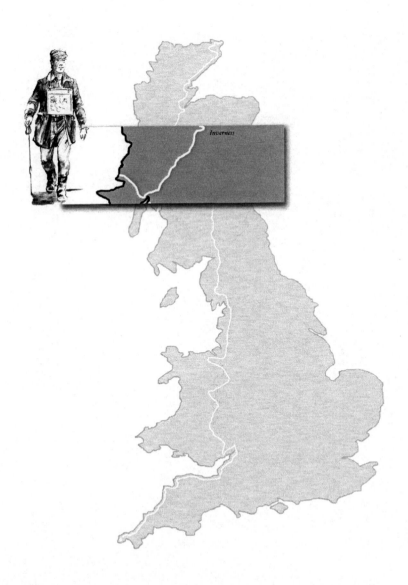

Day 90
22/9/13

FORT WILLIAM – INVERLOCHY – CAOL – NEPTUNE'S STAIRCASE – MOY BRIDGE –
GAIRLOCHY BRIDGE (INCLUDING CALEDONIAN CANAL)
(11 miles approx)

*A*fter a very good night's rest, and of course, the excellent full Scottish breakfast again, I resumed walking from Fort William from the points reached on Day 85 and included a tour of the town, so changing from the West Highland Way to the Great Glen Way, the Road to the Isles having been an excellent one-way detour in between. I am therefore now reverting to a north-easterly direction and still in old Inverness-shire.

The Great Glen Way is officially a 73-mile walk from Fort William to Inverness, following, sometimes, the Caledonian Canal or the shores of lochs or the mountains above the Glen. The Glen is a continuous valley right across Scotland, and I hardly need to say (as I say this sort of thing so often), stunningly spectacular. There is the continuous waterway link throughout, the Caledonian Canal linking between the tidal sea loch, Linnhe on the west, and the coastal estuary of the Beauly Firth on the east.

Starting out around 10.45, I walked to the plinth, the conspicuous monumental 'slab' of stone, which impressively denotes the start of the Way in the area of the ruins of the old fort itself, near the shores of Loch Linnhe. Today's weather was rather cloudy, the good old Scotch mist partly shrouding mountains, including Ben Nevis nearby. Drizzle came on later and eventually heavy rain.

Continued, on rural footpaths near the estuary of River Lochy, and enjoyed the sight of a steam locomotive again – this time, in railway sidings, steaming up and with two coaches in front. Clearly, loco and stock for the Mallaig runs. At Inverlochy, where I had a good view of the castle ruins, I crossed the River Lochy on a long wooden bridge (the Soldiers' Bridge). Passed Lochyside and followed the road to Caol, where the Way took me on the grassy banks by Loch Linnhe's shore and I paused to enjoy the views across this tidal expanse, made even better with the addition of iced cakes and ice cream! And mountains and showers all around – this went for most of today.

Near the 'exit' of the Caledonian Canal into the loch, I had to take a sharp turn left to join the canal tow-path. Here, and a little earlier, when I was trying to get my bearings, I met Scots guys who were extremely helpful to me. Earlier, one gave me quite a full geographical account of locations: now, this chap (walking his dog) accompanied me for a while on the tow-path, and pointed out locations of various points of interest, particularly Neptune's Staircase, the famous series of a considerable number of locks, immediately after each other. A memorable sight.

Just before, I diverted onto roads and crossed the railway. Then took the ascending tow-path beside the locks. I could entitle this part of the walk, 'Lots and lots of lochs and locks!'

The Caledonian Canal was generally pretty wide. The only boats I saw were moored. I did pass quite a lot of walkers and cyclists. One cyclist stopped and told me how much easier the 'going' was here compared with further north-east – 'the steep hills and rough paths'. (For me, what is to come.) But such conditions are usually more of an obstacle to cyclists than to walkers. They gain much on us where it's smoother. (The path followed with the canal on the left in 'my' direction.)

So, I continued through the beautiful, peaceful Glen, the tow-path before me, canal beside me, mountains above me – also, the River Lochy not far to my right. It was quite remote countryside, heather blooming, golden tints. Some areas pine-forested; some open. Eventually, I reached Moy Bridge, an attractive spot with picnic tables and a few good old stone wall buildings. And very soon after, arrived at Gairlochy Bridge and Bottom Lock, a similarly attractive spot to Moy but a little larger. And the rain was similar to Moy – but a lot heavier! Reached here about 3.15 pm

I now also had some extra walking to do – in the rain – but not part of the Way. A fairly long lane, south-eastward to the Commando Memorial at the main Inverness to Fort William road. Here I caught a fast coach via Spean Bridge to Fort William where I enjoyed sandwiches of bacon, chicken, cheese, tomato and other flavours, plus cup of tea in a restaurant.

Then walked back to relax in the jolly old guest house in my comfortable room, and to reflect on the wonderful day.

DAY 91
23/9/13

GAIRLOCHY BRIDGE – LOCH LOCHY (BUNARKAIG – CLUNES – KILFINNAN) – LAGGAN & LOCKS – LOCH OICH – ABERCHALDER BRIDGE (INCLUDING CALEDONIAN CANAL)
(18 miles approx)

*A*fter the enjoyment of a 'ditto' good night and a 'ditto' good breakfast, i.e. as good as ever, I walked into Fort William again, visited shops and continued to the railway station for a highly rewarding experience. The 10.15 steam train to Mallaig was due to depart. Smoke and steam were billowing from the locomotive, and after a series of shrill whistles and almost deafening 'snorts', from a 'grandstand' view at the end of the platform I saw the whole train, including the seven maroon coaches, proceed out of the station. It was packed with passengers and the dining coach looked very well 'laid out'!

I had a taxi waiting for me – the same firm as before. The very helpful guy's wife, and she is equally helpful, drove me on a most scenic and narrow and winding lane, which commenced at Neptune's Staircase and followed the Great Glen (on the slopes of hills and mountains), northern side, up to Gairlochy.

I began the walk about 11 o'clock and enjoyed sunny and dry weather today. Quite different to the last two! Met quite a number of walkers and the occasional cyclist. Saw a number of boats too. So the scenery, as described yesterday, was every bit as good today, enhanced by the weather. Shall I repeat it all once more? Lochs, mountains, canal, rivers, waterfalls, pine forests – I think that gives the picture as concisely as possible, sights of all these continuing throughout the whole day.

From Gairlochy the Way continued across the bridge at Bottom Lock, so I followed over to the other side of the canal, thus, and now left it on my right hand side at this picturesque little settlement already described and ascended a narrow lane up the pine-forested mountainside. Soon, the Way transferred to a downhill footpath, back to the waterside but this was the south-west end of Loch Lochy, after the Caledonian Canal's 'entry' into it. So, for a good many miles, I followed beside or near Loch Lochy (to my right), i.e., on its northern shores, banks and slopes.

Initially this was one of the most beautiful Glen walks I could imagine. You could certainly say a 'fairyland'. A very winding path in an autumn-gold coniferous forest and the autumn-gold bracken, with heather in purple bloom and masses of profuse bright green moss; rocks and boulders interspersed; and glimpses of the tranquil and extensive waters of the loch and the highland mountain slopes on the other side of it.

After a while the Way re-joined the narrow lane and through similarly beautiful scenery, I thus continued through the very small villages or hamlets of Bunarkaig and Clunes, which boasted some highly picturesque cottages and houses, large and small, and old and new – and still close to the loch shore.

From Clunes onward, until the far end of Loch Lochy near Laggan, I followed the Way on a fairly steeply undulating, wide forest track. I thus passed through Clunes Forest and South Laggan Forest and just near to the ruin Glasdhoire at the latter. Views across and above the loch typically good and the pine-covered mountainsides too (all around).

Eventually, the Way descended via Kilfinnan to 'water level' again, Laggan Locks, at the north-east end of Loch Lochy, from whence the Caledonian Canal resumed again. Continued on tow-path, which ascended to a woodland path above the canal and to its right. Thus I passed the pleasant area of Laggan village (South and North), to where the canal entered Loch Oich and I followed its southern shores, banks and slopes from its south-west, to north-east extents – a smaller loch, but as picturesque – through thick forest and woodland, partly on a disused railway course and partly on winding, woodland paths with exceptionally good, golden autumnal scenery to see both sides of the loch, and the trees gloriously reflected in the loch! So, I reached the main A82 road at Aberchalder Bridge (about 6 pm), end of loch; and scenic coach ride back (following the opposite shores of Lochs Oich and Lochy to the shores I walked) and via Invergarry, Laggan and Spean Bridge to Fort William. And walk back to B&B (snack in town on way; but no ice creams around today) – does that sound like an accidental poem of pleasure and lament?

I mentioned wonderful reflections in the loch. Finished at B&B with wonderful reflections on the day.

And so of course, tomorrow is the journey home. I again benefited from the helpful arrangements at the guest house, whereby I had cereals etc for early breakfast; then early taxi to station, the usual helpful guy driving; and then early train from Fort William. And another 'early' – the mist and clouds on and around Rannoch Moor resulted in novel views from the train of partial sights of Scottish mountains and at times, views of clouds below the railway! A group of young deer running across Rannoch Moor was a fine sight. And there were all the other usual fine sights. Route and stops basically as 20th September, except changed at Wolverhampton not Birmingham and other minor variations. Sunnier in south today. And what a great holiday again!

Day 92
26/10/13

ABERCHALDER BRIDGE – CULLOCHY LOCK – KYTRA LOCK – FORT AUGUSTUS –
BUNOICH – LOCH NESS, 'FIRST THIRD' – INVERMORISTON
(INCLUDING CALEDONIAN CANAL)
(13 miles approx)

To start with, no surprises to record that, on 25th October, I travelled by trains between Cosham and Fort William. Changed at same stations: Winchester, Birmingham and the two Glasgow stations, with taxi ride between – as per Days 89, 86 etc and as enjoyable as ever, always more or less the same route with its scenic highlights. Weather rather cloudy and evidence of recent heavy rain – the rivers were looking quite full. There was occasional heavy rain today too. Of course, it was now getting darker each time of travelling 'up' – I left Glasgow Queen Street in gathering dusk this time.

Interestingly too, the driver of the taxi to Cosham told me (I was talking about Scotland) that he used to work in catering at Balmoral for the Queen! He saw her on a number of occasions, usually when she was travelling to feed her horses on the estate. He much enjoyed exploring the countryside in the area too.

It was very good to reach the same excellent guest house, overlooking Loch Linnhe again, where I settled in for a very comfortable night.

But now to the walk next morning. Once again, the excellent full Scottish fried breakfast, and once again I toured Fort William town on foot. Weather sunny and windy until the very end of the walk when rain came on, and continued for the rest of the day.

I took the fast coach on the scenic route from Fort William and following the shores of Loch Lochy and Loch Oich to Aberchalder Bridge and commenced today's hike about 11.30. The first piece of entertainment was the mechanical swinging of the road bridge at the Caledonian Canal, stopping the traffic and allowing a boat through. I also enjoyed seeing the nearby Bridge of Oich, a nice little piece of history – it is the earlier bridge over the adjacent River Oich, well preserved but the traffic now uses its replacement very near it, the present A82.

Today's walk resumed from Day 91's end, at the point where Loch Oich 'ended' and the Caledonian Canal 're-started'. I followed the tow-path, initially with the canal on my left, but crossed at Cullochy Lock thereafter staying on the opposite side. River Oich ran close by to the left. I will make the usual understatement – the views were excellent. Autumn yellow/gold everywhere and I repeat yet again – I think I know it off by heart – Canal, rivers, waterfalls, burns, pine forests, mountains, and (later) Loch Ness. These were the themes of the day.

In due course, I passed Kytra Lock, and reached Fort Augustus. It was teeming with visitors – a busy village with interesting shops, souvenir-type especially, with a nice variety of Nessie (Loch Ness monster) postcards! I don't think I know of another place quite like it – here, the Caledonian Canal enters Loch Ness and a very impressive series of locks, similar to Neptune's Staircase (see Day 90), 'take' the levels downward, via the village and just before the loch. I don't think I need say any more about the Loch Ness monster, other than that I didn't see it (!) as the stories of sightings of the strange creature in, or near Loch Ness, are quite well-known. I can't seem to believe it exists!

The canal locks seemed to pass right through the delightful old village with its fine old stone cottages and quaint, narrow streets. I wandered around here and then resumed the Great Glen Way, which of course, I was following throughout today again. I followed a hilly lane past Bunoich to the start of a coniferous forest track, wide and undulating. Very good views down to, and across, Loch Ness. At times, the forests all around looked very dark and I thought of Enid Blyton's Noddy and Big-Ears stories – 'It isn't very good in the dark, dark wood', I think I recall! Later, due to tree-felling, I had to take an official diversion from the main track. Rather steep and slippery up and down paths – but no real problem. These came just before the final descent into Invermoriston, on the banks of River Moriston, with its very attractive waterfalls and rocks, in the area of Thomas Telford's fine old stone bridge, which follows across it. Invermoriston was a beautiful wee village very near Loch Ness. Arrived about 17.00, rain was increasing and I enjoyed eating some good cakes in the bus shelter. But I didn't locate any ice creams anywhere – again (oh dear!).

The coach soon arrived – it was a comfortable journey back in the wet and the dark. At Fort William, I walked back through the town to the good old guest house again. Another wonderful 'Great Glen Way' day.

Day 93
27/10/13

Invermoriston – Loch Ness 'second third' – Alltsigh – Grotaig – Ancarraig – Lewiston – Drumnadrochit
(14 miles approx)

Yet again, an excellent night, and breakfast as before. I then walked into Fort William and the same helpful taxi driver drove me through to Invermoriston, following the shores of Lochs Lochy, Oich and Ness again. A strong gale and heavy rain was forecast for the South and Midlands of England and Wales soon. We discussed weather, and he told me how he drove a heavy lorry in the 1987 gale – a very stressful experience. He didn't exceed 15 mph and fortunately he came to no harm. But he saw lorries that had overturned – many in fact did.

I started walking from Invermoriston about 11.30, and viewed the splendid River Moriston more closely – where the impressive waterfalls tumbled among large rocks and boulders – and I viewed Telford's fine old stone bridge again too. The weather was sunny for the earlier part today, but rain followed on toward the end. There were few walkers about today – and no monster! The autumn colours as good as ever, as were the forests and mountains, and the views to Loch Ness far below, and to the other side.

I followed a very steep, narrow lane out of the little village initially – well surrounded by pine forest. Having reached a good height, I then walked by tracks or paths, very winding at first and with plenty of ups and downs. I passed above Alltsigh, forest still all around. The track continued to rise very steeply in a series of zigzags, after which came some of the best views of the day. The village of Foyers was very clear on the opposite shore of Loch Ness. Then I followed more up-down-up-down forest paths, and I emerged from the trees on to a narrow lane, by the hamlet of Grotaig. Now the scenery was open and I followed the lane past fields, farms and cottages, but this part of the Great Glen Way (which I followed throughout, apart from very occasional minor diversions) ran rather more north of Loch Ness, which was not now visible for the rest of the day.

And so I continued on the lane, generally downward, past the settlements of Balbeg, Ancarraig and in forested area again, Woodend, and then down a very steep hill with hairpin bends and fine views of the villages in the valley ahead. I reached the first of these villages, Lewiston where I joined the A82 main road, which led me to Blairbeg and Drumnadrochit – arrival about 4.30 pm. It was something of a repeat performance of yesterday, in that the rain was coming on rather heavily, and I found refuge in a bus shelter. In fact it was wetter and darker than yesterday but the clocks 'changed' today, and this far north in Scotland, in winter, the darkness must be expected as I have commented before.

I returned by coach, passing the fine old Urquhart Castle at Strone Point on the shores of Loch Ness, and taking the 'usual' A82 route, back to Fort William. Then walk to B&B.

And no ice creams appeared today, at times when I might have had the opportunity to consume any. Two consecutive days and no ice creams. Oh dear! But there is still tomorrow (?). In the meantime, I must not panic. And, of course I have had another wonderful day anyway, enjoying myself.

DAY 94
28/10/13

DRUMNADROCHIT – URQUHART BAY – LOCH NESS 'THIRD THIRD' –
ACHPOPULI – BLACKFOLD
(11 miles approx)

The full Scottish breakfast having once again been much enjoyed, I set forth into Fort William again, well reinforced and boarded the coach at 10.30, more clearly of course, seeing the fine views than last night (rain and dark) – Lochs Lochy, Oich and Ness, and the various places en route all showed up well, and I alighted at Drumnadrochit, seeing too, the beauty of this fine wee village. Weather today was sunnier and chillier, the rain arriving later today after the walk! (I later ascertained that a strong gale and a lot of rain did sweep across southern areas of Britain today, causing considerable chaos, and sadly, a few deaths – and some injuries.)

Starting my walk at midday from Drumnadrochit I continued of course, on the Great Glen Way – firstly, along the valley beside the main A82 road past Kerrowdown Farm, reaching the shores of Loch Ness again at Urquhart Bay. Here I followed very steep, winding footpaths through thick coniferous forest – outstandingly scenic – but a few open areas early on provided excellent, though distant, views of the ancient Urquhart Castle, in its rugged stony glory. From it, visitors look for the Loch Ness monster! The castle is right above the shore.

My forest walk provided views of a most glorious mix of green and gold colours, and the ascents in this area were the most demanding of the whole Way, but the views of Loch Ness and all around, near the top of the mountain, most rewarding. The footpath had 'developed' into a forest track, in fact, well before the summit and (in the area of Corryfoyness) as yesterday the Way veered away from Loch Ness, more northward with no more views of the loch. The track was more stony, sometimes up and down across open moorland but more steeply downward in the forested area at Achpopuli. Here, I joined a downward forest lane, and a forest path, leading to another (more level) forest lane at Woodend. I followed this for some distance, emerging into open country again at Ladycairn and reached Blackfold. On this section there were some very inspiring views northward of quite distant mountains. I supposed I was now looking for the first time at some of the far north of Scotland. So at Blackfold, the time being about 5.30 pm, it was time to leave the Way and find a road with a bus stop. I therefore did walking additional to the 'official' walk as follows: I followed lane through forest going downhill, in the gathering darkness – descents which grew steeper and steeper.

Eventually, on low land, I joined the A82, with distant views of the lights of Inverness visible. In the circumstances it seemed wisest to follow this main road as far as the edge of Inverness, which I did, and I found a bus stop there. And a coach arrived straight away!

It is rather interesting that this is the second time I have entered Inverness on the walk project, before I have officially entered it on the walk! (See Day 74). I have visited the railway station, and now a bus stop but I have yet to record, hopefully, reaching Inverness 'properly'!

So I had a fast coach trip in the dark and wet, all the way back through the Great Glen to Fort William, and walk at end to B&B. Snacks again – very good – but, as I recorded yesterday, the same today, no opportunity for ice cream. (But, watch this space!) Meanwhile I stress – I've had yet another wonderful day. And the South has had a pretty rough storm. The North has been very fortunate. I do feel concerned for the South, but of course, it could have been a lot worse. A great mercy it wasn't. (One other point of interest – my walking has continued to be in the old county of Inverness–shire throughout.)

Next item of note – due to possible rail disruption southward after the storm. I spent an extra day and night in Fort William – so – 29th October: another full Scottish breakfast, followed by a walk to Inverlochy Castle (further to Day 90) for a 'close-up' of it – and I also noted snow had laid on Ben Nevis – and a walk round Fort William again, as well as a visit to the West Highland Museum there (plenty of interesting Scottish history). Enjoyed a vanilla ice cream, among many other good things at an excellent nearby café. Re my comments for preceding four days

— I now say 'Everything comes to those who wait'. Reminds me of a joke:

> A customer in a restaurant said to the waiter: *Do you realise I've waited here for 10 minutes?*
> The waiter replied: *That's nothing — I've waited here for 10 years* !

> And just another joke:
> A customer called out: *There's a fly in my stew!*
> Said the waiter: *Don't shout or let it get out. Or the others will want one too!*

Yes, today much enjoyed — colder, with sunshine and showers, and I kept active.

And of course, 30th October — a special early breakfast arranged again and the same taxi driver drove me to station again. Railways seemed back to normal and weather calm and bright. 'Usual' route home more or less, and the taxi ride at Glasgow again. Changed trains at Wolverhampton, not Birmingham as 25/10/13. Scenery was as good as ever, but little to see after Oxford as darkness fell. A satisfactory end to yet another most enjoyable holiday.

Day 95
30/11/13

Blackfold — Ness Islands — Inverness (including Caledonian Canal)
(7 miles approx)

Note: 1,332 miles since leaving Land's End: 74 of these are the Great Glen Way

*I*n contrast to my last journey 'up' on 25th October, there were 'surprises' on the route to Scotland this time. The train journeys of yesterday were as follows:

Took train Cosham to Winchester. Then changed to express, 'usual' route to Birmingham New Street and train continued calling at Derby, Sheffield, Doncaster and York, where I alighted. I then caught another express calling at Darlington, Newcastle and Berwick-upon-Tweed, before terminating at Edinburgh Waverley, where I changed to the Inverness express. This called at Haymarket, Kirkcaldy, Markinch, Ladybank, Perth, Dunkeld, Pitlochry, Kingussie and Aviemore en route.

The weather — a mixture of sunshine and rain, but often cloudy. But soon after Newcastle darkness fell! A long day of travelling of course — about 9 am to 9 pm and two of the railway staff were quite impressed by the length of the day's journey, as shown on my ticket. Also a lady passenger, sitting next to me at Perth was similarly interested, and when I told her about my walking project, she asked if I could send her a summary of my experiences as she was a story teller (lives in Aberfeldy). I, of course, happily agreed.

And some information as to the scenery. Up to Birmingham; as interesting as always. After this, I was back on the also-interesting routes to Edinburgh, which I had not 'done' for some time, including the scenic areas of the Peak District between Derby and Sheffield. Views at York, and particularly at Durham, including architecture were impressive. At the latter, a fellow-passenger who works in the city, pointed out to me, very precisely, the cathedral, castle and streets of the ancient areas. Views too, at Newcastle, especially of the River Tyne bridges were good. Berwick-upon-Tweed is of course a fine town to view, but I relied on the lights in the darkness! (The fine old town, the River Tweed and the grand old arches of the Royal Border Bridge.) The rugged coastal scenery and the fine city of Edinburgh too, were less seeable. The final 'leg' to Inverness, particularly beautiful, I hope to describe in my homeward day's account, in which comparative daylight should shine out! I can say for 'today', that the crossing of the Firth of Forth Bridge was a highlight, with many high (and low) lights around (!), so some good views. I saw little other scenery, of course, but travelled through grand mountainous areas (the Grampians and Cairngorms) and made my third 'unofficial' entry into Inverness (see Day 94)! And I have still not entered Inverness on the planned walk route.

I was met at Inverness station by the very obliging, friendly proprietor of the B&B. He drove me in his car, with another guest, to the accommodation, where I settled in very happily.

And now it's about time to write about today's walk. Very good night, very good breakfast, very good walk. Firstly, I walked into the centre of Inverness – the most northerly city in Britain – and took a taxi from this very fine city, using the main A82 route and 'connecting' lane (as walked after Great Glen Way Walk, 28th October) back to the Way at Blackfold, from whence I resumed the official Way about midday. Cold, fine and dry, and good sunny views today. Very scenic, as always. I entered a forest track leading off the lane, mainly coniferous (and gold-tinted) surroundings.

Excellent views of the Beauly Firth and distant mountains and Inverness. Descended, sometimes steeply, by tracks and paths past Dunain Hill right down to the edge of Inverness, valley level. I was now entering the city officially (see earlier comments on this 'Day 95')! Using roads and paths, and seeing golf course and football matches, I reached the Caledonian Canal (very wide here), and walked its tow-path to Tomnahurich Bridge, and followed a road to Floral Hall, to a path beside the River Ness wide and fast-flowing and surrounded by woods – a most beautiful part of the Way – including the crossing of three bridges 'via' two small islands (Ness Islands) to the opposite bank. Then followed paths and roads near the river (the magnificent old city all around me) and up to the grand old castle (stone, like so many high old Inverness buildings) to the plinth, the stone monument marking the end of the Great Glen Way! Views of this sizeable historic city below, ahead, both sides of river. So the Way completed, 74 miles with minor detours (it is officially 73!) I enjoyed very happy reflections. (Finishing time about 3.30 pm.)

Met a number of people today who showed interest in my walk, especially when I said I had started at Land's End, rather than Fort William! I learnt that the imposing castle dates from the 1700s, a conspicuous landmark on a hill above the River Ness, and it houses a museum and courts. Also toured the city on foot – fine streets and shops, fine river-bridges (I crossed one to see the also – fine old cathedral.)

And concluded with an excellent meal at a café (duck and salad, Victoria sponge and pot of tea). Outside, in the city street, I enjoyed the sight as darkness was falling of colourful Christmas lights coming on. Then walked back to the very good B&B, and enjoyed very good memories of the Great Glen Way etc!

SECTION 11

The far north of Scotland, including Wick & Thurso

203 miles

INVERNESS — CALEDONIAN CANAL, MUIRTOWN BASIN — BUNCHREW — INCHMORE
— KIRKHILL — LOVAT BRIDGE — BEAULY — WINDHILL — MUIR OF ORD
(16 miles approx)

*E*njoyed very good rest and breakfast, and the friendly company of my hosts — and guests too — before setting forth on the walk about 10.15. Weather quite cold — fine, dry and generally bright. Snow was visible on hills and mountains too.

And so for the far north of Scotland! I proceeded initially to the castle, then crossed a River Ness bridge and followed a main road which I assumed was the old A9 (which leads to Thurso, Wick and John O'Groats 'localities' — eventually) — but the 'new' A9 bypasses large sections of the original route, using more modern bridges near some firth estuaries.

My 'original main road' led me past Merkinch and across the Caledonian Canal at Muirtown Basin (quite a lot of boats), and then via Clachnaharry, from whence I followed westward (and, later northward), near the southern shores of the delightful Beauly Firth, with the tide high, and clear views across — views of distant mountains and also of the Kessock Bridge, which carries the 'new' A9 northward. I also had the pleasure of following the railway all day (the route which serves Kyle of Lochalsh, Wick and Thurso). Saw a number of trains of course. This road I was taking is recognised as a scenic tourist route and generally, there were good verges or banks to walk on.

I thus progressed via Bunchrew and Lentran to Inchmore, where I diverted onto quiet lanes for a while — through Kirkhill and a forested section around Ferrybrae, but rejoined the 'main' road just before Lovat Bridge. Soon after, I reached the village of Beauly itself (via Teawig). I had now completed the Beauly Firth section and was striking north, having also crossed the River Beauly.

Yes, Beauly was very attractive and its cakes are too. (About here I crossed from Inverness-shire into another Scottish county, 'Ross & Cromarty'.) Beauly seemed quite unspoilt, old and typically Scottish — relaxing to wander around — I saw the ancient priory and a selection of its shops, various stony buildings. But it was getting dark now.

So I quickened my pace, on via Windhill and past a golf course and industrial estate at Muir of Ord. The village centre was of attractive stone architecture (as I know I am so accustomed to say). Again, a pleasant feeling of history. I arrived at about 4.15 pm.

In due course, I caught a train back to Inverness, via Beauly and walked from the station to the excellent B&B. I settled in, thinking very happy thoughts about this very pleasurable day.

DAY 97
2/12/13

MUIR OF ORD — CONON BRIDGE — MARYBURGH — DINGWALL —
MOUNTGERALD — ARDULLIE — EVANTON — ALNESS
(18 miles approx)

*A*fter excellent night's rest and breakfast in the relaxing, friendly atmosphere of the B&B, I walked via the city centre to Inverness station. As an 'aside' I will record my favourable impressions of the station. It was a busy terminus, with plenty of people and trains coming and going. As far as I could ascertain, all the railways that were built to Inverness are still thriving there. Although Dr Beeching proposed, in 1963, to axe all routes north from the city, they were all reprieved. This meant that there are still four main railways in use, apparently:

1) To Edinburgh, Glasgow and the South via Perth
2) To Aberdeen, and Edinburgh via Dundee
3) To Dingwall and Kyle of Lochalsh
4) To Dingwall, Wick, Georgemas and Thurso

Although many lines not far away had been closed, Inverness seemed to retain the charm of a terminus of decades past, architecturally and as a hub of activity.

I took the 10.37, Wick and Thurso train, enjoying now the daylight scenes — the Beauly Firth and Beauly, and alighted at Muir of Ord.

Commenced walk at 11 am. Weather, as yesterday, was cold, fine and dry, and snow still visible on hills and mountains. I proceeded on the main road, again I assumed - as I have said - the old A9. Good grass verges or banks were again useful much of the time on this scenic route; and still near the railway. Walked to Conon Bridge, where it seemed appropriate to indulge in an ice cream. I enquired in the village but was rather surprised to be told that I should 'try the fish shop' (?) I wondered if new flavours, possibly mackerel or trout, might now be on the market. I found the shop in question, but it would appear that 'fish shop' is a local way of describing what is, in fact, an aquarium and café combined! The upshot of it all was that the vanilla ice cream was truly delicious.

I crossed the bridge over the River Conon and continued via Maryburgh and past Pitglassie, into the thriving little old town of Dingwall, on the shore of the Cromarty Firth. Had a nose around it — very pleasant, not least so the orange juice and chocolate and caramel cake slice I enjoyed in a café.

At Dingwall, I left the main road, taking an uphill route, which brought me onto a country lane on a hill ridge, which commanded excellent views of the Cromarty Firth and Black Isle beyond, and in due course the Cromarty Bridge which takes the present A9 across the firth.

I continued along this fine hill ridge, past Mountrich, Mountgerald, Woodlands, Lemlair; and gradually descended through Ardullie, Teanord, and past Milton of Katewell, to the pleasant little town of Evanton – back on the lower land again now.

It was now dark, and the road I had joined was the B817, very fortunate therefore that I was able to use a cycle track/footpath beside the road and partly in woodland. I duly reached Westford and then Alness, which in the darkness appeared to be a very attractive town, with beautiful blue Christmas lights illuminating the old main street. Arrival time, about 5.15 pm. I hope to see and describe Alness properly next visit.

An express bus was due – it whisked me back to Inverness, beside Cromarty Firth, over Cromarty Bridge, across Black Isle and over Beauly Firth on Kessock Bridge. I had a rather cold walk in strong winds from the bus station, through Inverness to B&B, which of course was very pleasantly, and contrastingly, warm. And very enjoyable reflections about today.

And now, of course, the 'next day' – the return home. Excellent packed breakfast provided for me for my early start by kind hosts. Incidentally, as to Inverness; as a young boy I well remember a Scotsman, quite elderly, who lived near us in the south of England, saying 'the best English is spoken in 'In – verr – ness'.' I think he had a point – perhaps the best English is Scottish!

After taxi ride to station, I caught the 7.55 express train, 'The Highland Chieftain', bound for London Kings Cross. It called at Aviemore, Kingussie, Pitlochry, Perth, Gleneagles, Stirling, Falkirk Grahamston, Haymarket, Edinburgh Waverley, Newcastle, Darlington and York, where I changed to train calling, I think, just Doncaster, Sheffield and Derby, before I changed at Birmingham New Street. Then train to Southampton Central, 'usual' route and stops to Winchester, then stop at Southampton Airport Parkway, before my 'final' change to semi-fast service to Cosham – then taxi home. A 13-hour day on trains!

Highlights! After a dark start, Scottish Grampians and Cairngorms Mountains so scenic but dawn did not break till about Aviemore – then fine views! So, I didn't see Slochd summit, but I did see Drumochter summit. The mountain passes were a grand experience – wild and rugged glory. And had good views of Edinburgh, and sea coasts after. Then on, scenery was as described on Day 95, but darkness fell around Birmingham.

What a wonderful holiday again!

ALNESS — INVERGORDON — SALTBURN — BARBARAVILLE — MILTON —
KILDARY — CALROSSIE WOODS — TAIN
(16 miles approx)

*E*ven more 'surprises' as to the route 'up' yesterday, in comparison to 29th November, 2013.

This time, took taxi to Havant station and 9.34 train calling at Petersfield, Haslemere, Guildford, Woking — and London Waterloo. Saw flooding in the Rowlands Castle area — also in various areas of northern Britain. (Today's weather was a mix of sunshine, cloud and showers.) Took taxi 'across' London — just to Kings Cross station. Particularly interesting — crossed River Thames on Blackfriars Bridge and had good views of the river and St Paul's Cathedral, the Shard and later, St Pancras International station — its fine original extensive historic buildings so well restored. Kings Cross was, of course impressive, as also was Waterloo — am I going on and on here? Railways, again (...)!

From Kings Cross, I was on the train for a long time! Departed midday and reached Inverness, where train terminated at 8.06 pm. It was the 'Highland Chieftain' express again, this time for its whole journey. Extremely fast-running — non-stop to York, and many station names not readable due to speed! I apparently travelled through, among other places, Hatfield, Welwyn Garden City, Stevenage, Hitchin, Biggleswade, Huntingdon, Peterborough — and the edges of Fenlands, Grantham, Newark, Retford and Doncaster — before York. After, stopped at Darlington, Newcastle, Berwick-upon-Tweed, Edinburgh Waverley and Haymarket (by now darkness had fallen), Falkirk Grahamston, Stirling, Gleneagles, Perth, Pitlochry, Kingussie and Aviemore — these sections of the route have already been described (Days 95 and 97).

One fellow-traveller, a gentleman returning home to Cromarty, sat near me all the way from Kings Cross (he had been visiting relations in the London area) and took quite an interest in my walking experiences, which I much appreciated. The proprietor of the B&B very kindly met me again at Inverness station, and drove me to the very welcome accommodation again, where of course, I had a very good night's sleep!

And so to today. After very good, ample breakfast and very friendly conversations with my hosts, who continued to show much interest in my project — and some entertaining playful activities by the pet cat and dog (the cat is the 'boss', the dog is a lively puppy) — I walked via the city to the station and took the 10.37 Wick and Thurso train via Beauly, Muir of Ord, Conon Bridge and Dingwall (stopped at each), to Alness. The views were clear and good, especially of the firths and more distant snow-covered mountains or bens. Indeed, the weather was clear and good, and dry and cold, and a crisp frost underfoot and what I would call a healthy Scottish winter's day.

I started walking around 11.30. Firstly, a quick tour of Alness, which looked so lovely last time, illuminated by Christmas lights. This time it was illuminated by bright sunshine and the old main street still looked very attractive. A wide, straight street, a good selection of shops and the typical fine old, stony architecture, so Scottish.

For most of the walk, I was near the railway; and as far as Barbaraville, I followed the shores of the Cromarty Firth, beside the B817 road, on paths, promenades and banks. Followed past Dalmore to Invergordon, a sizeable town with an impressive harbour. It is a deep sea port, reached by very large ships, including cruise liners which berth here to allow their passengers to disembark for coach trips to such places as Inverness. I continued beside the beach through Saltburn, Balintraid and Pollo, and Barbaraville. At times, this road was quite busy – I had to be very careful on sections where it became necessary to share it with the traffic. Passed Nigg Bay, and through Polnicol and Kilmuir. Then passed Tarbat Mains, Milton and Kildary. Here I joined the main A9 road, now well inland, and its very wide grass verges were most welcome. A busy but pleasant route.

So, via Shandwick and through the coniferous and deciduous Calrossie Woods, and I passed near Rosemount, Hilton and Aldie. Dusk fell in these regions, about 4.15 pm, and I enjoyed distant views of the lights of Dornoch ahead, beyond the Dornoch Firth. I turned off the A9 onto a local road, via Knockbreck to reach Tain, a fine Scottish town which much impressed me, and completed the walk around 5.15 pm.

I was just right for a bus to Invergordon, whence I transferred to an express bus to Inverness, using the Cromarty and Beauly Firth bridges. At Inverness, I enjoyed a bacon roll, cake and cup of tea at a café, just before they closed. Then walked to B&B to be greeted by a very lively puppy, again!

Certainly, another excellent day!

DAY 99
15/1/14

TAIN – MORANGIE- EDDERTON – EASTER & WESTER FEARN –
KINCARDINE – ARDGAY
(15 miles approx)

*T*oday, the walking took a more westward direction, to follow the southern shores of the Dornoch Firth – and the railway, closely. After another very generous breakfast, I walked to Inverness station, as yesterday, again taking the 10.37 Wick and Thurso train calling at all stations, also as yesterday and too, stopping at Invergordon, Fearn and of course Tain. Very good views again, including more of the Cromarty Firth.

A little rain today and some cloud, including Scotch mist, but good views continued for walk, especially of, and across the Dornoch Firth and of the bens, some still snow-capped beyond. I started out around midday, initially 'doing' Tain, which showed to great advantage in the daylight. It was indeed, another very delightful, typically Scottish old town – the usual assortment of imposing high, or less-high, stone buildings; a collection of quaint, hilly streets, some very narrow, some very wide; a good selection of shops, hotel accommodation, fine churches, and a museum.

Joined the main A9 road on the north side of the town and continued via Morangie, with its impressive-looking distilleries and at Ardjachie, left the present A9 (which proceeds north across the Dornoch Firth Bridge) and followed the 'old' A9, now A836, beside the firth and the railway. The tide was high, enhancing views across. Verges and banks provided for walkers again, but not at all points and it was quite a busy road.

Initially, I enjoyed views of high-rising coniferous forest on my left and Edderton Sands on my right. Continued past Redburn to the village of Edderton and on past Little Dallas (stopped nearby for cakes from rucksack). Views opened out more, woods and mountains all around the firth. Walked on via Dounie, Ardvannie, Easter Fearn and Wester Fearn. I think on this section I saw one of the many roches moutonnées (types of small rock outcrops) in a nearby field. (I had noted many previously in the English Lake District – see Day 61.)

And so, on through Ardchronie and Kincardine. Around this area, a sign informed me that I was now entering another Scottish county, namely Sutherland. (I have therefore completed 'Ross & Cromarty'.)

Soon after, I reached today's destination, another of the day's pleasant places to be noted – Ardgay (pronounced Ardguy). Arrival time about 5 pm. Also, I should record the last few miles approaching it were delightful – darkness having fallen, I enjoyed the twinkling lights ahead, not only of this village but also, and especially, of Bonar Bridge, the next place after, the other side of the firth and its illuminated bridge, which crosses the firth.

And further joys were in store for me. The first building I noticed in Ardgay was a café! I treated myself to egg mayo sandwiches with salad and crisps – a very good helping, and cups of tea and orange juice. People there, as often seemed to happen, took a kind interest in my walk. Many in these areas were walkers themselves – either locals or tourists - hence the mutual interest.

So, to conclude day – took train, stopping all stations as noted before back to Inverness and walked back to B&B, where I enjoyed talks with my hosts, before retiring to bed for sleepy reflections on yet another very happy day. Perhaps I got a little muddled in my dreams on the subjects of 'Train' and 'Tain'!

DAY 100
16/1/14

ARDGAY — BONAR BRIDGE — SPINNINGDALE — OSPISDALE —
CLASHMORE — DORNOCH
(*15 miles approx*)

*A*s yesterday, I will initially mention general direction of walking for today — eastward, i.e. the exact opposite! But this of course, was to ensure the enjoyment of the opposite side of the Dornoch Firth – above the northern shores – but the railway did not follow this area like yesterday.

Furthermore, perhaps of note, I observed today's heading – Day 100. I saw that on Day 50, I referred to celebrating the 'Day of Jubilee', having reached North Wales. Maybe I should celebrate two Jubilees having crossed yesterday into the 'next-but-one' most northerly county of Britain (Sutherland, see Day 99)!

After the very good night and the very good breakfast, I again walked to Inverness station, and again took the 10.37 Wick and Thurso train, in which I have become quite well known. Called at all stations to Ardgay — as yesterday evening, but opposite way of course — route already described. The shores of the Dornoch Firth, as applied to most of the journey, were so scenic but fog and mist partially obscured some areas. Indeed, the weather remained quite foggy all day. Please groan again at the following: views are mist (missed) (!) I must try to ration the puns. But I had seen the Dornoch Firth views clearly yesterday anyway – no problem. Weather too was cold and dry for the walk, creating quite an atmosphere. What I call, a sort of 'In the bleak mid winter' appeal, which I enjoy.

Started walking from the pleasant village of Ardgay, about midday. Continued on (I assumed) the 'old A9', with its good grass verges and banks much of the way, on this sometimes busy road. Followed across the flat valley 'floor' and over the fine, large bridge across the water, to the small township of Bonar Bridge, another pleasant settlement, and began the trek above the north shores of Dornoch Firth. The road rose steeply above the water to a considerable height, beside a coniferous forest. I continued via Little Creich and the ups and downs and bends of Spinningdale village. Fine woodland all around it, after which the road generally descended and I gained the one clear view of the day of the tranquil waters of the Dornoch Firth below me – the mist had cleared here. Some more forested areas followed and I passed via Whiteface, Ospisdale, and Overskibo, before joining the 'new' A9 near the scenic village of Clashmore. This road I followed through

203

coniferous Clashmore Wood – I had to watch out carefully for traffic, especially as darkness had now fallen!

Further on I turned right into a slightly less-busy road, into Camore and then Dornoch (arrival 5.15 ish) – a truly delightful town, as far as it was visible in street lights. It felt quite grand, not unduly large but spaciously laid out, with its fine impressive cathedral dominating its also fine and impressive Cathedral Square. A real sense of history, very 'touristy' and excellent high old Scottish buildings all around, including hotels, shops etc. I enjoyed a good meal at an inn – chicken, chocolate fudge cake with ice cream and a pot of tea.

Caught a bus from Cathedral Square, which conveyed me over Dornoch Firth Bridge ('new' A9) to Tain, where I transferred to train, stopping at all the stations back to Inverness: then walk back to the excellent B&B, where I met my hosts again before retiring to bed, with the usual pleasant reflections.

And of course 17th January, the journey home. As on earlier visit, 3rd December last year, I much enjoyed a very good packed breakfast and took taxi to station for the early 7.55 express 'Highland Chieftain' train. Weather – quite cold still, and cloudy with a little rain and some flooding to be seen between York and London. But it was dark to start with, of course, and also from London Waterloo onwards. Station stops were more or less the same as on the way 'up'; the routes (and speeds!) were the same. I took the train right through to London Kings Cross – no changes again of course, till then. (Route's highlights already described, Days 95, 97 and 98). Highlands are definitely highlights.

The taxi ride Kings Cross to Waterloo, around 4.30 pm provided good views from Waterloo Bridge this time, especially of the Houses of Parliament and Westminster Abbey; of the River Thames generally; and I noticed the Shard again.

And the train, Waterloo to Havant, called on this section of its journey at pretty much the same stops as the 13th January journey. Then taxi and home about 18.45. Plenty again to reflect on with much pleasure.

Day 101
13/2/14

Dornoch – Embo Street – Fourpenny – Skelbo – Loch Fleet – The Mound – Golspie – Dunrobin Castle entrance – Doll – Brora
(18 miles approx)

Yes, this heading reads 13th February, but as the journey 'up' now requires two days travelling, I start with 11th February. So – taxi to Havant station and fast 9.34 train as on Day 98 to London Waterloo. Flooding to be seen in the Rowlands Castle area again. Indeed, there is very extensive flooding in many areas of Britain at the moment – mainly the South and South-West and Wales; the Thames Valley and the Somerset Levels areas, particularly inundated. Today's weather for me started with wind and rain too. A further taxi took me over Waterloo Bridge so I had good views again of the Thames, Westminster Abbey and the Houses of Parliament etc. Alighted at London Kings Cross station, again admiring architecture of St Pancras station, too. (Day 98).

I also much enjoyed the impressive experience again of the ride on the 'Highland Chieftain' express train, midday from Kings Cross to Inverness (8.06 pm), as per Day 98. Same route, same stops, same speeds, same views, I think. Weather turned sunny, there was some degree of flooding in the north of England; darkness fell just after Edinburgh, and snow fell – and laid – from Falkirk onward, culminating quite significantly around Aviemore – quite a layer in the Highland regions. My host kindly met me at Inverness station again, we exchanged news and I settled in very comfortably, of course.

On 12th February, after, needless to say, excellent rest and breakfast, entertaining jokes and entertainment from the very lively puppy, I took a few exploratory walks around Inverness – down various streets and steps, into the city to visit shops and returned to the B&B from whence I was kindly driven again down to the bus station. So commenced my second day of travelling 'up'. Cold wind today, a little rain but quite bright, and good views. (I am getting reports of continuing floods and gales in the South.) I was conveyed to Dornoch over the Kessock and Cromarty Bridges, above the firths; and on to Tain etc and the Dornoch Firth Bridge (routes covered before, opposite direction), then into Dornoch itself.

I booked in at an impressive hotel in the afternoon – spacious, in pleasant grounds, of castle-like appearance. Staff very helpful. Enjoyed a late walk before dusk to see the town 'properly' (see Day 100). As I then recorded – 'Truly delightful'. I did Cathedral Square and the main streets again and also walked by lanes in the Littletown area, to the coast (sands) and the famous Royal Golf Course, before settling in for the night at the hotel.

And now, I think it's about time to write about the walk of 13th February itself! After very good night and breakfast, I began walking at 9.30, via Dornoch town again. A real mixture of weather, starting with 40 to 50 mile-an-hour gales, the tail end of gales from the South! Nothing compared with weather they had had down there though – exceptionally severe, mainly south-west, to north-west England via Wales, torrential rain, severe flooding and train services very disrupted, as much else is. For the morning, I was buffeted with heavy rain and painful hail, too. After that cloudy, and then blue sky and showers, but not too cold. A little snow was lying, but higher up on the bens and around them. Snowdrops were in bloom, quite profusely – a very appealing sight! And I have to add that at times today I was very near the railway – also a very appealing sight to me! Oh, yes, one other 'item' – I was now on a generally northward course again.

I left Dornoch by a pleasant lane through undulating, open country via Achinchanter and Embo Street, to more wooded areas at Fourpenny and Skelbo (where there is an attractive ruined castle, and where I commenced following the scenic shores of tidal Loch Fleet). High bens ahead and around now – mountainous scenery not far off for the rest of the day. I joined the main A9 road near Cambusavie Farm and followed its banks and verges for the remainder of today – busy but grassy – and superb views.

Crossed The Mound, a bank which formed the more westerly end of Loch Fleet, and continued via Kirkton into Golspie, a fine Scottish town with a pleasant beach and an assortment of shops. Then crossed the pretty Golspie Burn and reached the entrance to the grand drive to imposing Dunrobin Castle and its own small railway station adjacent. Continued near the coast for the rest of today and a little further on, had a distant but fine view of Dunrobin Castle, with its high towers including turrets I thought – of a 'magical, fairy tale' appearance. Most impressive!

Scenery became more open later and I continued past Strathsteven and Doll, into the fine town of Brora and explored its river, harbour and beach areas, as well as streets and shops - again, a pleasantly, typically Scottish spot. Arrived about 3.45 pm, enjoyed coffee at a cosy pub by a warm fire. Then, train back to Golspie, where a very reliable and obliging taxi driver who took a friendly interest in my walks, met me and drove me back to the comfortable hotel at Dornoch.

Needless to say, a very lovely day.

DAY 102
14/2/14

BRORA — GREENHILL — LOTHBEG — CRAKAIG —
LOTHMORE — PORTGOWER — HELMSDALE
(14 miles approx)

Walking continued on a generally northward course today. And weather was really most pleasant – bright, sunny, a little cold, dry and calm, excellent clear views all around. Amazingly more reports were coming in about the exceptionally severe weather 'down south'. More extreme flooding, transport disruption and structural damage – even, very sadly several deaths. Seas exceptionally rough, and similar areas to Day 101 references were again affected.

After good night and breakfast, and interesting conversations with staff about my walking, I exited the hotel front door to find the 'same' driver in his taxi, ready and waiting for the drive to Golspie station where I alighted, after interesting conversations with him again of course, re walking etc. I took the train on to Brora on this scenic coastal line.

I duly started the walk about 9.45 and followed the pleasant A9 main road nearly all the way, using the grassy roadside mostly. This route followed close to the sea coast and the railway pretty well throughout. High bens and mountainous scenery dominated the horizon – in snow-capped splendour. Also plenty of snowdrop flowers abounded again today. The route was quite hilly at times.

So I proceeded past East Brora Muir and Greenhill, Kintradwell, Lothbeg and Crakaig, before taking a short 'lane detour' to enjoy views of some scenic architecture – dwellings in further small settlements – the areas of Whitchill and Lothmore. Then back to the main road, which I followed to Portgower. Here, an interesting development occurred. This was a very pleasant little village by the coast, but the road was very narrow, and in addition, there were major road-works, which were causing long traffic queues; single file traffic was controlled by traffic lights. It left me no room to walk and too, a notice instructed pedestrians to phone a certain number! I thought what happens if I phone and I'm told I must wait for a vehicle, which would be provided to take me through? Then I will have cheated, and not walked the entire route! But this might be difficult to explain.

An ideal option became apparent on consulting the map – it also provided an alternative very scenic route. I turned back to a lane that led very steeply upward, inland from the village and by taking a series of paths and tracks which led over high viewpoints – vistas of the sea, way ahead and below – enjoyed this unspoilt countryside, bypassing Portgower and picked up more beautiful lanes, equally steep but downward, back to the main A9, with all its traffic queues. I followed this back all the way to Portgower, before resuming my northerly route along it to Helmsdale. Just shows how sometimes what might appear to be set-backs can turn into a bonus!

I soon reached West Helmsdale, and then Helmsdale, by way of coastal A9 and enjoyed a walkabout taking in the harbour – I love these good old Scottish fishing ports – such a lovely, fishy, briny, windy, wild atmosphere!

Also toured the beach, sands, streets and shops, concluding happily, around 3.30 pm at a delightful café, where I indulged in the joys of a pot of tea, and a doughnut, and ice cream.

By now of course it was getting dark, but there was not long to wait for my train, where some of the staff remembered me from my earlier travels in the area. We had interesting talks on the journey about my northward walking. I thus returned via Brora to Golspie, where I was promptly met by the helpful taxi driver again, and enjoyed talking about my day's progress en route back to Dornoch, where I settled in happily at the hotel.

And of course very happy reflections on the day. I suppose to pick up a favourite theme, I should include not only reflections on the ice cream but also reflect on the doughnut as it was a particularly good one. Cakes too, of course have featured quite prominently in my accounts of experiences.

And so this led me to the following story I was once told: A young boy was going out to tea. His mother told him to be sure not to have more than one cake. The lady providing the tea pressed him to have a second cake. He said 'no' and that he had promised his mother he would only have one. She tried to persuade him again, and he felt he would have to relent, so he devised a compromise and replied, 'Well, I think it would be alright. My mother would have been happy for me to have two – if she had realized how small the cakes were.' (!)

Day 103
15/2/14

Helmsdale – Navidale – Ord of Caithness – Berriedale – Newport –
Borgue – Ramscraigs – Castle Hill – Dunbeath
(18 miles approx)

Again, the walking was in a generally northward direction today. After a comfortable night and welcome breakfast, I was driven by the very helpful taxi driver again to Golspie station – a very pleasant ride of course. Also a very pleasant train ride via Brora to Helmsdale, where I enjoyed the coastal views to great advantage (it was dark on this section yesterday of course). I talked to a retired nurse from the area on this journey – she was able to point out the best views and showed me a delightful rocky location, where you sometimes see seals basking in the sunshine.

Alighting at Helmsdale, my first impression was of a powerful, penetrating wind – and strong and cold indeed. Perhaps the train had been too cosy! But the weather was still nothing like as rough as in southern Britain, according to news I had heard. (See comments of yesterday.) Later today I seemed to be in more sheltered areas often, but it continued to be decidedly cold – conducive to brisk walking – there were short sharp showers, but good clear views, including vistas of snow on distant mountain regions again; and of coast at times; and high, rugged cliffs. Snowdrops continued to 'oblige'.

I started walking about 10.30, seeing the streets and shops again and ascended on the main A9 through East Helmsdale (no coastal railway today). The grassy roadsides were very handy for most of the walk. Interestingly, I seemed to detect generally that my memories way back at the start of this project in Cornwall, suggested that the scenery there did quite resemble this far north of Scotland. Open, rugged, wild, unspoilt …

I was soon ascending a long steep winding incline. I also soon transferred from the county of Sutherland to the county of Caithness. Exciting that Caithness is the most northerly county of mainland Britain. Via Navidale and Ord of Caithness, with more bends and climbs – and descents too – ups and downs are mostly pretty steep – and through more open (also some forest though) country, but truly panoramic views, and past Ousdale and Borgue Langwell. And then the really dramatic part - Berriedale! Warning notices abounded – and escape route arrangements! It was an extremely steep descent to the foot, near the sea, followed immediately by a very steep ascent, complete with hairpin bends throughout! Very scenic little village, wooded slopes and gurgling burn rushing through deep valley.

Up on the other side, I was back in high, open country where I diverted for a short distance onto a pleasant lane, through the small village of Newport, with attractive dwellings. Resuming the A9 again, I continued via Borgue and Ramscraigs, small farms and settlements all around, and after the summit of Castle Hill descended past Balnabruich into the byways of Dunbeath (which is bypassed by the A9). Another good old Scottish fishing port – I soon did village, harbour and beach, so completing the walk around 3.30 pm (including the Portormin part).

Enjoyed a snack at a restaurant (just above the village) consisting of considerable quantities of crisps and orange juice. Interestingly, it is easy, it seems, in these less populated parts of Britain to inadvertently become in a sense slightly 'famous', not of course in any true sense of fame! During today's walk, some three cars passed me at various points and 'toot, toot, toot' from their hooters, and 'wave, wave, wave' from the occupants. They may or may not have been people I had met. I suppose folk may have begun to recognise the one lone walker, devotedly following the A9 for days. Conspicuous with hi-vis jacket, cap, stick, rucksack and map case! Indeed, at the Dunbeath restaurant, some folk came in and asked how the walk was going - they'd passed me at Portgower on foot and in their car today. They had said in the car, 'Oh! There's that man again. He's still walking again today!' And they kindly offered me a lift back but I'd already booked the taxi. I told them about my project! I do like the Scots very much — for their friendliness and hospitality. As indeed is the case, of course, with the helpful taxi driver, who soon arrived and took me all the way back to Dornoch. A dark but much enjoyed ride, to the good hotel. It's certainly been a great day again!

And so to the two days of travelling back south. Very good rest and breakfast, interesting conversations re Scotland with staff and a couple from the Orkney Islands; and the chap very kindly drove me and all my luggage down to Dornoch Cathedral Square. Then pot of tea and scone and jam at hotel there, and I took express coach back to Inverness by very direct route using the Dornoch, Cromarty and Beauly Firth Bridges etc … similar to Day 101. Cold with short, sharp showers but sunny views, and snow on bens. My host again drove me to B&B, had entertaining conversations, and fun with the dog, I took a walk back to the city, afternoon (tea and cakes in café), then back to B&B again for pleasant evening. I heard the floods were still severe 'down south'.

And too, the second day of travelling home. Enjoyed good packed breakfast – then early taxi to station for the 'usual' 7.55 'Highland Chieftain' express. Again, usual route, stops, speeds and views, I think. This time though, I enjoyed daylight all the way – especially appreciated for the early part – I saw clearly the views from Culloden Viaduct; Slochd summit; and Highland mountain scenery up to Aviemore area. Excellent scenery, especially too, the beautiful Cairngorms mountains, well covered in snow. Clear views! Sunny! Some flooding en route in England. Darker after London. Taxi from Kings Cross to Waterloo, using Blackfriars Bridge, views of Thames, Shard and St Paul's Cathedral good. Fast train Waterloo to Havant, taxi home. *Superb* holiday – I shall soon run out of adjectives!

Day 104
18/3/14

Dunbeath – Knockinnon – Latheronwheel – Latheron – Lybster – Clyth – Bruan – Ulbster – Thrumster – Hempriggs – Wick
(22 miles approx)

As with Day 101, I firstly have two days travelling 'up' to describe. So here goes. On 16th March I took taxi to Havant, but took a different train route this time, from thence. The weather was different too – mainly bright and sunny, that is, until it got dark, of course! It was quite a cold day – also I had developed a cold, just as I left home, if you please! The fast train called at Emsworth, Southbourne, Chichester, Barnham, Worthing, Shoreham–by-Sea, Hove, Burgess Hill, Haywards Heath, Gatwick Airport, East Croydon and London Victoria. Clapham Junction and district were omitted due to engineering works. I travelled on other lines in the Tulse Hill, Herne Hill and Brixton areas. Took taxi past Hyde Park and Marble Arch, to London Kings Cross. Plenty of good architecture to admire, as previous times.

The 'Highland Chieftain' express, middayish, conveyed me thence to Inverness, as impressively as ever, also following a minor diversion in the Hertford North area, though. Otherwise the route was the same and as fast, and the stops more or less the same. Clear views prevailed through all daylight hours. Today only minimal flooding compared with last time. Edinburgh and other places of course, were great highlights. Darkness fell around the Perth/Pitlochry areas, and there was comparatively little snow on the high bens of Scotland. My host, as obliging as ever, met me at Inverness station and drove me to B&B where I enjoyed a good rest and comfortable quarters!

And so to day two of travelling up, (17th March). Again needless to say, excellent night's sleep, and breakfast, and jokes, and fun with the puppy! Then, as usual, conveyed to the station for an outstandingly fascinating train journey, views showing up well, amid sunshine and showers and cold winds, but very little snow, if any at all. The route was so long and circuitous, through wild, remote and extremely scenic country – The North Highlands of Scotland. A mix of coastal or inland, with glorious glens, burns, gorges, lochs, firths, moorland and mountainous terrain, forests, rugged landscapes, remote indeed, the wee hamlets and villages with their tiny old stations – often unstaffed halts – all so charming. Over four hours from Inverness to Wick, so a real treat, although of course I had already travelled on some of the more southerly sections. The train left Inverness at 10.37. Stations including unstaffed halts often not called at were: Inverness, Beauly, Muir of Ord, Conon Bridge, Dingwall, Alness, Invergordon, Fearn, Tain, Ardgay, Culrain, Invershin, Lairg, Rogart, Golspie, Dunrobin Castle, Brora, Helmsdale, Kildonan, Kinbrace, Forsinard, Altnabreac, Scotscalder and then Georgemas Junction, where train reversed and proceeded to Thurso, reversed again there, proceeded to Georgemas Junction again and on to Wick.

I was met at Wick station by the lady who runs the nearby B & B in the town. She drove me to the very pleasant and comfortable accommodation. I enjoyed food and drink, and settled in very happily

And so now to the walk itself. I still have the cold and cough, but the great outdoors seemed to help, and sunny (and showery) cold, windy weather proved to be just what the doctor ordered! After very good night and breakfast and enjoyment of hospitality, plus interest in my project by my kind hosts, I took the bus from Wick down the A99/A9 coast roads to Dunbeath, much enjoying the very northern Scottish accents of fellow travellers, some of which I could not really follow!

Started walking from Dunbeath around 10.30. I used the main coast roads I had just travelled on nearly all the way, so returning to my northward walk route, from where I reached on 15th February. Views good and clear; near cliffs and sea throughout; snowdrops, daffodils and gorse in bloom (spring was in the air!); and good grassy verges for scenic roadside walking, most of the time. High up and quite hilly till latter part. (No railway today but I couldn't complain after the last two days!) But now less mountainous than previous walks, the landscape opened out more.

So proceeded forth on the A9 via Inver to Knockinnon, where I detoured onto a short scenic lane for a while and then resumed A9 to Latheronwheel and Latheron, both significant, attractive villages. Now I took the A99 to remain near the coast. Via Swiney to Lybster, where I enjoyed a snack from my rucksack in the pleasant main street of this small typical Scottish town. Then on via Occumster, Clyth, Bruan, Ulbster, Borrowston, Gansclet, Thrumster, Hempriggs, (passing Loch Hempriggs) and Whiterow, before entering Wick, and returning to B & B (6 pm) – all very – let's have a change of adjective – 'jolly stuff'! As to Wick, I hope to explore the town properly tomorrow, for by the time I arrived it was too dark to comment adequately.

I enjoyed a relaxing evening in my room, and partook of further snacks and coughed and sneezed somewhat; but felt all the better for the day out and the quality of the B&B, and reflections on the joys of the walk itself.

DAY 105
19/3/14

WICK – CASTLE OF OLD WICK – MILTON – HASTER – BILBSTER – WATTEN – LAREL – GEORGEMAS JUNCTION
(20 miles approx)

Duly refreshed, after another very good night and breakfast, I set forth on foot at 9.45, and firstly 'did' Wick. Cough and cold were improving. The weather proved to be highly memorable – initially, in the shelter of the town, I was 'merely' aware of a cold, gusty wind crossing my path. But more was to follow.

I found Wick to be a really delightful town – to put it simply, just so Scottish. The typical northerly feel - another fishy briny port; a sense of history; the tall solid grey stone buildings; a sizeable town with a good range of streets and shops. I found a walk out to the Castle of Old Wick especially interesting, but now a ruin, set above cliffs and rocks on the wild rugged coast. Also included in the 'tour', Wick Bay, harbour and beach. The Wick River area, especially where a sizeable older stone bridge crosses over, was impressive too and views as throughout today are clear and good.

I next set forth in a north-westerly direction on the open road, the A882. Open is the right word. Once through the Janetstown part of Wick, I was in open country and views of the landscape opened up. I was quite near the railway all day and finding grass banks on the roadside very useful much of the time. But when I had left the shelter of the street buildings, I was suddenly aware of the full force of a very strong gale. If I had been taken by surprise, I feel the gusts might have blown me off my feet. I have not in my whole walk from Land's End experienced winds like these! My progress was certainly delayed. Eventually the gale ceased after an hour or two, but it returned to some extent toward the end of the walk. Looking back on it, it was fun! There was also some cloud and a little rain. But of course it was because of the geography of this part of Scotland that gales felt so strong. Mountains were only to be seen in the distance, southward. Some people would call the landscape bleak, but I loved it – countryside was open and undulating. Weather, I suppose from the Atlantic, came at me without interruption!

And so I continued through Milton, Haster and Bilbster, to the larger village of Watten where the signboard informed me that this was the 'Birthplace of Alexander Bain, Inventor of the Electric Clock.' Interesting. After this, I had good views of nearby Loch Watten; I also saw some very delightful, frisky little lambs, some white, some black and white, the first I have seen this season. I then passed Oldhall House, and between Upper and Lower Larel to the junction of A882 and A9 roads, and followed the A9 southward for a short distance to Georgemas Junction station, a remote outpost on the North Highlands railways indeed. (Arrived about 5.15 pm.) I referred to this station by the way, Day 104 'in my travels'. It certainly had very much the atmosphere of the 'railways of old'. Little must have changed over many years. And with the shrill wind whistling over on this cold, wild March day, the station building appeared like some kind of ancient fortress of the railway world, if I'm not exaggerating too much!

From here I caught a train back to Wick, along the scenic route. The conductor remembered me from earlier visits on more southerly sections of this line. She showed a kind interest in my walking experiences again. And from Wick station, I took the short walk to my B&B where I felt very welcome again. I ate and drank snack-wise, in my room. I still coughed and sneezed at times, but nothing like the noise of today's gales! A day I won't forget, but most well-worth doing, and lots of air!

And a closing paragraph, which I think fits in with today – some remarks by the 'certain lady' I sometimes quote from. On one occasion, when I happened to spend most of the day indoors, she said, 'But there was one thing about it, you did manage to get out in the evening and get some fresh air, when you had to unblock the drain.'(!)

Day 106
20/3/14

Georgemas Junction – Roadside – Thurso – Mountpleasant – Murkle – Castletown
(14 miles approx)

Well 'reinforced' again at B&B with due rest and a breakfast to keep me going for the immediate and foreseeable future, I think the first thing to impress me as I entered the street, was that it was distinctly less windy than yesterday, an impression which continued throughout the day. Weather was quite cold, quite sunny and minimally showery now and again. But views were showing up well.

I took a short walk to the main bus stop, whence I was transported via Watten to a point very near to Georgemas Junction station, to which I also walked. I then started the walk 'proper' at 11 o'clock and followed beside the A9 road using the obliging verges, banks and occasionally the gutters; never far from the railway and River Thurso. As yesterday, I enjoyed the, as I call it, glorious bleakness of the unspoilt, open, undulating countryside all around, and mountains far distant.

Proceeded through Roadside, an apt name I thought; and then, referring back to the map, a place called 'El Sub Sta' – rather remarkable was my impression, until I realised it was presumably an abbreviation for 'Electricity Sub Station'! Then I reached Millbank and Thurso. The latter was the birthplace of Sir William Smith, founder of the Boys Brigade.

Thurso like Wick, was indeed an impressive, typically Scottish town. I crossed the fine, sizeable main bridge over the River Thurso, and continued to the town centre, with its spacious, high old stone buildings – shops, houses etc and wide well-laid out streets. I also saw a café with some well-laid out cakes and strawberry milk shakes, which I was delighted to take possession of. Then walked onto the cliffs and sands of Thurso Bay, with excellent views of at least one of the Orkney Islands – Hoy certainly – across the Pentland Firth. All this showed up very well.

Something that is of particular interest to me is that I had a great grandfather (who I never knew though) who was a coastguard at Thurso. My grandmother was born in Thurso – I well remember her – but I think she was too young to remember Scotland. They moved to the South of England. Although the family were not Scottish, my grandmother was very proud of her association with that country and, like myself held the Scots in high regard.

I move on (literally). At Thurso the direction of my walking altered from approximately north-west to north-east. I followed beside the A836 road – an ideal route. Quite busy, but grassy 'sides' again, pretty straight, but so good for getting the best views all around, especially of the coast, Pentland Firth, the Orkney Island of Hoy – and Dunnet Bay and Dunnet Head which are further along Scotland's mainland coast. The road has regular ups and downs, but not extreme.

I continued past Mountpleasant and via Stitley and Murkle, into delightful Castletown, of moderate size, with attractive architecture – old buildings abounding. (4.15). And just right for a bus ride back via Thurso, Halkirk and Watten, to Wick, where I shopped for more 'eats', to be enjoyed in the comfort of my room at the B&B in the evening. As my host reminded me, there is a saying – 'Feed a cold' (opposed to 'Starve a fever'). It seemed to be working.

Another 'jokey' piece seems relevant here. I had mentioned being noticed on my roadside walking – this is continuing still, somewhat (waving and hooting) – see Day 103. I suppose I am rather conspicuous, particularly the bright yellow high-vis jacket (a wise precaution). Indeed, on more than one occasion when wearing this 'apparel' at railway stations, I was approached by anxious travellers, 'Could I direct them to the correct platform for the next train to (wherever)'? The penny eventually dropped – I realized my image was rather too 'official'!

Which reminded me of another incident I was once told of. During wartime, a man who previously worked in a quite different capacity was put on police duties. He was provided with a very smart policeman's uniform, of which he was duly proud, but it was easy sometimes to forget the new career and its requirements and to revert, in his mind, to the memories of his earlier career. When on one occasion, someone asked him for directions to somewhere, he replied, to the astonishment of this member of the public – 'I'm afraid I really have no idea. I think the best thing you can do is go and ask a policeman.'!

But, back to today again. Just to say how wonderful the walk has been and too, how wonderful the rather calmer weather!

Day 107
21/3/14

Castletown – Dunnet – Mey (Including castle, east & hill areas) –
Gills Bay – Huna – John O'Groats
(17 miles approx)

Note: 1,535 Miles since leaving Land's End

Yes, you see from reading the heading, where I ended up today! Now I don't expect you to believe the following, any more than I do.

'I suddenly had the idea today, as I seem to have nearly reached the
end of Britain. Remembering that the walk began at Land's End, why
not go to John O'Groats? After all, I seem to be awfully near it!'

Seriously now – of course, ever since I left Land's End, I always hoped I would reach John O'Groats – a distant dream for a long while, but it has been kept an open secret. I 'titled' the first journal *'A Book about a Walk'*, as quoted Day 1. Then, and up to now, I have throughout, been deliberately evasive in references to destination and length of the Walk – I have virtually avoided such subjects! No more guessing – read on:

I left the comfortable B & B, cough and cold under control, feeling the benefit of the rest and breakfast of course; taking a taxi via Bower, across to Castletown, well driven on the fast open road and purchased bottled water and fruit pastilles at a local shop.

Started walk about 10.45, my direction progressing from north-east to east today. The subject of weather was particularly happy. A very strong wind, again, but behind me all the way – I felt like I was exceeding the speed limit! But it was cold – and dry and sunny, and views were very clear again. Daffodils and bleating black lambs added to the feeling of spring.

Enjoyed the beauty of Castletown again before progressing with very pleasant road walking (the A836 still with its grassy edges and good views all around, always near or fairly near the coast, moderately hilly, but with more bends than yesterday). The landward vistas were of the undulating, delightfully open countryside; those seaward were of the rugged coast, Pentland Firth and Hoy, and other Orkney Islands.

So I followed near the sands and rough seas of Dunnet Bay, partly sheltered by gigantic sand dunes with views across to Dunnet Head, before passing through Dunnet village and near to St John's Loch. Then for a while the road turned more inland, so views of sea, white horses, huge breakers became more distant. I continued via Corsback and Rattar to Mey, a scenic and noteworthy village because of the Castle of Mey, which I diverted down a narrow lane to see, rather distantly but a good view gained. (It was closed to the public – Winter Season.) It was of course, the Queen Mother's residence, where she enjoyed quite a lot of her time I am told, walking the remote beaches or watching rough seas or stormy weather from the high viewpoint of her castle room. The wild setting, the views of coast and Orkneys and the ancient, imposing structure of the towering castle itself cannot fail to impress.

I returned to the A836 route and walked through East Mey and down Mey Hill to coast and cliffs again. Continued past Gills Bay, Kirkstyle and Huna – all attractive village locations – and then, yes – John O'Groats! A great sense of excitement! Arrived at 3.45 pm. I really seemed to sense the atmosphere, and what a scenic spot too.

The view of the rugged Island of Stroma, not far north, was excellent – also more distant islands of the Orkney group showed up well. Too, the rugged mainland coast, the harbour and pier, village centre and tourist attractions (museum and craft centre, hotels and cafés...) and I had my photo taken by a waitress at the John O'Groats sign. Enjoyed orange juice and shortbread – the ice cream season did not seem to be 'yet', in this cold wind, but no matter – 'it's where I am', I was thinking! And I thought back to Land's End on 16th August, 2010 (!), as I noted too (Day 103), Cornwall does somewhat resemble Caithness – open, rugged, wild and unspoilt.

(Jan de Groot was I understand, a Dutchman, who reached land, where I now am – hence the name John O'Groats – just to add basic relevant information about the origin of the place.)

I took the bus back via Keiss to Wick and B&B, and was also welcomed by my host who very kindly celebrated the day with me, taking a great interest in this journal, and she gave me a chocolate cake! I soon phoned my brother to celebrate the news with him – so plenty of enjoyment. Words really almost fail me now! It's been just such a really, really happy day!

And now the first of two days travelling back. Excellent rest, breakfast and conversations; cough and cold much better. Had a walk around Wick again and very kind host took my luggage to the station by car, where I took it over. Cold, sunny and showery weather, fine views and a little snow on the bens. The very fascinating scenic, long train ride to Inverness, was of course as good as it was on 17th March, opposite direction, otherwise 'ditto'. Inverness host most kindly met me again – so to excellent B&B!

And second day, journey home. Much interest from my hosts re walk completed – and much fun as before, jokes etc, and drive to early 'Highland Chieftain' express train. Usual stops, plus Carrbridge, Newtonmore, Blair Atholl, Dunkeld & Birnam, Dunblane and Berwick-upon-Tweed. *Very* scenic, with snow laying deep, mountain areas, as far as Pitlochry – and good sunny views all journey; Edinburgh and coast areas particularly good, too. Usual route to London Kings Cross and similar taxi route (in dusk now) as 16th March, to London Victoria, then similar route and similar stops to Havant, and taxi home. Excellent breakfast at B&B of course, and plentiful snacks later.

I most gladly reiterate again – what a very, very happy experience the whole Land's End to John O'Groats walk has been!

How very fortunate I am. (And now I must decide about my next ice cream!)

LAND'S END – ST IVES – HAYLE – PORTREATH – PERRANPORTH – NEWQU
– BUDE – HARTLAND POINT – CLOVELLY – WESTWARD HO! – APPLEDOR
MARTIN – LYNTON & LYNMOUTH – PORLOCK – MINEHEAD – WATCHE
– FLAX BOURTON – BRISTOL (TEMPLE MEADS) – WESTBURY-ON-TRYM
SEVERN – GLOUCESTER – WESTBURY-ON-SEVERN – CINDERFORD – F
MONMOUTH – PANDY – LLANTHONY PRIORY – BLACK MOUNTAINS – F
– WELSHPOOL – OSWESTRY – LLANGOLLEN – RUTHIN – DENBIGH –
– CHESTER – HELSBY – FRODSHAM – WARRINGTON (BANK QUAY)
LEYLAND – PRESTON – GARSTANG – GALGATE – LANCASTER – MOR
WINDERMERE – RYDAL WATER – LAKE GRASMERE – AMBLESIDE – KI
– CARLISLE – GRETNA GREEN – LANGHOLM – TEVIOTHEAD – HAWICI
– GOREBRIDGE – NEWTONGRANGE – EDINBURGH (WAVERLEY, PRINCI
DALMENY – FIRTH OF FORTH BRIDGE, SOUTH SIDE – SOUTH QUEENSF
– STIRLING – CARRON BRIDGE – KILSYTH – KIRKINTILLOCH – MILNG
– INVERSNAID – INVERARNAN – FALLS OF FALLOCH – CRIANLARICH
GLEN COE – KINLOCHLEVEN – FORT WILLIAM – THE ROAD TO THE
LOCH EILT – LOCHAILORT – LOCH NAN UAMH – BEASDALE – BORRO
MALLAIG (END OF THE ROAD TO THE ISLES) – CAOL – MOY BRIDGE –
BRIDGE – FORT AUGUSTUS – INVERMORISTON – LOCH NESS – GROTAIC
– KIRKHILL – BEAULY – MUIR OF ORD – CONON BRIDGE – DINGW
BONAR BRIDGE – DORNOCH – LOCH FLEET – GOLSPIE – BRORA –
– LATHERON – LYBSTER – WICK – WATTEN – GEORGEMAS JUNCTION
LAND'S END – ST IVES – HAYLE – PORTREATH – PERRANPORTH – NEWQU
– BUDE – HARTLAND POINT – CLOVELLY – WESTWARD HO! – APPLEDOR
MARTIN – LYNTON & LYNMOUTH – PORLOCK – MINEHEAD – WATCHE
– FLAX BOURTON – BRISTOL (TEMPLE MEADS) – WESTBURY-ON-TRYM
SEVERN – GLOUCESTER – WESTBURY-ON-SEVERN – CINDERFORD – F
MONMOUTH – PANDY – LLANTHONY PRIORY – BLACK MOUNTAINS – F
– WELSHPOOL – OSWESTRY – LLANGOLLEN – RUTHIN – DENBIGH –
– CHESTER – HELSBY – FRODSHAM – WARRINGTON (BANK QUAY)
LEYLAND – PRESTON – GARSTANG – GALGATE – LANCASTER – MOR
WINDERMERE – RYDAL WATER – LAKE GRASMERE – AMBLESIDE – KI